Residential Tourism

TOURISM AND CULTURAL CHANGE
Series Editors: Professor Mike Robinson, *Centre for Tourism and Cultural Change,*
Leeds Metropolitan University, Leeds, UK and Dr Alison Phipps, *University of Glasgow,*
Scotland, UK

Understanding tourism's relationships with culture(s) and vice versa, is of ever-increasing significance in a globalising world. This series will critically examine the dynamic inter-relationships between tourism and culture(s). Theoretical explorations, research-informed analyses, and detailed historical reviews from a variety of disciplinary perspectives are invited to consider such relationships.

Full details of all the books in this series and of all our other publications can be found on http://www.channelviewpublications.com, or by writing to Channel View Publications Ltd, St Nicholas House, 31–34 High Street, Bristol, BS1 2AW, UK.

TOURISM AND CULTURAL CHANGE
Series Editors: Professor Mike Robinson, *Centre for Tourism and Cultural Change, Leeds Metropolitan University, Leeds, UK* and Dr Alison Phipps, *University of Glasgow, Scotland, UK*

Residential Tourism
(De)Constructing Paradise

Mason R. McWatters

CHANNEL VIEW PUBLICATIONS
Bristol • Buffalo • Toronto

Library of Congress Cataloging in Publication Data
A catalog record for this book is available from the Library of Congress.
McWatters, Mason R.
Residential Tourism: (De)Constructing Paradise / Mason R. McWatters. 1st ed.
Tourism and Cultural Change: 16
Includes bibliographical references and index.
1. Retirement, Places of-Latin America. 2. Tourism-Latin America. I. Title. II. Title:
Residential Tourism: (De)Constructing Paradise. III. Series.
HQ1063.2.L29M39 2008
307.3'360846098-dc22   2008012847

British Library Cataloguing in Publication Data
A catalogue entry for this book is available from the British Library.

ISBN-13: 978–1–84541–091–9 (hbk)
ISBN-13: 978–1–84541–090–2 (pbk)

Channel View Publications Ltd
UK: St Nicholas House, 31–34 Hight Street, Bristol BS1 2AW.
USA: UTP, 2250 Military Road, Tonawanda, NY 14150, USA.
Canada: UTP, 5201 Dufferin Street, North York, Ontario M3H 5T8, Canada.

The policy of Multilingual Matters / Channel View Publications is to use papers that are
natural, renewable and recyclable products, made from wood grown in sustainable
forests. In the manufacturing process of our books, and to further support our policy,
preference is given to printers that have FSC and PEFC Chain of Custody certification.
The FSC and/or PEFC logos will appear on those books where full certification has
been granted to the printer concerned.

Typeset by Saxon Graphics Ltd, Derby
Printed and bound in Great Britain by the Cromwell Press Ltd

Contents

List of Figures

Chapter 1
Understanding Residential Tourism

Introduction

In 2005, *Forbes* magazine published an article, entitled 'Paradise Found: Where to Retire Abroad', which opened with the following introduction:

> Who can resist the fantasy? Instead of catching the early-bird special in Florida, wouldn't it be more fun to sip away your sunset years in Provence? Such thoughts often occur on vacations. During a pastis-induced haze, you think, who needs Target or Oreo cookies or 100 cable channels to make life enjoyable? I could live here forever. You nurse the dream, lingering over real estate ads in a local café. But soon you realize that your nest egg isn't going to let you buy one of those overpriced villas and live like Peter Mayle for the rest of your life. Before you know it, the vacation is over, and so is your reverie. Don't fret. We found five idyllic places – from Patagonia to Phucket – where you can still live like a king on what you've saved. So dream on. (Kratz, 2005)

Indeed, who can resist the fantasy of living like a king in paradise? In *The Shape of Utopia*, Robert Elliott writes that ideals such as paradise, utopia and the golden age are 'projections of man's wishful fantasies, answering to the longings for the good life which have moved him since before history began' (1970: 7). In recent years, for a growing number of retired-aged North Americans and Western Europeans, a desire for the good life has, quite literally, moved them to the ends of the earth. For the chance to live like royalty in paradise, these individuals voluntarily surrender their rooted identities and their physical ties to a stable home and community in exchange for a new beginning in a truly foreign and faraway place.

One of these places that has quickly assumed an international identity as an emerging retirement destination is Boquete: a rural, coffee-growing district of less than 20,000 inhabitants, located in the verdant highlands of western Panamá. Incredibly, within just a five-year span, the foreign population in this community has mushroomed from under two dozen to over 500 inhabitants; and, according to Rubén Lachman Varela, a prominent Panamanian economist, this foreign population is projected to increase exponentially into the thousands within the coming decade. While these foreigners, whom I will refer to as residential tourists, represent only a fraction of the total population of the district, the social, cultural and economic impacts of their presence have permeated the entire fabric of this place, dramatically altering its identity in short order. Within just a few years, Boquete has been thrust into a crossroads between its provincial, agricultural-oriented past and its imminent future as an international destination for residential tourism.

The ultimate aim of this book is to examine Boquete at this crossroads and to investigate the social impacts of residential tourism on place and community at the local level, by directly exploring how its inhabitants – both native and foreign – experience their shared place of residence. How these residents experience their surrounding world, both physical and human, is significant because it offers a window into their unique identities, values, and desires for their lives in this place. In addition to understanding the meanings that residents assign to themselves and their surroundings, by exploring how these ostensibly diverse residential groups experience a shared place of home, there exists an opportunity to learn about how these residential groups interact with each other and their immediate world. Furthermore, by investigating foreign and native residents' experiences of Boquete at this critical juncture, there exists an opportunity to investigate how a complex, transformative and little understood phenomenon such as residential tourism affects places and communities at the local level.

The findings that will be presented in this book suggest that native Boqueteños and foreign residential tourists experience Boquete in fundamentally different ways. This experiential divide is so great it is as if these two groups were living in two distinct worlds, or two separate realities, despite the fact that they literally share common ground. Whereas native Boqueteños experience Boquete as a *place* to which their entire beings are fundamentally fused, residential tourists predominantly experience Boquete as a *landscape* from which they are, in many ways, distanced and alienated. Central to this experiential exploration is the contrast between the ideas of place – a durable, profound and organic entity shared and cared for by community – and landscape – a selective and ideological vision of one's surroundings which remotely mediates subject and object.

This dualism between place and landscape, however, does not tell the entire story of residential experiences in Boquete during this momentous era of foreign-led growth and development. Indeed, as the institution of residential tourism increasingly permeates the fabric of Boquete, both groups of residents begin to express that their respective relationships with Boquete are rapidly changing, each for dramatically different reasons. As the dynamic intervention of residential tourist growth and development continues to remake the dimensions of place, community and landscape in Boquete, both the place native residents know and the landscape residential tourists desire seem to be disappearing.

Residential Tourism

Before continuing any further, let us pause to consider the relatively obscure concept of residential tourism, around which this book is oriented. Terminological difficulties abound when attempting to label a complex, heterogeneous and newly emerging phenomenon such as this. For this work I conceptualize residential tourism, in the absolute broadest context, as the enduring practices and lifestyles which result from a channeled flow of consumption-led, permanent or semi-permanent migration to a particular destination. Within the specific socio-geographical context of this work, residential tourism may be more precisely characterized as the lasting effects which result from the process of international, consumption-led migration undertaken by individuals – primarily by retirees – from North America and Western Europe to Latin America. Paramount to residential tourism are two components: it is comprised of a lifestyle that is oriented around patterns of leisure and consumption, in which work imperatives are minimal or nonexistent; and it takes place permanently or semi-permanently in a particular *destination*, outside one's traditional socio-geographical milieu. As such, the term is also applicable as an identity (residential tourist) and as a descriptive identifier (e.g. residential tourist destination, lifestyle and so forth).

On the surface, it may appear that the mere decision to employ the term residential tourism creates a fallacious, deterministic framework that presupposes certain lifestyle behaviors for this practice. Certainly, some degree of judgment is being cast by choosing to use the weighted term 'tourism'; however, its use in this work is neither arbitrary nor deterministic.

Within the compound identity of the residential tourist, the latter word certainly carries a great deal of symbolic currency in Western cultures. Indeed, according to Dean MacCannell, the tourist has become a morally loaded identity among critical theorists, who often have 'derided' this identity for 'being satisfied with superficial experiences of other peoples and other places' (1976: 10). (This, despite MacCannell's own insistence that the tourist possesses an inherent desire for 'deeper involvement' with other cultures and societies.) However, while acknowledging the moral baggage that accompanies the terms 'tourist' and 'tourism', my motivation to use these terms derives purely from the associative value they hold as a comprehensible identity and practice with which most readers can relate. I desire to imbue these terms neither with the negative connotations awarded by MacCannell's critical theorist opponents, nor with the positive connotations awarded by MacCannell himself. Their uses are principally part of an operational strategy to overcome the great terminological difficulties that a complex, heterogeneous and newly emerging phenomenon such as residential tourism presents.

I selected the terminology of residential tourism in the absence of an agreed-upon vocabulary among the residents of Boquete – both foreign and native – to describe this emerging phenomenon. In particular, I selected this terminology after much discussion with the foreign residents of Boquete concerning their own identity. Prior to conducting my fieldwork, I often referred to this group as 'expatriated retirees'; however, upon arriving in Boquete, I quickly learned that a significant number of residential tourists found this term personally offensive. Several residential tourists downright despised the term 'expatriate' because they felt it conveyed an extremely negative political connotation and misrepresented them as unpatriotic individuals who had shunned their native countries. While I am sure that not *all* residential tourists are completely at ease with the terminology I have chosen, I am confident nevertheless that it is the most appropriate and representative language available.

Residential tourism, in fact, is a term with an established scholarly tradition, albeit one that is nascent and, thus far, limited in its application in research scholarship. For at least the past decade, Spanish scholars in the social sciences have utilized residential tourism to describe the permanent or seasonal residence of (mostly elderly) northern Europeans along the Costa del Sol region of southern Spain (e.g. Casado-Diaz, 1999; Clavé, 1998; Raya, 1994; Rodriguez, 2001; Vera, 1997). In all the works that employ this term an emphasis is made regarding the links between vacation tourism and residential tourism. Indeed, geographer Vicente Rodriguez finds that residential tourists' 'pattern of behaviour, their perception of the area where they live and their appraisal of environmental events are mainly tourist orientated' (2001: 60). Among this group of scholars, Rodriguez offers the most explicit conceptual definition for the residential tourist identity. He does this by identifying four main criteria that characterize residential tourists as a social group:

> They constitute a concrete *human group* (retirees; the elderly); they exhibit different *patterns of mobile behavior* (permanent migration, temporary migration or simply mobility); they demonstrate a *tourist motivation* with an individual basis (satisfaction in enjoying free time) and economic dimensions (in terms of consumption, real

estate markets and services); and they create territorial *effects* (53, emphases in original).

Rodriguez's four main criteria provide excellent anchors for a logical and accommodating conceptual framework for residential tourist identity. In addition to affirming a distinct and incontrovertible correlation between short-term vacation tourism and long-term residential tourism, his conceptual definition rightly emphasizes the immense significance of the territorial effects that residential tourism creates. The inclusion of this final criterion is important not simply because it is an important focus of this work; in a broader sense the recognition of residential tourism's territorial and, I would add, social effects is very significant because of the awesome transformative power the phenomenon of residential tourism possesses. Simply put, residential tourism is meaningless until it is situated in a socio-geographical context and explored as a dynamic phenomenon which alters the identities of the places and communities with which it becomes associated.

However, despite Rodriguez's valuable contribution to articulate four cornerstone criteria of residential tourist identity, I find several of his paren-thetical descriptions of these criteria to be somewhat underdeveloped and misleading. The first concerns the *human group* criterion. Simply owing to the wide-ranging subjectivity that the fluid terms 'retired' and 'elderly' can denote, I am opposed to Rodriguez's suggestive contention that residential tourists are categorically retired, elderly or both. While most residential tourists tend to be retired, older individuals, there simply are no practical barriers to prevent younger individuals from undertaking a lifestyle of resi-dential tourism. Even more problematical, there is no possible way to delimit concrete, definitional boundaries for terms as arbitrary as 'retired' and 'elderly', particularly the latter. Instead I conceive residential tourists – independent of their exact vocational statuses or ages – to be a distinct social group with a relatively homogenous set of intentions and motivations for undertaking a consumption-oriented way of life in socially selected destina-tions beyond their traditional socio-geographical milieus..

My second exception to Rodriguez's conceptual framework concerns his claim regarding residential tourists' *patterns of mobile behavior.* Whereas he seems to suggest that residential tourists' patterns of mobile behavior may reasonably vary across the entire spectrum of mobility, I contend that residential tourist identity *must* be restricted only to those patterns of mobility that are capable of accommodating either permanent or semi-permanent residence in *one* particular location. Indeed, without some standards of residential (semi-)permanency what criteria remain to differentiate short-term vacation tourists from residential tourists? This issue only highlights the lack of clarity and inherent difficulties that arise when one attempts to distinguish among a variety of identities along the continuum of tourist typologies; a problematical issue with which several scholars have engaged with limited success (e.g. O'Reilly, 1995; Vera, 1997; Williams *et al.*, 1997).

Despite the detailed modifications I have proposed above, I find that the four main criteria which Rodriguez proposes to conceptually define the residential tourist identity remain fundamentally sound and exceedingly insightful. However, I do find it necessary to include a fifth main criterion in order to distinguish definitively the residential tourist identity from a variety of other tourist identities. This additional criterion is that residential tourists possess a distinct *intention* to make a lasting home in their host destination. From a practical standpoint, this new criterion that I propose would undoubtedly be more difficult to assess than the existing criteria because understanding one's intentions for undertaking a specific action are not always manifested as empirically evident. Rather, understanding one's intentions for pursuing a specific course of action – in this case, migrating to a particular destination outside of one's traditional socio-geographical milieu – is a subjective enterprise that requires qualitative assessment and personal engagement. Yet despite the difficulties of assessing this additional criterion, I find that *intention* is a powerfully influential dimension of residential tourist identity. It resonates to affect every minute aspect of how the residential tourist perceives and experiences his new environment and constructs his new reality in the host destination. This criterion of *intention* directly relates to the *residential* ambitions of the *residential* tourist; it concerns the symbolic, experiential declaration of the residential tourist to reestablish the inimitability of 'home' in a new place. Simply having the intention, or plan, to recreate 'home' in this new place acts as a powerful lens of perception which uniquely influences how one views himself and his encounters with the social and physical environment in this place. Thus, while in theory a vacation tourist and a residential tourist may both have the same superficial experiences upon arriving at a particular host destination – disembarking from the same airplane, walking through the same airport terminal, seeing the same sights while driving away from the airport, and so forth – the experiential significance of the residential tourist's intention to make a lasting home in this place is powerful enough to wholly differentiate his perceptions and experiences from those of all other tourist identities. This correlation between intention and perception, with regard to establishing the distinct identity of the residential tourist, cannot be overstated.

In addition to the established use of 'residential tourism' in academic scholarship, my decision to utilize the terminology in this work also derives from the fact that it is popularly employed by Panamanians to refer to the growing number of foreign residents, who are overwhelmingly North American retirees, that have migrated to their country during the past decade. In fact, the official name for the type of visa that the Panamanian government issues to the majority of this foreign residential cohort is called the *turista pensionado*, or the 'pensioned tourist' visa. Furthermore, Panamanian media outlets, such as the daily newspaper *El Panamá América*, have increasingly adopted the term *turismo residencial* to describe this growing residential phenomenon which, more and more, is affecting the everyday lives of the Panamanian population at large. Likewise, Varela and colleagues employ this term in their recently published educational booklet, *Economía de Panamá para Todos*, which aims to provide a basic understanding of economics to the general Panamanian citizenry. In the eight pages devoted to the discussion of residential tourism, Varela presents his interpretation of the emerging phenomenon as follows:

> If the definition of conventional tourism, for example the one utilized by the World Bank in their statistics, identifies a tourist as someone who ... lives less than a year in a country which he visits, then how does one define a tourist that comes to our country and never leaves, and whose income comes from abroad and, therefore, from the point of view of the national economy his expenditures are service exports of Panamá? What if we call this segment Residential Tourism? Perhaps this sounds strange, but there are many people who no longer wish to continue living in their country of origin, and when they retire, or even before, they decide to try their luck in another place. This other place, as it relates to us, might be Panamá. In this country there are an estimated 2,500 families of this type. (Varela *et al.*, 2005: 127–8)[1,2]

That Varela and his colleagues devote an entire section of their booklet to a discussion of residential tourism and its economic implications for Panamá demonstrates residential tourism's growing impact on the everyday lives of Panamanians.

When the contributing process of migration comes into focus within the larger context of residential tourism there exist several points of intersection with similar phenomena, similar fields of research and similar terminologies. In the broadest of terms, Henry Buller and Keith Hoggart (1994) conceive of two main branches of migration: labor-oriented and consumption-oriented migration. For the latter branch of migration, scholars have provided a number of synonyms including amenity migration, quality of life migration and lifestyle migration. Migration scholars also have teased out a number of subtypes within this branch of migration, among them counter-urban and retirement migration. Regardless of which term is being employed or which subtype is being discussed, consumption-oriented migration shares several fundamental links with tourism.

Indeed, tourism itself is a subtype of consumption-oriented migration; granted that vacation sojourns lasting a month or less, which are by far the most common form of tourism, are *very* temporary forms of consumption-oriented migration. Perhaps the strongest conceptual link associating short-stay vacation tourism with more permanent forms of consumption-led migration is articulated by Allan Williams, Russell King, Anthony Warnes and Guy Patterson (2000). In essence, they insist that the establishment of short-stay, consumption-oriented migration flows to a particular area contribute to the secondary creation of more permanent forms of consumption-oriented migration flows into that area. This contributive link between temporary and permanent consumption-oriented migration has two distinct geographical facets. The first concerns what they describe as the 'definition of search spaces' (2000: 35). This idea espouses the theory outlined above: that flows of permanent or semi-permanent, consumption-oriented migration to a particular destination more often than not arise out of pre-existing flows of short-term vacation tourism to that destination. In other words, consumption-oriented migrants usually formulate the idea and acquire the desire, knowledge and confidence to relocate either permanently or semi-permanently to a particular destination only after having visited that destination as vacation tourists. As such, vacation tourism often functions as a springboard propelling individuals into more permanent forms of consumption-oriented migration.

The second geographical facet concerns what these authors express as the 'provision of basic infrastructures that facilitate in-migration' (Williams 2000). Whereas the first facet concerned the identification of destinations and flows of consumption-oriented migration to these destinations, this second facet deals with the accumulation, or development, of desirable consumer-oriented amenities and services in specific regions and local destinations. In a nutshell, the idea here is that short-term tourism provides the impetus for the development of consumer-oriented amenities and services in a particular area, which, in turn, begins to make the area appealing as a destination for more enduring forms of consumption-oriented migration. This notion closely relates to R.W. Butler's (1980) groundbreaking theoretical model for a resort destination's cycle of evolution, which sets forth a life cycle of stages of development and decline for a resort area. This notion also relates to subsequent applications of Butler's model which have been applied to retirement destinations (e.g. Foster & Murphy, 1991; Hovinen, 1982; Truly, 2002). All of these ideas dovetail with the basic premise that consumption-oriented migration to a particular destination and the development of consumer-oriented amenities and services in that destination are provocatively related stimuli in a feedback loop that generates the progressive development of a tourist industry in a destination. In other words, more tourists prompt the creation of new and improved consumer-oriented amenities and services. These new and improved amenities and services, in turn, serve to attract more tourists; and, like this, the feedback loop of consumer-oriented growth and development evolves in this destination until the limits of capacity are attained, at which point the cycle stalls into stages of stagnation and decline. Erik Cohen's (1972) work serves as an excellent complement to this discussion, as he helps to explain how both the absolute volume and overall social identity of tourists visiting a particular destination also evolve over time through several distinct phases as the destination matures. The overall point to be emphasized here is that there exists a well-documented and established correlation between the evolution of short-stay vacation tourism, the development of consumer-oriented amenities and services, and the creation of distinct flows of more permanent forms of consumption-oriented migration to a particular destination or area. It is at the end of this chain of correlation where I wish to situate the phenomenon of residential tourism, which is the resulting lifestyle and practices of a particular type of (semi-)permanent, consumption-oriented migration.

Moving beyond this consideration regarding how short-stay vacation tourism relates to residential tourism, it becomes necessary to explore residential tourism's close association with another specific type of consumption-oriented migration: international retirement migration (IRM). While IRM and residential tourism share many practical similarities, they must be treated as two distinct theoretical phenomena for several important reasons. To illustrate their conceptual differences I will utilize certain contextual elements from the Boquete case study, so that in the process I may also begin to illuminate some demographical information about Boquete's residential tourist population.

First, it is valid to say that the majority of the residential tourist cohort in Boquete undertook a process of IRM to reach Boquete. The overwhelming majority of residential tourists in Boquete are of retirement age, being between 50 and 70 years of age. They are also predominantly retired from professional careers and, therefore, generally rely upon retirement savings and/or pension funds to provide for their living expenses in Boquete. However, there are notable exceptions among this cohort. These include several residential tourists who are significantly younger than what is generally considered to be 'retirement age', as well as residential tourists who, despite having retired from their professional careers and in the absence of pressing financial imperatives to work, have created small businesses or cottage industries in Boquete. As such, a critical problem with IRM as a label for the phenomenon taking place in Boquete is that 'being retired' simply does not apply to the entire residential tourist cohort.

While international retirement migration effectively describes the initial *process of migration* which most residential tourists undertake in order to reach Boquete, the terminology of IRM simply is not adequate to refer to the lasting *residential experiences, effects* and *identities* which continue to develop and persist long after the physical process of migration has occurred. In this way, I interpret the domain of IRM and similar forms of consumption-orientated migration to relate to the transitory processes and phenomena directly associated with migration, while the domain of residential tourism is better suited to refer to the enduring consumer-oriented practices and experiences, as well as the general effects, of this particular type of foreign residence.

Despite these differences, the existing body of literature concerning IRM theory and practice is quite helpful for establishing the contextual foundations of residential tourism. In fact, given that the body of IRM scholarship is much more established than that of residential tourism, there is much knowledge to be gained from a brief overview of IRM theory. While IRM theory does not critically and directly inform the direction of this work, it nonetheless provides important insights into the forces and motivations that draw residential tourists to destinations such as Boquete.

Contributions of IRM

According to Williams, King and Warnes, in the most general of terms IRM may be regarded as a 'highly selective migration process which redistributes [retired] individuals – and their concomitant incomes, expenditures, health and care needs – across international boundaries' (1997: 132). Similar to other types of consumption-oriented migration, the practical nature of IRM is such that its migrants generally flow in geographical directions which directly contrast patterns of labor-oriented migration; hence consumption-oriented migration is often referred to as 'counter-stream migration'. As such, while labor-oriented migration in the European and Pan-American contexts generally flows in a south to north direction, from lesser to more developed geographical regions,

IRM typically flows in the opposite direction, from north to south, towards areas with two desirable attractions: a warm, pleasant climate and a relatively lower cost of living. Essentially, this is the purpose of IRM (and the drive behind residential tourism): to achieve a higher quality of life for a lower cost of living.

Significantly, within the past decade IRM has experienced both an impressive expansion, in terms of the spatial scope of its reach, as well as a pronounced increase, in terms of a growing number and diversity of individuals participating in this type of migration. This is important for our case study, given that the overwhelming majority of residential tourists have migrated to Boquete only within the past five to seven years. Only two or three decades ago IRM was considered either a luxury of the socioeconomic elite – such as the custom of wealthy, older European elites who famously retire to the Spanish, French and Italian rivieras – or otherwise a downright socially unorthodox act – such as the occasional North American retiree relocating to a hippie or artist community in México. In both cases the absolute volume of IRM flows was small and the geographical scope of host destinations quite limited. Today, however, IRM has evolved not only to accommodate a larger socioeconomic group (including more individuals from the middle class), but also to become a more socially acceptable practice among mainstream retiree populations, particularly in North American and Western European societies (Williams & Patterson, 1998). Furthermore, IRM flows have expanded impressively in geographical scope just within the past few years. This is perhaps best reflected in the geographical diversity of regions represented in *Fortune* magazine's list of its five 'idyllic' retirement destinations for 2005. Included in this list are previously obscure destinations in Argentina, Croatia, México, Thailand and, incidentally, a small highland community in Panamá named Boquete.

In abstraction, IRM, similar to residential tourism, is both product and agent of the ubiquitous phenomena of globalization and modernization. To be precise, however, scholars cite a number of factors, which, taken as a cumulative whole, help to explain why IRM has gained impressive momentum in recent years. It is important to understand that no single factor is capable of fully accounting for IRM's recent increase in popularity; rather the reasons are multiform and interwoven. First, retirees of the 21st century generally are healthier, younger and more active than their predecessors. The average retirement age has progressively fallen throughout Europe and North America since the Second World War (Williams *et al.*, 1997). When concomitant advances in health care and medicine during the same period are also considered, the resulting implications are that, in addition to there being more 'young old' retired persons today, there are also more retired persons who are leading more active and healthier lives further into old age (King *et al.*, 1998; Williams & Hall, 2000).

Furthermore, over the past 50 years, social attitudes and perceptions regarding what it means to be retired have also undergone an evolutionary process of extraordinary proportions. Gerontologist Anthony Warnes contends that 'old age has been converted from a short "empty" period marred by ill health and physical or mental incapacities, to a "third age" of life during which new social and recreational activities are pursued' (1992: 181). Indeed, increasingly, retirement is evolving into a period of reward for one's lifelong career of hard work, as mainstream social views begin to regard retirement as a 'golden age' of leisure and consumption.

In addition, several scholars contend that the recent boom in IRM is the deferred result of increasingly mobile lifestyles, which have developed during the lifetime of the baby boomer generation; a colossus generational cohort – consisting of roughly 77 million individuals, or approximately one-quarter of the total population, in the United States alone – which, at the start of the new millennium, began to take its first steps into the life stage of retirement (MetLife Mature Market Institute, 2005). Certainly, the baby boomer generation's sheer size alone may partially account for IRM's increase in volume during the past decade. However, equally influential, if not more so, are the monumental social transformations of mobility, tourism and retirement that this generation has witnessed over its lifetime. This generation is, in many ways, a social vanguard introducing a new and dynamic brand of retirement living. To be sure, this was the first generation to grow up during an age of mass international travel, both for business and for pleasure. The collective personality of this generation is perhaps best characterized by the AARP in its introduction to a baby boomer travel study that the organization recently published:

> Boomers see themselves as younger than their age might imply and a majority consider themselves adventurous. They certainly consider themselves more adventurous than their parents. Findings from the current study suggest that a fair percentage of boomers have traveled to exciting and exotic destinations. Many have participated in adventurous activities not only while on adventure travel but also as a part of their leisure activities. (Davies, 2005: 3)

Given that the baby boomer generation is accustomed to highly mobile lifestyles, in which 'adventure' is often the desired outcome of travel, it is not surprising that even a small percentage of this massive generation will seek to continue these lifestyles of mobility and adventure well into retirement. This, of course, relates back to the earlier discussion of vacation tourism's strong connections to consumption-oriented migration, IRM and residential tourism.

Furthermore, in identifying factors which might help to explain why IRM has gained impressive momentum within the past decade, scholars have pointed out that many of the mobility and communication barriers that previously deterred IRM on a widespread level have been conquered in recent years. The dawning of hyper-efficient transportation and communication technologies – such as the increased availability of daily, non-stop international flights, as well as the ubiquity of the internet, and satellite television and telephone technologies – now allow transnational identities to flourish with ease like never before. According to John Urry (1995), this march towards greater interconnectedness is part of a larger process of 'global miniaturization,' which implies not only greater ease of international connectivity, but also greater ease of procuring the comforts of home – in the form of familiar amenities and services – throughout the globe.

On a similar note, increased labor mobility during the baby boomer generation's lifetime has, as Allan Williams and C. Michael Hall contend, 'contributed to the geographical dispersion of friendship and family networks,' which provide retirees of the 21st century with less of an incentive to remain 'at home' during their retirement years (2000: 8). In fact, Urry argues that increased residential mobility, an expanding spatial dispersion of family and social ties and, by extension, a weakening of place-based communities in advanced capitalist societies all culminate in the growing 'de-traditionalization' of social life. According to his theory, the 'stripping away of the centrality' of traditional social institutions rooted in place now allow individuals and groups more freedom to establish 'new sociations', or social institutions, that are not hamstrung by conventional socio-spatial constraints (1995: 220). Applying this theory to the present context, IRM may be seen as a means for retirees to establish new sociations in idealized destinations located beyond the limits of traditional socio-geographical boundaries; new sociations which coalesce around tourist-like lifestyles of leisure and consumption in 'exotic' and unconventional destinations. In this regard, the social practice of residential tourism may very well be a strategic, 21st century response by the 'third age' to the deterioration of the cohesive nuclear family and the disintegration of tight-knit, place-based communities 'back home'. Residential tourism may very well serve as a practice to invigorate with new meaning and purpose the realities of retirement in a time of diffuse socio-spatial relationships.

Towards New Understandings

Despite the relatively small number of scholars devoted to exploring IRM and residential tourism, the theoretical and practical advancements made within the past 10 to 15 years have been impressive and unconditionally illuminating, as evidenced above. Nevertheless, much of my motivation for pursuing this research endeavor arises from what I perceive to be significant knowledge gaps and regional biases in IRM and residential tourist studies.

Regarding the latter deficiency, with only few exceptions, IRM and residential tourist scholarship, to date, has primarily existed as the exclusive domain of European scholars investigating these phenomena in their European contexts (e.g. Buller & Hoggart, 1994; Casado-Diaz, 1999; Clavé, 1998; King *et al.*, 1998; O'Reilly, 1995; Raya, 1994; Rodriguez, 2001; Vera, 1997; Warnes, 1992, 1994; Williams *et al.*, 1997, 2000; Williams & Hall, 2000; Williams & Patterson, 1998). In fact, despite the voluminous flows of IRM currently channeling into Latin America, despite the decades-old presence of residential tourism in countries such as México and Costa Rica, and despite its recent emergence in countries like Argentina, Belize, Guatemala, Honduras, Nicaragua and Panamá, there exists only one published work of research-supported scholarship concerning these issues in the Latin American context. This is geographer David Truly's (2002) research paper, in which he presents a conceptual matrix of IRM, and briefly explores changes to the social composition and attitudes of the expatriate community in Lake Chapala, México. It goes without saying that we know very little about IRM and residential tourism in the Latin American context beyond superficial data, even though we can be certain that these dynamic phenomena create significant impacts upon the places and people they affect. Indeed, Kevin McHugh certifies retirement migration as 'nothing less than a grand social experiment in escapism and community, an experiment in progress with profound social, cultural and political implications' (2003: 173). This is especially true at the local level, where population growth and economic development initiated by retirement migration and residential tourism possess the catalytic potential to wholly remake places and dramatically alter the social fabric of communities. Thus, by exploring residential tourism in Boquete, I hope to begin the monumental and important work of examining the impacts of IRM and residential tourism in Latin America at the local level, so that a regional bias in the study of these emerging topics may begin to be corrected. As these phenomena promise to become more prevalent and influential throughout Latin America in the coming decades, it is critical that we immediately begin to explore their social, cultural, economic, political and environmental effects.

A second contribution I hope to make with this work is, at the very least, to probe and illuminate the depths of experiential gaps in knowledge regarding social interactions and place experiences among inhabitants of residential tourist destinations. To date, the bulk of IRM and residential tourist research has tended to focus on quantitative and socio-demographic lines of inquiry. Certainly, these research endeavors are valuable and necessary first steps into emerging fields of research such as these topics present. However, for all of the strengths that the existing bodies of IRM and residential tourist literature provide, few, if any, of these works present any insight into what daily life is really like in emerging destinations for IRM and residential tourism, such as Boquete.

Building a Framework[3]

From the beginning this research project has aimed to explore the nature of everyday interaction between two ostensibly diverse groups of residents inhabiting a shared living space in which residential tourism was developing. In the case of Boquete, the primary residential groups are the mestizo-dominant, Spanish-speaking native residents and the white-dominant, English-speaking foreign residential tourists. In addition to the obvious linguistic, racial and cultural differences existing between these residential groups, they are further distinguished by vast socioeconomic disparity and diverse social patterns and lifestyles. When all of these considerations are situated in the spatial context of intimate residential coexistence, it becomes clear that this situation bears the distinct potential for class and cultural conflicts to develop. However, this dynamic and novel context of residential coexistence also presents possibilities for positive intercultural exchange, productive modernization and development, and the creation of a vibrantly diverse community of inhabitants with an impressive variety of backgrounds, traditions and tastes. What then are the everyday contexts of living and socializing like in these dynamic places where residential tourism is emerging? To be certain, the only way to explore this question is through a qualitative study of residents' actual perceptions and personal experiences of their immediate socio-spatial realities.

In retrospect, while this book does not squarely confront the question posed above, it does shed a great amount of light on residents' everyday realities and experiences in places where residential tourism has taken root. By remaining flexible and evolving with the direction

that the research process led me, I came to discover residents' multiform experiences of and meanings for place to be a critical issue of
importance and an indirect path for exploring my question posed
above. Indeed, place experience is a channel of illumination through
which people articulate greater ideas about their social and individual
identities, as well as a frame through which the researcher may understand his subjects' perceptions of and values for themselves and their
surrounding world.

Given that my research agenda for this work required qualitative
research methods, I felt a strong burden, as Norman Denzin and Yvonna
Lincoln advocate, to 'study things in their natural settings, [to attempt] to
make sense of, or interpret, phenomena in terms of the meanings people
bring to them' (1994: 2). With this self-imposed obligation in mind, I
quickly came to the realization that in order to engage *all* residents of
Boquete in a common discussion about their daily lives, experiences and
social interactions, I had to locate a common experience to which all residents could relate and about which they could all authoritatively speak. It
quickly became clear to me that place was this unifying experience, which
literally bound all of Boquete's diverse residents together despite their
many differences.

By exploring the range of place experiences and place meanings among
these inhabitants, there exists an opportunity to learn about residents'
situated identities, values, social interactions, daily routines and meanings for their lives in this place. Furthermore, there exists an opportunity
to learn about how Boquete's residents frame and articulate their values,
experiences and perspectives of their lives in this place. Indeed, Edward
Relph asserts that the 'meanings of places may be rooted in the physical
setting and objects and activities, but they are not property of them –
rather they are property of human intentions and experiences' (1976: 47).
Building on this idea, I began to redirect my research focus towards
exploring place identity as a means to learn more about the everyday
residential experience in places affected by residential tourism. However,
'place is not a simple undifferentiated phenomenon of experience that is
constant in all situations, but instead has a range of subtleties and significances as great as the range of human experiences and intentions,' Relph
(1976: 26) further contends. As such, my line of inquiry continued to
evolve towards an exploration concerning *why* these coresidential groups
share a place of residence, *how* each group experiences daily life in this
place differently and *what* meaning this place holds for each. Yet, again,
Relph tells us that it is 'not just the identity *of* place that is important, but
also the identity that a person or group has *with* that place, in particular

whether they are experiencing it as an insider or as an outsider,' (1976: 45, emphases in original). Accordingly, I expanded my line of inquiry so as to incorporate an investigation into how these inhabitants' relationships with their place of residence is changing over time, within the temporal context of this tumultuous era of residential tourism growth and development in Boquete.

Out of this evolving process of revision I produced the following four primary research questions, which I will directly explore in this book. How do native and foreign residents experience their shared place of residence? What prevailing meaning does this place hold for each residential group? In a social context, what is being created and what is being destroyed during the contemporary process of residential tourist growth and development? And lastly, within the context of residential tourist growth and development, what is the evolving nature of residents' relationships with their place of residence? By exploring these four basic questions, this book endeavors to investigate a number of – hitherto unexplored – social, cultural and spatial effects of residential tourism at a local level.

Book Overview

In the next chapter I undertake a detailed theoretical analysis of the concepts of place and landscape, exploring the socio-historical contexts and repositories of meaning that each concept embodies. To assist in this exploration, I engage in a thorough, interdisciplinary review of the varied significances of place and landscape, most notably in cultural geography. Here I also examine how the entities of place and landscape – part physical objects, part social creations – are experienced from a diverse range of social perspectives including, most importantly, insiders and outsiders. This chapter ultimately aims to establish the theoretical lens through which I will explore, interpret and analyze residents' experiences of Boquete in subsequent chapters.

In Chapter 3, I complement the theoretical framework constructed in the previous chapter by establishing the practical geographical, socio-economic and historical contexts of Boquete. This expansive exploration of the origins, historical development and present-day context of life in Boquete reveals a dynamic community whose overarching identity is the product of a unique fusion of foreign and local influences that have blended together over the past century. This analysis of the various contexts of Boquete rightly establishes the proper foundation for investigating the impacts of residential tourism on place and community in upcoming chapters.

In Chapter 4, I advance from the contextual platform established in the previous two chapters to a qualitative investigation of residential tourists' actual experiences of Boquete. This chapter begins by analyzing the promoted image of Boquete as a residential tourist destination, which is marketed and advertised to the outside world through print and Internet media. From this analysis I identify four main tropes which characterize how Boquete is promoted to outsiders as an idealized destination for residential tourism; the sum of these tropes I term the 'promotional grand image' of Boquete. This promotional grand image serves to establish a conceptual basis against which residential tourists' actual experiences of Boquete are compared in the following section. In this second section, I present and analyze residential tourist informants' actual experiences of Boquete, as articulated during one-on-one interviews. I find that their experiences fundamentally evince an alienated relationship with their surroundings as landscape, which ultimately holds important implications regarding, among other issues, their patterns of social interaction with the native community and their attachment to Boquete as a permanent and meaningful place of home.

Subsequently, in Chapter 5, I complement the analysis of residential tourists' experiences of Boquete by examining how native residents experience their place of home. I find that while native residents have traditionally maintained secure ties to place and a strong sense of community, subsequent residential tourist growth and development appear to be contributing to degenerative processes that are estranging native inhabitants from place and community. In particular, I identify three distinct processes of estrangement: the experiential alienation of individuals from community, the commodification of familial land into alienable real estate property and, in the most extreme, the permanent and physical displacement of inhabitants from their homes in Boquete.

Following the detailed, qualitative exploration into how residents articulate their experiences of Boquete during this era of residential tourism growth and development, the final chapter begins with a reexamination of the overall phenomenon of residential tourism. I argue for a theoretical understanding of residential tourism as a complex, multidimensional phenomenon whose numerous impacts are both destructive and constructive for the places and communities it affects. In the second section, I return to the present state of affairs in Boquete, where the previous two chapters left off, to speculate on three possible scenarios for the future of Boquete and its fragmented identity. In addition, I propose the idea of landscape nomadism, which I intend to characterize a particular segment of highly mobile residential tourists who move from place to place in pursuit of an elusive landscape of residential tourist paradise. Finally, I conclude with some suggestions for future research and a final note regarding the significance of landscape to the residential tourist experience. In the end, I argue that landscape affords its beholder the indulgence to transcend, if only in his mind, the imperfect world around him in order to arrive at an ethereal vision of what he wishes this world to be. However, this detached perspective is an irresponsible relationship with one's immediate world because it excuses the beholder of his responsibilities to this world around him by obscuring his inescapable interconnectedness *with* it.

Conclusion

As both an agent and product of the processes of globalization and modernization, residential tourism is an experiment in progress that is taking places and people towards unprecedented futures. At the global level, residential tourism is but a minor function of these ubiquitous, earth-changing processes. However, at the local level, it is a potent, transformative force capable of wholly remaking places through tremendous acts of creation and destruction within the brief span of a few years. A powerful force such as this, once set in motion, becomes difficult to manage and control.

The first residential tourists arrived in Boquete less than a decade ago. Among the coffee farmers and verdant mountain slopes, they set out to create permanent homes and establish enduring roots in this place. Less than 10 years later, amidst an underdeveloped region of Panamá, Boquete is rapidly growing and wildly developing beyond expectations and beyond control. Gated communities for the emerging class of super-rich residential tourists are being erected alongside working coffee farms employing indigenous workers who live in an anachronistic, harsh reality of poverty, institutionalized discrimination and malnutrition. Land prices in the district have skyrocketed by as much as 500% within the past five years, creating a bona fide real estate frenzy. Meanwhile, the residential tourist population is increasing exponentially, having surged by roughly 2000% within the last decade.

Less than 10 years ago, amidst a terrible economic crisis, native Boqueteños welcomed residential tourism with open arms as the community's economic savior. However, within just a few short years, the savior they welcomed now threatens to remake the district into an aesthetic- and consumption-oriented landscape and uproot its inhabitants from their meaningful links with community and place. Controlled by no one, yet propelled by many, residential tourism is rapidly leading Boquete into an unknown future. Incredibly, this is but a fragment of the extraordinary chronicle of residential tourism's coming of age in Boquete to be explored in this book.

Notes

1. 'Si bien la definición del turismo convencional, por ejemplo aquella que utilice el Banco Mundial en sus estadísticas, identifica a un turista como alguien que … vive menos de un año en el país que visita, cómo definir a un turista que llega a nuestro país y nunca se va, y cuyos ingresos provienen del exterior y que, por lo tanto, desde el punto de vista de la contabilidad nacional sus gastos son exportaciones de servicios de Panamá? ¿Qué tal si a ese segmento le llamamos Turismo Residencial? A lo mejor te suena extraño, pero hay mucha gente que no quiere seguir viviendo en su país natal, y cuando se jubilan, o antes, deciden probar suerte en otro lado. Ese otro lado, en el caso que nos incumbe, puede ser Panamá. En este país se estima que hay 2,500 familias de ese tipo.'
2. All in-text English translations appearing in this work are courtesy of the author.
3. See Appendix 3 for complete methodological research notes.

Chapter 2

Spatial Interpretations: Seeing Landscape, Sensing Place

Introduction

The primary aim of this chapter is to establish a firm theoretical foundation for subsequent chapters in which I will present and analyze the various ways that residents experience Boquete during the present era of residential tourist growth and development. These experiences are fundamentally channeled through two spatial mediums: landscape and place. As such, in this chapter I engage a collection of interdisciplinary literature, albeit primarily geographical in focus, in order to establish precise and thoroughly differentiated theoretical interpretations for the concepts of landscape and place.

First, I explore landscape as a complex idea with layers of material, cultural, perceptual and representational meaning. Owing to this multilayered significance, landscape manifests itself in a variety of forms, both tangible and intangible. While the idea of landscape over time has become explicitly dissociated from much of its original meaning, the concept, nevertheless, continues to carry implicit ideological significance. As such, I explore landscape as a historical creation ideologically associated with certain ideas regarding power, perspective, property and nature. Ultimately, this section builds toward an interpretation of landscape as an alienated and ideologically informed 'way of seeing' the surrounding world.

In oppositional terms to landscape as an alienated, visual experience, place is constituted as an intimate, multisensory experience. In particular, the experience of place is explored as shared meaning at the collective level of community and in the context of a multidimensional and all-enveloping experience of complete fusion between subject and object. From this interpretation of place, the analysis then widens in scope to explore the conditions of placeness and placelessness, so as to situate a particular notion of place, as set forth above, among a wider range of place experiences.

Landscape

...as an idea

'Landscape is at once patently obvious and terrifically mystified' writes Don Mitchell. 'The more the word landscape is used, the greater its ambiguity' (1996: 2). Indeed, in the academic domain alone, the term has been variously employed to denote an entire spectrum of conceptions, ranging from a geographical unit of area with physical and cultural dimensions (e.g. Sauer, 1967) to a purely ideological symbol (e.g. Cosgrove, 1984, 1985; Daniels & Cosgrove, 1988). Enumerating a few of the concept's various meanings Mitchell states that landscape may be understood as 'a picture representing a view, the art of depicting that view, the (human and natural) landforms of a region, a "way of seeing", or the area that can be comprehended in a single view' (1996: 2). In an effort to reconcile the multiple significances of the concept, Denis Cosgrove argues for an understanding of landscape as having various layers of meaning and different meanings depending on the context.

Striving to formulate a basic conceptual definition for landscape, which will apply to all the various layers of meaning, Cosgrove arrives at a unifying principle:

> [The] unifying principle derives from the active engagement of a human subject with [a] material object. In other words landscape denotes the external world mediated through subjective human experience in a way that neither [the terms of] region nor area immediately suggest. Landscape is not merely the world we see, it is a construction, a composition of that world. Landscape is a way of seeing the world. (Cosgrove, 1984: 13)

By this reasoning, Cosgrove directs the idea of landscape away from a fundamental entity grounded in the material world and towards an understanding of landscape as a product of human perception: an image of the land. In concordance with this shift, Malcolm Andrews asserts that the modern notion of landscape possesses more currency as culturally and subjectively informed concept than as an objective, physical entity. It is precisely this conceptual significance of landscape that we will explore in this section by surveying the works of some notable advocates of this interpretation.

Moving beyond Cosgrove's unifying principle, as the least common denominator, or core layer, of significance, the landscape idea has multiple layers of meaning which build one on top of the other and interact to create a complex and intricate conceptual whole. First, there is a *material* layer to the notion of landscape, as landscapes on a most fundamental level imply a human relationship with the physical world. Constituent to the notion of landscape are the objective forms, whether encountered or created, which exist 'out there' in the world and which serve as the material referents to our perceptual formation of landscapes.

Indeed, there are certain cultural geographers, such as James and Nancy Duncan (2004), who endeavor to demonstrate how material landscapes – as land that has been shaped and transformed in accordance with certain aesthetic conventions – come to symbolize and showcase certain ideologies of power, class and taste. This material layer of significance directly relates to an object being appropriated by a human subject, such as in the subject-object relationship that Cosgrove describes above. In this relationship, the object is those material and observable things in space which one may appropriate – either physically or visibly – to create a landscape. In certain instances, a material object is the outcome of the production of landscape, such as in the case of landscape paintings, photographs, postcards, manicured lawns, ornamental gardens and so forth. This material transformation of land into landscape – which Raymond Williams (1973) calls the 'self-conscious development of landscape' – carries social currency because of a second layer in landscape's meaning.

In a closely related, second meaning, landscapes also are *cultural* products: the material and perceptual consequences of a 'collective human transformation of nature' (Cosgrove, 1984), in which landscapes assume significance according to their culturally agreed-upon iconological values. This is what Andrews means when he discusses the cultural construction of landscapes:

> [We] carry culturally prefabricated mental templates with us wherever we go and ... what we see and reflect upon is continually adjusted to those templates. What is new is always accommodated to what is familiar. ... A landscape, then, is what the viewer has selected from the land, edited and modified in accordance with certain conventional ideas about what constitutes a 'good view'. (1999: 4)

According to this constructionist interpretation, the value of landscapes are not so much inherent to the external scenes and objects as they are created and imbued with meaning by the perceiver according to his existing set of cultural values. This cultural layer of significance refers to our internal landscape manuals, or templates, which help us to distinguish and appreciate discrete landscapes from among the seamless and infinite panorama of spaces, sights and scenes that we encounter in our everyday lives (ibid). This layer of significance fundamentally relates to the variation of cultural values concerning aesthetics and, in particular, the visual composition of a 'good' or extraordinary view.

However, that landscape ultimately must be perceived by an individual's faculty of vision accommodates a third, highly subjective *perceptual* layer of meaning. Despite the cultural 'templates' that help us to recognize and appreciate distinct landscapes, much of the process of seeing landscapes nevertheless is a personal and, therefore, subjective visual experience. Discussing the subjective qualities of landscape that art illuminates, Cosgrove writes that, 'the artistic use of landscape stresses a personal, private, and essentially *visual* experience' (14, emphasis in original). In fact, this visual component of the landscape idea is made clear throughout Cosgrove's (1984) work, in which landscape is fundamentally explored as the subjective illusion of the surrounding world and those who appear in this world, as perceived by an individual, detached observer.

While in theory it is important to differentiate between the cultural and perceptual layers of landscape's meaning, in practice these layers virtually function together so seamlessly that the process of landscape perception encompasses both personal/visual and cultural elements at once. The blending of these two layers – and, indeed, the material layer as well – is evident below, as Andrews describes the 'intricate process of discrimination' in our everyday perception of landscapes:

> We are selecting, editing, suppressing or subordinating some visual information in favour of promoting other features. We are constructing a hierarchal arrangement of the components within a simple view so that it becomes a complex mix of visual facts and imaginative construction. The process of marking off one particular tract of land as aesthetically superior to, or more interesting than, its neighbours is already converting that view into the terms of art; it is what we do as we aim the camera viewfinder. (1999: 3)

Here, in another reference to landscape's close relationship to art, Andrews conceives of landscape as: 'mediated land, land that has been aesthetically processed. It is land that has arranged itself, or has been arranged by the artistic vision, so that it is ready to sit for its portrait' (1999: 7).

The cultural association between landscape and art, a relationship bridged by aesthetics, in fact points to a fourth layer of meaning: a *representational* layer in which landscape is interpreted and represented through cultural texts, such as paintings, films, novels, photographs, and the like. While not all manifestations of landscape produce material objects, it is important to note that all landscapes indeed are representational texts, or symbols, encoded with moral, political, social and cultural meaning that signifies a particular ideological interpretation of the observable world. Stephen Daniels and Denis Cosgrove affirm this idea, declaring that a 'landscape park is more palpable but no more real, nor less imaginary, than a landscape painting or a poem' (1988: 1). The critical value of landscape, then, lies not in its represented form, its symbolic shell, but rather in its underlying, representational meaning.

Figure 2.1   René Magritte: *La Condition Humaine*, 1933. Image courtesy of the Board of Trustees, National Gallery of Art, Washington.

Taken together, the idea of landscape contains material, cultural, perceptual and representational layers of meaning. Two important points regarding the fundamental idea of landscape are worthy of explicit reiteration here.

The first is that landscapes are not inherently material objects; rather they are mediated, representational symbols, sometimes abstract, sometimes concrete. The second important point is that all landscapes, by definition, are human creations and, in particular, cultural products. Landscapes are made, not encountered. Sometimes their manufactured origins are obvious, other times their artificial origins are deceptively encoded or obscured from plain sight. Andrews alludes to these two points concerning the idea of landscape during his endlessly fascinating analysis of René Magritte's painting, *La Condition Humaine* (Figure 2.1). Discussing Magritte's perceptual play with the representation of a landscape appearing almost seamlessly across two distinct spatial planes, Andrews conjectures that:

> This is Magritte's literalizing of a cultural change in our perception of landscape. Or is 'nature' simply an idea we need to construct for that which is *beyond* the painted, framed object? Perhaps the 'original' has in some respects never been other than a construction, a fabric of our perceptions determined by cultural conventions and changing human needs. To what extent does the formal framing of a view of the natural world – the window view of Romanticism as much as the framed, painted landscape – not just enhance but produce the sense that there is such a thing as unframed landscape? Is that sense of a real, wild landscape beyond the frame just as much an illusion as the framed, painted view of it? And is *that* unanswerable question, graphically posed in Magritte's painting, what he means when he entitles it 'The Human Condition'? (127, emphases in original)

That unanswerable question brings us back to Cosgrove's original idea regarding the equivocality of the landscape idea. Landscape perception is fundamental to the way that many people relate to their surroundings, yet the implications for how this 'way of seeing' (Berger, 1977) affects place experience and situated human interaction remain deeply obscured from our everyday collective consciousness (Cosgrove, 1984; Mitchell, 1996).

It is because of this mystification that landscape remains such a rich fountain of encoded cultural, social, and spatial significance. Cosgrove argues that:

> Indeed it is in part precisely the dual ambiguity which purchases landscape's continued value in a geography which aims to comprehend terrestrial space as both subject and object of human agency, in a geography which finds its aims and methods more closely aligned to those of the humanities and their hermeneutic modes of understanding than with the natural sciences. (1984: 15)

Landscapes, as deeply encoded cultural texts, are fascinating precisely because they are infused with ideological significance that affects how we experience and relate to our surroundings and to each other.

Important to landscape's socio-cultural value as a text is Cosgrove's claim that 'the landscape *idea* is a visual ideology'. This 'visual ideology' acknowledges that landscape is a social construction – a way of seeing that is manifested in a variety of different forms and through a variety of media – as well as a reservoir of meaning that reflects perceptions and influences beliefs. It also acknowledges that landscape, as a way of seeing, is a particular way of relating to the external world which carries specific political and moral views about this external world and the spectator's relationship with and role in it (Cosgrove, 1984). D.W. Meinig has something very similar to this 'visual ideology' in mind when he contends that, 'any landscape is composed not only of what lies before our eyes, but what lies within our heads' (1979: 34). This is because even landscape as a material object is fundamentally a cultural symbol that must be effectively read and deciphered in order to be properly understood in its most basic form as a representational symbol (Andrews, 1999).

That landscape in all its forms represents and is informed by an ideological way of seeing, subtly alludes to conceptual origins that are quite political in nature. Indeed, as we shall see, landscape is a socio-cultural convention that arose out of a specific historical–cultural context and, over time, has developed close cultural associations with the ideals of nature, the countryside, utopianism, artistic representation and the aesthetics of a 'good view'.

...as historical creation

The origin of the term landscape, in its modern English form, may be traced back to the 15th century Germanic word *landschaft*, denoting land immediately adjacent to a town (Andrews, 1999) or, alternatively, 'an area of known dimensions like the fields and woods of a manor or parish' (Cosgrove, 1984: 16). Despite a rich etymological and conceptual written history of landscape, for brevity's sake I shall confine my examination here to a brief review of three salient works (Andrews, 1999; Cosgrove, 1984, 1985) which probe landscape's conceptual evolution and meaning.

Significantly, the landscape idea emerges, at the historical intersection of need and capability, within the context of two thoroughly revolutionary processes dawning in Western Europe during the late 15th and early 16th centuries: the socioeconomic transition from medieval feudalism to modern capitalism, and the philosophical birth of renaissance humanism

(Andrews, 1999; Cosgrove, 1985). With regard to the latter process, the
original significance of landscape drew upon humanist advances in geom-
etry, and linear perspective techniques in particular, in order to achieve
visual and representational control over the surrounding world in a way
that complemented and, in many regards, surpassed the capabilities of
cartography. For the rational humanist, the ability to create a two-dimensional artistic representation of scenes from the surrounding world with a
stunning degree of geometric accuracy and visual depth served to demonstrate man's rational conquest over the domains of space and nature. If
maps functioned to representationally objectify territories in limited
detail, then landscape representations were their artistic, high resolution
counterparts. Landscape allowed the rational humanist the ability to
objectify and therefore exert control over his immediate environs.

    With regard to the contemporary emergence of capitalism as the new
social order, landscape quickly became appropriated as an ideological tool
of the landed, socio-political elite to exert their influence and absolute
authority as landowners over property and labor. Collectively, landscape
was employed to reinforce the emerging capitalist hegemony that was just
beginning to be defined and implemented throughout Western Europe.
Indeed, landscape was employed by political elites to naturalize the new
and inequitable politics of the capitalist system of labor, to legitimize
increasing socioeconomic stratification between the landed and landless
classes, and to solidify a nascent hegemony in which land had become
alienable, private property with new rules concerning its use and rights of
access. As a representational symbol of the capitalist hegemony, the idea
of landscape finds efficacy as an ideological technology deployed to visually represent in a concrete and illustrated form the abstract notions of
property and the new order of labor relations. To this end, Cosgrove
contends that landscape gave landowners an 'illusion of order and
control,' which not incidentally, 'complemented a very real power and
control over fields and farms' (1985: 55).

    Just as a picture is worth a thousand words – particularly at a time when
literacy was a privilege of the elite – landscape emerged as a critical
medium through which the capitalist system of land ownership and labor
relations were disseminated and naturalized as apolitical, equitable and
benevolent progress. The importance of landscape to establishing the new
hegemony is evident when Cosgrove states that, 'in painting and garden
design landscape achieved visually and ideologically what survey, map
making and ordnance charting achieved practically: the control and domination over space as an absolute, objective entity, its transformation into
the property of individual or state' (1985: 46). By materially representing –

and thereby solidifying – their claims to power, the socio-political elite literally succeeded in *real*-izing their ideological vision of the way the world and social relations in it ought to be.

Indeed, if this visionary medium concerns itself with the representation of powerful moral and socio-political *ideals*, then just as much, if not more, of landscape's rhetorical potency derives from what is *absent* or *not* represented than what is (re)present(ed) on the surface. The reality is that landscape's facade (or positive image) obscures a dark, textual underworld – or negative image – of absence, distortion, manipulation and escapism; what is left out of versions of our world represented through the medium of landscape is akin to a backroom where undesirable, diametric versions of the world are cut from view like the waste from an editor's cunning scissors.

Over successive centuries, as landscape has evolved from its original context, been elevated to a form of fine art, and become appropriated by popular culture as an aesthetic end in and of itself, landscape representations in the modern, everyday world have largely become irreferential symbols dissociated from their original context and meaning. For the most part we, as Westerners, consciously appreciate landscape only on a superficial, aesthetic level; uncritically reading only what is represented on the immediate surface, and neglecting to comprehend that, as a visionary representation, landscape ultimately is a rhetorical text which carries encoded ideological significance.

However, while most modern landscape representations may not explicitly broadcast ideological messages, Andrews cautions:

> Landscape in art can express a set of political values, a political ideology, when it is least seeming to invoke political significance. The very concept should make us wary of assuming that any representation…is wholly without programmatic content. (1999: 156)

Herein lays the deceptive nature of landscape. On the surface of landscape there is a seductively simplistic and organic facade purportedly representing a faithfully precise reproduction of the way things are in the 'real world'. However, behind each landscape there is a maker, who is interpreting, editing, framing, coloring and filtering the world as he sees it until the resulting creation of landscape becomes a fantastic blend of empirical observation and personal ideology. Indeed, no two perceptions or representations of landscapes are alike.

As we have explored above, since its nascence, the underlying purpose of landscape has been about the representation of social, political and moral ideologies concerning how our world and human relations in this world ought to be. However, as the concept of landscape has evolved over time, much of this ideological 'programmatic content' has descended into landscape's hidden conceptual undercurrent, banished from the surface, as landscape has increasingly come to be, quite literally, taken at face value as an aesthetically pleasurable 'good view'. Indeed, it seems that efforts to naturalize and apoliticize this 'programmatic content' through representations of harmonious and apolitical landscapes were so effective that, at some point, landscapes came to be valued primarily for their superficial facades or artistic forms; their abilities to represent harmonious and apolitical scenes with an emphasis on aesthetic style. What has become obscured in this growing preoccupation with landscape as a 'good view' is the absent image of implicit political references to commerce, civilization, inequitable human relations and, most recently, the alienating effects of industrialization and urbanization. Instead, what has become paramount to the modern conception of landscape as a 'good view' are its references to those spaces and settings that are least likely to explicitly invoke this absent image. Indeed, Andrews argues, as does Cosgrove (1984) and others (Cox, 1988; Lowenthal, 1982; Porteous, 1996; Williams, 1973), that over the course of landscape's history, the idea has evolved to develop primary associations with the concepts of nature, the countryside, and an imagined rural idyll. According to Andrews, this is because:

> In a natural landscape, any kind of marker of human presence and human usage – a bridge, a road, a milestone, a castle, an isolated monument – inflects that landscape, connects it however vestigially with the insignia of human control and organization. Pictures of wild scenery, without a trace of cultivation or human presence, and without any declared emblematic intent, appeal largely *because* they dramatize that landscape's own untrammeled liberty. Such landscapes constitute a gesture of defiance to what is felt to be an oppressive expansionist civilization, and are therefore infused with political meaning. Images of landscape, pastoral or sublime, are images of retreat, refuge, retirement. They are places where politically life emphatically is *not*, and therefore remind us of what is absent. (1999: 156, emphases in original)

Here is a reasonable and attractive theory to account for the intimate association between the ideas of nature and landscape, as well as to explain our collective preference for natural landscapes. Natural landscapes, indeed, allow us to escape, if only in our minds, the burdens of our civilization. However, while our collective indulgence in natural landscapes derives from our desire for escapism and retreat, I contend that we are significantly less focused on and cognizant of what we are escaping from, or, what is absent – an oppressive urban environment, political life, civilization and so forth – than what we are retreating towards, or, what is present in these landscapes: harmonious scenary, coherent expanses of open space, surreal 'nature' and so on.

Thus, while absence certainly is an important part of the composition of landscapes, in our everyday encounters with landscapes only rarely do we consciously acknowledge or explicitly understand how the absence of certain visual references to our civilization is crucial to the overall significance of how we preceive landscapes. To some extent, we can attribute our collective disregard for the role that absence plays in our appreciation of landscapes to our willful desire to appropriate landscape as a medium for escaping the imperfect and oppressive realities of our everyday world and retreating to peaceful and morally simplistic havens. We choose not to dwell on the ideological mechanics of landscape composition so as not to spoil the fantasy. However, to a certain extent, our collective mystification regarding what is absent and how it contributes to landscape's concealed ideological significance is a product of being progressively more experientially out of touch with the world around us. The more we become experientially isolated from our immediate spatial and social contexts, the more we rely on remote visual perception to make sense of the world around us.

...as power

Already it is becoming evident here that the landscape idea implies the imposition of order and control over the external world, as based on the perceiver's viewpoint regarding the way things ought to appear. In *The Lie of the Land*, which is intently concerned with the politics of landscape, Mitchell offers a simple and candid appraisal of this way of seeing: 'truly, the production of landscape is about the reproduction of power' (1996: 56). Differing slightly from Cosgrove's assertion that the landscape idea is a visual ideology, Mitchell disputes what he perceives to be a 'misguided project' in cultural geography: the notion that landscapes are '*only* representations, *only* ideological'. Instead, working off Henri Lefebvre's (1991) thesis on ideology, Mitchell argues that 'it is impossible to talk about ideology ... without examining and explaining the spaces that give that ideology currency and serve as its referent' (1996: 5).

Indeed, landscapes must be examined in their spatial contexts, not as floating and abstract ideological texts, but as referential and situated texts relevant to specific social, spatial, and temporal contexts. Having already established the critical importance of absence to the meaning of a landscape, it logically follows that in order to critically understand the full ideological significance of any particular conception of landscape, one must first understand what is missing from this particular socio-spatial representation of our world. This necessarily implies situating any representation of landscape amidst its larger social, spatial and temporal contexts; expanding the conceptual frame to explore the various contexts in which this landscape in situated from a variety of perspectives. It demands examination of who are the shapers or perceivers of this representation of landscape; and what are their beliefs, desires, and motivations for creating this representation. It further demands we examine who and what are being perceived; what are the alternative experiences of and meanings for these places and people; what are the histories of these places and people; and how do they relate on a larger socio-spatial scale to a greater world.

Having established this caveat, Mitchell goes on to effectively demonstrate how landscape is work: a work of art, worked land and, significantly, also an erasure of work. In this vein, Mitchell contends that:

> [t]o ignore the work that makes landscape, it seems to me, is thus to ignore a lot of what landscape *is*. In this manner, the production of landscape is quite similar to the production of nature that Neil Smith (1990) describes: it is a hugely mystified, ideological project that seeks to erase the very facts of its (quite social) production. (1996: 6, emphasis in original)

Indeed, Mitchell makes an excellent point here to propose that *erasure* – the erasure of work involved in manufacturing landscape – is the source of much of landscape's appeal. This idea squarely relates to the above discussion regarding the centrality of escapism and retreat to the idea of landscape. Examining the perceptive processes that frame, edit and modify land – and those who appear on the land – into landscape, Mitchell declares that these processes are the 'reckless erasure of the lives of ordinary people in order to celebrate [the landscape] as a visual spectacle' (1996: 20–21). The process of making and perceiving landscapes is much about indulgent deception; that is, crafting a manipulated and ideological interpretation of our world, then erasing evidence of its artificiality so that it appears natural, 'authentic' and, above all else, pleasurable. This requires erasing, overlooking or obscuring from view any unpleasant elements or symbols that might remind us of the social, political and economic inequalities and disharmonies upon which our world is constructed. As it relates to his historical analysis of

California's agricultural landscapes, Mitchell elaborates on his main thesis, stating that:

... images have been repeatedly called up to valorize and celebrate the 'way of life' that California agriculture had become by the turn of the century. *Only* by erasing – or completely aestheticizing – the workers who made that way of life is its celebration possible. *Only* by seeing California purely as a landscape view can we see beauty without understanding the lives of the damned who are an integral part of that beauty. And that move, erasing the traces of work and struggle, is precisely what landscape imagery is all about. (1996: 20, emphases in original)

Raymond Williams similarly makes this point regarding the politics of landscape and the erasure of the contexts of its production when he writes about the elaborate gardens and parks – the 'arranged landscapes' – of Enlightenment-era England:

Indeed it can be said of these eighteenth century arranged landscapes not only, as is just, that this was the high point of agrarian bourgeois art, but that they succeeded in creating in the land below their windows and terraces what Jonson at Penshurst had ideally imagined: a rural landscape emptied of rural labour and of labourers; a sylvan and watery prospect, with a hundred analogies in neo-pastoral painting and poetry, from which the facts of production had been banished: the roads and approaches artfully concealed by trees, so that the very fact of communication could be visually suppressed; inconvenient barns and mills cleared away out of sight ... ; avenues opening to the distant hills, where no details disturbed the general view; and this landscape seen from above, from the new elevated sights; the large windows, the terraces, the lawns; the cleared lines of vision; the expression of control and of command. (1973: 124–25)

Through a manipulated image of order, landscapes obscure, suppress, and refute social tensions and the politics of human civilization. In this regard, Cosgrove categorically asserts that landscape is a 'controlling composition of the land rather than its mirror' (1984: 270). In Williams' illustrative description, the estate owner's view of the arranged landscape serves as a visual symbol of his real power over the land and those who work this land. The landlord's possession of this naturalized view of his estate from an elevated position perfectly represents and reinforces this power. However, without knowing the contexts of this landscape's production, whose 'unnatural' or undesirable visual elements have been carefully 'emptied out', 'concealed' and 'banished' from view, there are no indicators to alert visitors to the highly contrived nature of this scene; a manufactured image of natural order, social harmony and agrarian bourgeois ideals. As Mitchell and Andrews have demonstrated, power relations – including elements of control, order, domination and oppression of one dominant group over another – and the context of the landscape's production are often obscured and mystified to outsiders who know this scene only visually and, therefore, only superficially. Owing to this alienated relationship, John Berger maintains, 'landscapes can be deceptive' (1977: 13).

...as alienated perspective

As has been made apparent above, the faculty of sight is critical to the creation and perception of landscapes. This visual appropriation of the land and those who appear on the land creates a distant relationship which makes understanding these objects limited at best. Along these lines, Yi-Fu Tuan reasons that, unlike the intimate sensations of touch, taste and smell, sight tends to be a detached experience in which objects are surveyed from a distance. Furthermore, unlike many senses which function involuntarily, sight can be easily negated by closing one's eyes or adjusting one's field of vision. As such, 'vision and attention are discriminating', Edward Relph (1976: 124) alleges. 'There are gaps in our experiences of landscapes – settings and scenes which we effectively screen out because we do not like them or do not understand them or have no interest in them'. This process of screening and framing our visual encounters with the world to create a landscape is what Andrews (1999) characterizes as a constructionist approach to landscape perception. Importantly, this constructionist approach supports the conclusion that landscape is a subjective, cultural creation that we construct, rather than an objective, natural creation that we simply encounter and observe.

An uncritical and aesthetically oriented experience of landscape is what John Punter (1982) terms the 'visual quality paradigm'. He describes this model of landscape experience as the 'aesthete's approach in its preoccupation with beauty and the formal or artistic qualities in building and the landscape, and its emphasis on subjective "sense activity" as the basis of art and beauty' (1982: 108). This paradigm contrasts with two other models that Punter articulates regarding the experience of landscape: the 'landscape perception paradigm', which is characterized by a socially conscious cognitive approach to understanding how individuals read and interpret landscapes; and the 'landscape interpretation paradigm', which is concerned with critically deconstructing the significance of landscapes as elaborate socio-cultural symbols or texts. While the latter two paradigms generally are reserved for the deliberate and critical analyses of landscape perception and meaning, the visual quality paradigm appropriately characterizes how the majority of people in advanced capitalist societies experience both everyday and exotic landscapes in their daily lives.

Commenting on this visual quality paradigm, Punter contends that this common way of seeing 'tends towards the ultimate in terms of detached external perception of the landscape' (1982: 109). This type of detached, visual experience is informed by an 'ideology of sight, distance and separation,' Cosgrove (1984) asserts. He elaborates on this claim, stating:

> Landscape distances us from the world in critical ways, defining a particular relationship with nature and those who appear in nature, and offers us the illusion of a world in which we may participate subjectively by entering the picture frame along the perspectival axis. But this is an aesthetic entrance not an active engagement with a nature or space that has its own life. (1985: 55)

Indeed, to the extent that landscape is a subjective and estranged socio-spatial experience, Andrews explores how the Western tradition of landscape art over the past six centuries stands as a record of many societies progressive disengagement with the land and a shift in emphasis from its productive value to its aesthetic value. To be sure, the distinctions between how we value land and how we appreciate its idealized representations as landscape art are ever diminishing.

Related to this idea is the transformative way that the popular diffusion of the personal camera has affected the way we experience new places and exotic landscapes. Andrews (1999), Cosgrove (1984) and Urry (1990) all suggest that this device and the way of seeing it has popularized effectively the function to commodify our encounters with new parts of the world into a series of exotic and/or aesthetically significant landscapes. Indeed, increasingly the modern practice of tourism in many ways is more about capturing and consuming images of landscape – via personal photography and sightseeing – than it is about direct social engagement and cultural interaction in these places. To this effect, Relph comments that, 'for many people the purpose of travel is less to experience unique and different places than to collect those places' (1976: 85).

Informed by this theoretical nexus of tourism, sight and consumption, Urry (1990, 1995) argues that this way of experiencing the world as consuming tourists pervades our everyday experiences in advanced capitalist societies. In these societies, Urry theorizes, hyper-mobility has had 'radical effects on how people actually experience the modern world...changing both their forms of subjectivity and sociability and their aesthetic appreciation of nature, landscapes, townscapes, and other societies' (1995: 144). With increasingly mobile lifestyles, our interactions in space become wider in scope but thinner in experience; the resulting 'tourist gaze', as Urry (1990) terms it, encourages us to become spectators and consumers of the world, collecting signs and images – as a substitute for other, more meaningful forms of interaction – as we quickly move about in a state of hyper-mobility from place to place.

The nexus of all of these ideas underlies an increasing alienation from an active, direct engagement with the places and people we encounter in our daily lives. It also indicates an institutionalized way of remotely sensing our surroundings based on an ideology of sight, distance and separation, as Cosgrove proposes. All of this points towards the singular conclusion that our experiences of the surrounding world – both physical and human – have become increasingly impersonal, experientially ever more distant and appraised more and more in aesthetic terms. As a passive and alienated visual experience of our world replaces an active and direct engagement with this world, we are required to invent meaning for the people, places and objects, from which we are dissociated. In the absence of direct, first-hand knowledge about the meaning of these places and people, we are left to color in meaning through remote observation, inference, and imagination. In essence, landscapes are becoming more and more a way we experience the world around us in advanced, post-industrial societies.

... as Commodity

It has also been implied above that landscape has increasingly evolved into a commodity to be consumed. The consumption of landscape as an aesthetic amenity relates to Urry's discussion of the tourist gaze; it takes place when we are playing the part of modern-day explorers touring new places and collecting new signs and images. In discussing modern-day tourists and their practice of commodifying landscapes, Andrews states that:

> [t]hey see a grand stretch of lakes and mountains, use the camera to frame a section of the spectacle, and take this picture, supposedly fixing it in all the softness of its living colours. Then they get it developed and printed and offer it for sale, and these terms 'take', 'capture', and 'fix' all belong to the language of appropriation. (Melvin, 2004: 82)

Aside from the dubious claim that tourists routinely sell their landscape snapshots, Andrews certainly hits the mark in describing what tourism has become for many people: a journey to foreign places so that beautiful scenes may be captured by a mirrored lens in a fraction of a second and materially appropriated as a fixed image. While this appropriation of landscape is perhaps more abstract than the creation of landscape art, both essentially have the same meaning in commoditizing and controlling an image of the land and its natural and human environment. Indeed, what could be a more deliberate and contrived creation of landscape than the meticulous actions of an inspired tourist who, with camera in hand, jockeys at a designated scenic overlook for that perfect vantage point from which he may fastidiously capture the 'naturalness' of the scene by carefully framing out of view the surrounding automobiles, trash cans, electrical lines, cigarette butts and chain-link fencing that might otherwise betray the artificiality of this snapshot of 'natural' landscape?

Landscape as a commodified image or as an aesthetic amenity is essentially the same regardless of whether it is captured as a material representation through the camera lens or whether it is captured as a mental perception through the naked eye. Indeed, in Andrews' (1999) chapter entitled, 'Framing the View', he explores how the different landscape forms are accentuated through a variety of frames, all of which effectively achieve the same function: to mediate an inside–outside, subject–object relationship, whereby an objectified image is remotely appropriated by its perceiver.

The aesthetic value of landscape can also be commodified into quantifiable monetary value as real estate property. While a 'good view' provides nothing in the way of productive or material dividends, this visual consideration nonetheless is one of the most important criteria for determining the monetary value of land in advanced capitalist societies. This is precisely what Cosgrove (1984) and Andrews (1999) have in mind when they claim that the landscape concept implies an emphasis on land for its aesthetic value rather than for its productive value. For D.W. Meinig, this modern 'speculation in land' – as 'primarily a form of capital' to be appraised based on its aesthetic value and landscape view – is a way of seeing 'landscape as wealth' (1979: 41). Individuals who see the external world from this perspective, according to Meinig, 'are wont to look upon every scene with the eyes of an appraiser, assigning monetary value to everything in view' (1979: 41).

... as restrictive 'good view'

As established earlier in this chapter, the concept of landscape is inextricably tied to a visual, detached and aesthetically oriented way of seeing the surrounding world. We have also explored above how the concept of landscape has evolved to acquire intimate cultural associations with the equally cabalistic concept of 'nature'. Indeed, Andrews (1999) argues that landscape has come to acquire a cultural currency that is generally synonymous with a 'good view' of the natural world. Cosgrove enhances this interpretation of landscape as a 'good view' by arguing that the alienated experience of our physical and human surroundings via the landscape perspective signifies a 'restrictive way of seeing,' which greatly diminishes our ability to experience the surrounding world through other, more meaningful forms of interaction. This restrictive way of seeing the world limits not only *what* we see, but also *how* we see it. Meinig (1979) implies that this way of seeing – and appraising – one's surroundings, based primarily on aesthetical considerations, fundamentally neglects to consider what non-aesthetic values, functions and meanings our physical and human surroundings might hold for others. Describing this as a 'landscape as aesthetic' perspective, Meinig contends that, 'there are many levels and varieties to this view, but all have in common a subordination of any interest in the identity and function of specific features to a preoccupation with their artistic qualities' (p. 46).

Landscape as an aesthetically oriented, yet experientially restrictive 'good view' typically corresponds with particular scenes of the emptied-out countryside, where overt political emblems are less visible, may be framed out of view or benignly naturalized into the scene, as was discussed previously in this chapter. As Andrews (1999), Cosgrove (1984) and Tuan (1998) have noted, landscapes have evolved to acquire cultural associations with leisure, relaxation, escapism from civilization and romantic ideas about 'nature' as Edenic, utopian, and morally superior to the corrupting influences of the city. Indeed, Andrews contends that the natural countryside is most often associated with landscape precisely because it is most readily perceived as harmonious and comprehensible. Of course, this (mis)reading of rural landscapes as pleasant and harmonious spaces are possible because, in a particular sense, the contexts of their production are often obscured to us as passers-by and, in a more general sense, the political significance of absence in an emptied-out landscape is often lost on us, as discussed above.

In spite of the concept's earliest implication to property, landscape in more recent times 'often *is* that which transcends human interference, which repairs division and unifies segregated territory', Andrews (1999: 157) explains. 'Landscape may include signs of property divisions but, in the Romantic mind, it will transcend these'. The 'good view' constructed is often an endless, coherent stretch of countryside disappearing into the horizon, with fences and other socio-political symbols which represent division and property having been perceptually, or perhaps even physically, excised from the scene. This 'good view' often is one not only devoid of artifacts, but also one often devoid of human presence (Melvin, 2004).

Thus landscape, as a restrictive 'good view', not only implies an ideology of sight, separation and distance, but also a deep-rooted, implicit desire to de-politicize and de-historicize a visual experience of the world so that it becomes benignly simple, thoroughly enjoyable and morally good. This is what Andrews means when he declares that landscape can 'mask' the land. This is also what Berger intends when he equates landscape to a 'curtain' behind which 'struggles, achievements and accidents' take place (1977: 15).

...as rural idyll

'As we become more urbanized and mechanized,' writes Andrews, 'the greater our appetite for landscapes without human presence, or signs of human presence – unless, that is, the human presence is organically sympathetic to landscape, such as shepherds, cottages, or cornfields' (cited in Melvin, 2004: 82). This preference for 'rural' and/or 'natural' scenes, as it is addressed above, is fundamentally based on these scenes' symbolic value as an antipode to the city, urban living and the politics of civilization. While rurality and nature are concepts with histories as convoluted and ambiguous as the landscape idea, for brevity's sake I shall employ but one scholarly interpretation for each. Respectively, these are: 'an idealized lifestyle emphasizing small-scale built landscapes, community, unhurried quietness and localism,' as Harvey Perkins (1989: 62) defines the former concept; and the nonhuman world 'out there', which is a 'profoundly human construction,' as William Cronon (1995: 25) defines for the latter.

Andrews' previous quote regarding landscape preference implicates both rurality and nature. Signifying the latter, he tells of preferred landscapes 'without human presence'; signifying the former he describes preferred landscapes with an 'organically sympathetic' human presence, such as 'shepherds, cottages, or cornfields.' While natural and rural landscapes each carry significance in their own rights, both share a fundamental commonality in that they are human constructions that represent idealized and highly nostalgic versions of a bygone world; they are, Andrews writes, 'utopian vision[s] of a world innocent of history and political meaning' (1999: 151).

If we conceptualize the city as the epicenter of civilization, and pristine 'nature' as the untouched spaces of wilderness, or the antidote of civilization, the in-between space, then, could be thought of as a 'middle landscape' (Porteous, 1996; Tuan, 1998). Elaborating on this concept, in *Escapism*, Tuan writes:

> Between the big artificial city at one extreme and wild nature at the other, humans have created 'middle landscapes' that, at various times and in different parts of the world, have been acclaimed the model human habitat. They are, of course, all works of culture, but not conspicuously or arrogantly so. They show how humans can escape nature's rawness without moving so far from it as to appear to deny roots in the organic world. The middle landscape also earns laurels because it can seem more real – more what life is or ought to be like – compared with the extremes of nature and city.... (1998: 24–5)

This utopian 'middle landscape', which is virtually synonymous with the notion of the 'rural idyll' (e.g. Buller & Hoggart, 1994; Thrift, 1987; Williams, 1973), is more an imagined space – fertile ground where our idealized conceptions of landscape can come to creative fruition – than it is a particular scene of landscape in and of itself. It is an abstract, golden-hued setting where our dreams of bucolic, utopian living take root in the collective imagination. This imagined space is saturated with cultural meaning, alternatively signifying: a 'reservoir of scenic values' (Thrift, 1987); a 'premium' space associated with safety, health, vigor (Perkins, 1989); a higher quality of life and slower pace of life (e.g. Beyers & Nelson, 2000; Buller & Hoggart, 1994); and a simple, moral alternative to the chaos and disorder of urban civilization (e.g. Andrews, 1999; Cox, 1988; Williams, 1973). In addition to these spatial attributes, the ideas of middle landscape and the rural idyll also connote temporal attributes, which recall with nostalgia a bygone era. This dimension of temporality is evident as these ideas are described as frozen in 'some kind of Golden Age'; a pre-modern, pre-industrial 'natural order' from which humanity has regrettably strayed (e.g. Andrews, 1999; Lowenthal, 1982); or a 'preferred', 'mythic' or 'valued' past which has been 'sanitized' of its history and its contexts of production (e.g. Lowenthal, 1982; Porteous, 1996; Williams, 1973).

Given the wealth of cultural significance bestowed upon the rural idyll, located in the collective imagination between the poles of 'nature' and urban civilization, it logically follows that this alluring nexus of imagined time and space is where our ideal landscapes find fertile ground to thrive in the collective imagination. The moral, social and cultural values encoded in the notion of the rural idyll are exactly what J.B. Jackson contends that middle- and upper-class Americans seek in an ideal landscape:

It comprises those spaces and structures and relationships which people of those classes are familiar with and find pleasant as a setting for their way of life. It is a spacious rural (or semirural) landscape of woods and green fields (plowed fields are suspect, hinting at mechanization or, worse yet, commercialized farming). It is a landscape of private territories, admission to which is by invitation only. The houses, substantial and usually architect-designed, are self-sufficient and somewhat withdrawn from too close a contact with their neighbors, and are surrounded by a buffer zone of lawns and shrubbery and trees. Not far away is a small forest or miniature wilderness area, tacitly recognized as the exclusive playground of the local families. Life proceeds according to a fixed schedule from one territory to another: from private house to private tennis club to parish church and private school. To pass through a gate, a portal, or a front door, or to park in a private driveway is more than merely entering: it affirms membership in a well-established group. As in a Jane Austen novel, nothing of significance happens in the public realm, and with little traffic and no sidewalks, the streets are like country roads all eventually leading to privacy and home. (1997: 72–3)

This rural idyll that Jackson conjures up closely resembles other landscape scholars' conceptions of the ideal American and British landscapes (see, respectively, Porteous, 1996; Buller & Hoggart, 1994). It also underscores the idea that landscapes may also signify romantic or utopian visions of an idealized way of life, which, almost without exception, are founded upon feelings of nostalgia for a bygone time and place. In this way, landscape is also a canvas onto which individuals in advanced capitalist societies paint their dreams and moral ideals regarding what life *ought* to be like.

In fact, there are scholars who study consumption-oriented migration from the premise that individuals will voluntarily uproot themselves from their established homes and communities, and forfeit their rooted identities to relocate over great distances in pursuit of the rural idyll manifest on earth. Two such scholars are Henry Buller and Keith Hoggart (1994), whose study explores the trend of international counter-urban migration of British residents to the rural French countryside. In this particular form of consumption-led migration, Buller and Hoggart find that what essentially motivates the British to expatriate to rural France is the lure of a perceived rural idyll and an Arcadian way of life that is not available in Great Britain:

In this context, France has come to represent the rurality that Britain is increasingly unable to provide; a rurality that is at one and the same time both an alternative to the contemporary British experience and a throwback to an idealized rural past. Furthermore, the rural dream is an essentially middle class consumption oriented one, in that it is founded upon aesthetic and non-productive notions of the role of rural space. Here, Britons moving to rural France bring with them a cultural notion of rurality that is very different from that held by the majority of existing residents. (1994: 129)

Significantly, the final sentence of the above statement underscores the idea that the image of the rural idyll has been cast over – or imposed upon – a real living place and community. This brings us back to landscape as a restrictive way of seeing which can 'mask' the land, and towards the idea of landscape as an outsider's perspective.

Outsiders and Landscape/Insiders and Place

Just as Buller and Hoggart's findings demonstrate, what is experienced as an aesthetically pleasant landscape by one individual or group may be experienced by another as a *place* of home with a wholly distinct identity and set of meanings. These contrasting experiences of a singular spatial context inform Cosgrove's (1984) dichotomies of outsider/insider and landscape/place. To illustrate these distinctions, Cosgrove appropriates an anecdote written by David Lowenthal concerning two unique responses, one by a 'sophisticated traveller' and the other by a 'responsible landowner', to a forest clearing in Appalachia during the colonial era:

> For the former the clearing was a chaotic and visually offensive scar of the pristine majesty of the forest. For the latter it was a record of pioneering effort and a symbol of his family's and the nation's future. The place was invested with a personal and social meaning that had little to do with its visual form. ... To apply the term *landscape* to their surroundings seems inappropriate to those who occupy and work in a place as insiders. Herein is a clue to the status of the landscape concept. (1962–63: 19, emphasis in original, as cited in Cosgrove, 1984)

For the insider this is not a scene to be appraised for its form; rather it is a *lived-in* and *worked-in* place that functions to shelter, sustain and provide the basic foundation for life. Unlike the outsider, Cosgrove contends that the insider cannot readily separate himself psychologically and emotionally from the scene, so as to *see* it purely in aesthetic terms as a landscape. Similar to this, Williams asserts that 'a working country is hardly ever a landscape. The very idea of landscape implies separation and observation' (1973: 120). This implies for the insider an inalienable sense of and attachment to place; a synthesis of subject and object to such a degree that they each constitute a meaningful part of the other.

Relph shares this conception of the outsider/insider dichotomy of spatial experience, contending that, 'from the outside you look upon a place as a traveller might look upon a town from a distance; from the inside you experience a place, are surrounded by it and part of it' (1976: 49). Both Cosgrove and Relph conceive of outsideness and insideness as an absolute dualism, much in the same way that absence and presence imply mutual exclusivity. While there are different degrees of outsideness and insideness (one may be physically inside but still remain experientially outside, Relph contends) and while one may cross over from outsideness to insideness (thus, the significance of thresholds, both physical and experiential) individuals are always either on one side or the other.

However, consideration of Tuan's sensory exploration of place raises one significant wrinkle in this distinction. In the 'Intimate Experiences of Place' Tuan argues that a profound experience of place is multisensory, involving 'our whole being, all our senses' (1977: 146). This intimate knowledge of place evokes phrases such as the 'texture of place' and the 'warmth of home'. Whereas the remote experience of landscape requires nothing more than the faculty of vision, the intimate experience of place requires the full sensation of immersion. As such, one cannot know place in a meaningful way from the outsider's perspective because this alienated experience denies an individual the opportunity to become intimately immersed in the experience of place.

Yet, significantly, one *can* sense landscape from a position of meaningful insideness. Indeed, just as place is multisensory, the visual sensing of one's surroundings is a very real and necessary component of the experience of place. In the anecdote above, Lowenthal allows for this by declaring that: 'The visible forms and their harmonious integration to the eye may indeed be a constituent part of people's relationship with the surroundings of their daily lives, but such considerations are subservient to other aspects of a working life with family and community' (cited in Cosgrove, 1984: 19). Certainly, landscape is an integral component of place; the ambient setting with which cherished memories and meaning become associated. For instance, Kathryn H. Kavanagh's study of the Navajo cosmology reveals that the Navajo perceive their surrounding landscape to be imbued with a 'living presence' and 'mythic and spiritual meaning' (2005: 33), which gives important meaning to their sense of place. However, it must be emphasized that for the Navajo their surrounding landscape is not appraised simply as a series of aesthetic forms from which they are experientially disconnected, but rather as a window, or visual entrance, into a repository of collective meaning concerning their unique heritage, history, spirituality and meaningful ties to the land as an ancestral place of home.

As such, while landscape is certainly a constituent part of place, its significance is interwoven with and inseparable from a larger network of multidimensional meaning, which taken as a whole constitutes the significance of place. Thus, while landscape can be sensed from within place, place fundamentally cannot be meaningfully sensed from the perspective of experiental outsideness. In addition, while landscape comprises a *part* of the meaning of place, and vision a *part* of the sense of place, place and sense of place ultimately imply a greater degree of meaning, experiential depth and collective social negotiation than the outsider's experience of landscape could ever allow.

Place

Meaning and context

While the concept of place is perhaps more intuitive than that of landscape, a concrete definition for place is no less obscure. Indeed, Tuan asserts that 'most definitions of place are quite arbitrary' (1996: 455); 'place can be as small as the corner of the room or [as] large as the earth itself'. In addition to this wide spatial range, place also elicits a broad experiential range that stretches across the entire spectrum of human interpretation. However, the specific context of place I wish to explore here is intermediate in scale on Tuan's range above, and uniquely experienced as an inimitable place of home. This is place at the local level of community; place as a field of care.

Before providing a more concrete definition of place in this context, I think it necessary to make a note of distinction concerning my use of the terms place and community in this book. In the context of this work, I intend both place and community to imply spatial as well as social significances. However, I distinguish between these two concepts based on whether the emphasis is primarily spatial or social. With place, of course, the emphasis rests on the spatial qualities of the various relationships between inhabitants, their environment and each other. With community, the emphasis of significance is social in nature; it fundamentally relates to the interactions of a defined, place-based social group, as well as their collective values and shared identity.

Having established this subtle distinction between place and community, in the context of this work, let us now proceed towards a more concrete understanding of the idea of place. Perhaps the best detailed conception of place at the level of community, and in conceptual contrast to the idea of landscape, is found in Tuan's discussion of stability and place:

> To be always on the move is, of course, to lose place, to be placeless and have, instead, merely scenes and images. A scene may be of a place but the scene itself is not a place. It lacks stability: it is in the nature of a scene to shift with every change of perspective. A scene is defined by its perspective whereas this is not true of place: it is in the nature of place to appear to have a stable existence independent of the perceiver. (1996: 447)

Important to the idea of place, then, is that it is a stable, enduring and rooted entity that supersedes any individual conception or representation. Unlike the two-dimensional facade of landscape, place is rich in depth and complexity. Furthermore, unlike landscape, place is something that is shared and recreated on a daily basis through social interaction. Place also implies a profound fusion of subject and object, as has been implied above. While landscape is 'out there', alienated and distanced from direct human experience, place, for those who experience it most profoundly as insiders, is intimate and all-enveloping.

An intense experience of place is most often associated with the idea of home, which is 'the foundation' of our identity as individuals and as members of a community, the dwelling-place of being,' Relph reasons (1976: 39). It is the 'central reference point of human existence', as well as 'the point of departure from which we orient ourselves and take possession of the world' (pp. 20, 40). From an experiential perspective, home is the center of one's known universe.

However, just as place can signify warmth and security, like a hearth, place also can feel oppressive and confining, like a prison. Relph calls this the drudgery of place, which he describes as the onerous experience of being held captive by the all-too-familiar qualities and repetitions of a place; of not having the means for escape. In this way, it is important to keep in mind that the intense experience of being rooted in place may not always be comforting and desirable.

At the community level, home is a neighborhood or town, or what Tuan calls a 'field of care'. Fields of care, Tuan asserts, 'do not seek to project an image to outsiders; they are inconspicuous visually' (1996: 447); 'they can be known in essence only from within' (p. 451). Place as a field of care implies that its inhabitants, or caretakers, share a rich collective history that acknowledges and is built upon the traditions and experiences of past generations. Furthermore, place as a field of care suggests that its inhabitants possess a strong sense of place; a sense of belonging and identifying with this place. Indeed, place as a field of care means that the identities of a place and its people are reciprocal creations. This means that inhabitants' identities are rooted in and defined by place, just as the identity of place ultimately is the product of its inhabitants. Importantly, place provides the spatial context for individual and social identities to exist. Place as a field of care also elicits strong feelings of attachment from its inhabitant caretakers. This attachment implies two dimensions: having *roots* in place over time, and sharing social *bonds* or kinship ties within the community (Hay, 1998; Riger & Lavrakas, 1981).

With regard to *bond*edness, place on the level of community is fundamentally a social creation that must be lived-in and recreated through daily interaction in order to persist. While components such as location and landscape are essential to the constitution of place, community undoubtedly is the critical ingredient to place as a field of care. The importance of community as *the* vital component of place becomes clearer in Alan Burnett's description regarding what constitutes a local community:

> [S]haring common interaction and involvement (activities) and having a sense of common identity and interests (attitudes) are significant ingredients [to community]. Interaction refers to the social network of face to face relationships amongst friends, relations, acquaintances and neighbours which may occur in a local area with varying degrees of frequency and intensity. Involvement implies the active participation in institutions and organisations (and assumes their existence). Identity consists of those feelings of belonging and attachment for places ... Finally, interests refer to common or at least compatible values and needs which people feel they share on a number of issues which confront them. When a group is integrated and its activities and attitudes tend to converge in the same local area, then this constitutes a local community. (1975: 6–7)

Within the context of place as a field of care, community – as the aggregate of individual activities, attitudes, interactions, identities and interests – is the fine-spun texture of place which can only be sensed intimately and experienced from within. 'In this context places are "public" – they are created and known through common experiences and involvement in common symbols and meanings,' Relph declares (1976: 34). The stronger one shares in these common experiences, symbols and meanings, the greater the sense of belonging, or being rooted in place and bonded with community. Of course, this statement underscores the important point that experience of place is not absolute; rather place can be sensed in

varying degrees of intimacy along a spectrum between absolute insideness and outsideness.

... and placeness

To have a sense of place, any place, is to be experientially 'on the inside',
or in Relph's terms, to experience placeness. Placeness, in the extreme, is
an authentic attitude towards place and an unselfconscious sense of place
(Relph, 1976). Authentic and unselfconscious placeness evokes similarities to inhabitants' attitude towards place as a field of care because both
suggest a profound degree of investment in and care for a particular place.
Authentic and unselfconscious placeness implies a wholly organic and
uncontrived fusion of subject and object. For Relph, an authentic attitude
towards place is:

> understood to be a direct and genuine experience of the entire
> complex of the identity of places – not mediated and distorted
> through a series of quite arbitrary social and intellectual fashions
> about how that experience should be, nor following stereotyped
> conventions. It comes from a full awareness of places for what they
> are as products of man's intentions and the meaningful settings for
> human activities, or from a profound and unselfconscious identity
> with place. (1976: 64)

Experienced at this most profound level, authentic placeness is what
Relph terms 'existential insideness', which is 'knowing implicitly that *this*
is where you belong' (p. 55; emphasis in original). Relph insists that existential insideness denotes an unselfconscious sense of place because one's
belongingness and constituency to place are inherently ingrained in one's
everyday reality. This experience of existential insideness is similar to
Williams' (1973) experience of the 'knowable community' ('a whole
community, wholly knowable') because both imply a profound insideness
and sense of belonging that approaches the limits of human ability to
relate to place and community.

Interestingly, both Relph and Williams look to pre-industrial, agricultural society to locate examples of existential insideness and the knowable
community. While Relph explores a farming town depicted in Steinbeck's
Grapes of Wrath to illustrate qualities of the former, Williams writes about
the decline of the latter as follows:

> There can be no doubt, for example, that identity and community
> became more problematic, as a matter of perception and as a matter of
> valuation, as the scale and complexity of the characteristic social

organisation increased. Up to that point, the transition from country to city – from a predominantly rural to a predominantly urban society – is transforming and significant. The growth of towns and especially of cities and a metropolis; the increasing division and complexity of labour; the altered and critical relations between and within social classes: in changes like these any assumption of a knowable community ... became harder and harder to sustain. (1973: 165)

The essential argument that both scholars make is that opportunities for people living in technologically advanced societies to cultivate and retain a meaningful sense of place have been significantly compromised due to new and accelerating patterns of mobility, and a general deterioration of the significance of place as a field of care. Indeed, Relph asserts that, 'while for the primitive hunter or medieval artisan a sense of belonging to this place imbued his whole existence, for the modern city-dweller it is rarely in the foreground and can usually be traded for a nicer home in a better neighborhood' (1976: 66).

Relph does allow for other authentic forms of placeness, albeit forms which are deliberately self-conscious and less intimate than that of existential insideness. If we imagine the condition of insideness as a continuum, fading away from the extreme of existential insideness the next, less acute form is empathetic insideness. Empathetic insideness involves acknowledging the unique characteristics of a place's identity, possessing thoughtful awareness of its environment, and respecting it as a meaningful entity. However, while the intentions towards place are authentic, the attachment and sense of belonging are contrived and self-conscious. In the context of this work, this experience is perhaps best illustrated by Ulf Hannerz's (1990) cosmopolitan personality, who possesses a stance of openness towards diverse peoples, places and cultures, and a willingness to engage them on their own terms. Fading away even further on the continuum is behavioral insideness, which is nothing more than possessing a conscious awareness of one's physical presence in a particular place. Relph argues that this is the most common form of insideness in advanced industrial and post-industrial societies, as we acknowledge our presence in certain places only because we are aware of their distinct qualities or location.

... and placelessness

Relph theorizes that in advanced (post-)industrial societies, place and sense of place have deteriorated even further into a condition he terms 'placelessness'. This post-modern condition describes 'both an environment without significant places and the underlying attitude which does not acknowledge significance in places' (1976: 143). As an attitude it has much to do with changes to the value of 'home'. Home in former times, such as the era illustrated in Lowenthal's anecdote of the Appalachian settler, implied stability and permanence; a fixed point of reference. 'To build a new house or to settle in a new territory [was] a fundamental project, equivalent perhaps to a repetition of the founding of the world' Relph affirms (p. 83). 'But in contemporary society' he asserts, 'home is the location of your house and that can be changed every three to four years with little or no regret.' This exchangeability of homes is perhaps the most common manifestation of placelessness; the ultimate consequence of which is the devaluation of the meaning of 'home'. As the significance of home deteriorates and, in general, places become more insecure and transitory, the world of belonging and being in place grows smaller and smaller so that more and more of our experiences of the world are passively perceived from a disaffected distance, mediated by the perceptual frames of windows, screens, lenses and the like. In this way, placelessness implies outsideness.

Placelessness also characterizes a 'uniformity and standardization in places' as the distinct identities and uniqueness of places can erode without a stable community of authentically invested caretakers to maintain and renew place on a daily basis (Relph, 1976). Placelessness can also imply place destruction through the expropriation and redevelopment of place. By these acts, the material and symbolic forms of place are destroyed, remade or demolished altogether.

Conclusion

Ultimately, all of the ideas explored above – from landscape and place, to insider and outsider, to placeness and placelessness – imply not only different ways of relating to one's physical and human environment, but also diverse intentions and meanings for this immediate environment. These concepts all relate in one form or another to notions of land, home, community, identity and the dichotomy of rootedness/mobility.

In contrast to the projected image of landscape, the meaning of place is not projected outward; rather it is experienced from within. While the flimsy image of landscape changes with the turn of a shovel, the blink of an eye or the stroke of a brush, the stable entity of place is both enduring and durable; changing only slowly over time as its caretakers negotiate and renegotiate the terms of their collective, place-based identity, as well as the terms of their relationships with the land, their surroundings and each other. Tuan asserts that, 'space is transformed into place as it acquires definition and meaning' (1977: 136). As such, place is an entity rooted in space and time, bonded into meaning by its inhabitants who share place collectively as a community. Place is a multidimensional and multisensory entity that is experienced only from inside by becoming a part of it.

As a way of seeing, the landscape idea is about more than simply the faculty of vision. While vision, indeed, is an important way of sensing and perceiving landscapes, this 'way of seeing' is also about one's intentions for his or her surroundings, one's social position or identity and one's cultural perceptions. Landscape implies a complex layering of meanings which interact across various levels so that landscape becomes manifest in a variety of forms, ranging from material land to mental images. However, in all its forms, landscape is a cultural artifact which is fabricated by a visual ideology based on Cosgrove's principles of sight, separation and distance. As it fundamentally is an ideological creation, landscape is an interpretative text which can be deconstructed to reveal many hidden and implied social, political, moral and cultural values. If place is a defined and meaningful metamorphasis of space, then landscape could be considered as the projection of meaning, ideals, and imagery onto or over spaces and places encountered through visual perception. From a position of existential insideness, landscape is merely a 'backdrop' to one's experiences of place as a field of care, Relph insists; however from a position of experiential outsideness, landscape often functions as a 'curtain', to use Berger's term, which serves to obscure the situated and collectively held meanings for and identities of place and its caretakers. Beginning in chapter four, we will explore how these dynamic human experiences of landscape and place that were established in this chapter fundamentally relate to the context of residential tourism in Boquete.

Chapter 3
Locating Boquete in Space and Time

Introduction

As is the case with so many places upon close examination, Boquete possesses a supremely unique identity, comprised of subtleties, contradictions and a richness of depth that make this place impossible to define concisely. Slice it one way and Boquete appears to be the prototypical quaint and provincial Central American community organized around an agricultural way of life. Its inhabitants live by modest means, cultivating coffee and other produce on land that has been passed down from generation to generation. Slice it another way and Boquete is revealed to have an exceptional history as a place of refuge and retreat for a variety of travelers, wanderers and migrants: from the enigmatic Dorasques who sought refuge in Boquete's hidden valley to escape the ravages of colonialism, war and disease in the 16th century; to the European labor émigrés who defected to Boquete following the failed attempt by the French to dig a Panamá canal in the late 19th century; to the American workers of the successful second attempt who came to Boquete for rejuvenating holiday retreat and wilderness adventure in the early 20th century; and, finally, to the present wave of residential tourists who seek in Boquete a comfortable climate, low cost of living and experiences of exotica.

The purpose of this chapter is to establish the proper geographical, historical and socioeconomic contexts for the subsequent examination of present-day residential tourist growth and development in Boquete in later chapters. Particularly in this chapter, I wish to reveal the nuances of Boquete's present identity as one built upon a history of native and foreign influences blending together over time to create a distinct social fabric of community. At the same time, however, residential tourism presents Boquete with a host of challenges and implications that are without precedent in its history. Likewise, residential tourists' identities, behaviors and motivations for living in this place are fundamentally distinct from those of the previous generation of foreign settlers.

Geographical Context

Situated in the interior highlands of Pacific western Panamá, Boquete sits amidst a lush evergreen forest between 3000 and 4000 feet in elevation. Located just 11 kilometers to the southeast of Volcán Barú, the highest peak in Panamá, Boquete is an official district of Chiriquí, the most agriculturally productive province on the isthmus. Boquete rests on the southern slope of the crystalline junction of the Cordillera de Talamanca and the Serranía de Tabasará mountain ranges, which abut roughly at the 11,250-foot high Volcán Barú.

A vista from the towering summit of Volcán Barú offers observers a truly unique perspective: it is the only place in all of the Americas in which both oceans – the Caribbean-Atlantic to the north and the Pacific to the south – are visible from a single vantage point. T.F. Meagher, an Irish-American surveyor hired by a group of New York businessmen to negotiate transoceanic transit rights and mining concessions with Costa Rica during the 1850s, wrote of this unmatched panorama in a travel essay published in *Harpers* in 1861:

> Looking down through the drizzly clouds, and for miles over the sloping forest, we beheld the valley out of which we had come, and the vast plain we had traversed from Davíd to the foot of Boquete. Beyond that again – separated darkly from it by what appeared to be a narrow belt of palm, but in reality by an unmeasured tract of that glorious tree – the golden Pacific seemed to pulsate in the sun. Nearer to us by ten leagues – jutting right overhead, indeed, so close did they appear – were the cloven heights of the volcano, ever the great central figure of the scene, reared in steep black masses against the cloudless sky. Turning toward the north – on the extreme verge of a whole world of mountains, all buried in what seemed to be an impenetrable forest, and barely discernible through the hazy atmosphere – the waters of the Atlantic, hushed within the islands of the Chiriquí Lagoon, glimmered in the twilight of the horizon. But the cold up there was piercing – we were on the highest ridge of the great dividing range and the dense mist, in a few minutes, had drenched us thoroughly. So, taking a last look at that transcendent scene, turning from the Atlantic to the Pacific, and from the Pacific to the Atlantic waves once more, we rapidly descended. (1861: 120)

The 'vast plain' that Meagher describes between the settlements of Boquete and Davíd is known geologically as El Francés, an impressive alluvial slope that gradually descends southward from the mountainous apex-like spine in the center of the western isthmus down to the Pacific coastal plains.[1] This gentle slope declines more than 3000 feet in elevation over the course of the 40 kilometers separating Boquete from Davíd, its larger neighbor to the south and the provincial capital of Chiriquí, located on the coastal plain.

Long before Boquete was established as a permanent settlement in the latter half of the 19th century, this area was well-known nonetheless as '*el boquete*' among travelers and inhabitants throughout the Pacific western region of the isthmus. This appellation, signifying 'narrow gap' in Spanish, owes its origin to the distinctive geographical feature found here, in which an impressive section of the sloping cordilleras is funneled through a constricted, bottleneck pass located in the present-day district of Boquete, before spilling open onto the wide llano of El Francés to the south (Figure 3.1). Just inside this narrow and crooked *boquete*, immediately to the north, rests a depressed highland basin (Boquete's hidden valley) encircled by towering mountain slopes, whose summits range from 5000 to 6000 feet in elevation. Eusebio Morales, an ardent nationalist who helped compose the country's declaration of independence from Colombia in 1903, recalls in extraordinary detail his northward journey through these natural features, during a visit to Boquete in 1907:

The entrance to this region is situated thirty miles from Davíd and the road is an inclined plain that the traveler ascends without realizing it, until [he reaches] an altitude of 3500 to 4000 feet. The ascent is so smooth that one only realizes the accomplishment upon looking back and seeing in the distance the ocean and the islands near adjacent coast. ... A short distance from the most narrow part [of el boquete], the plains widen again only to end, shortly thereafter, at an abrupt cliff from which one may see, below, the town of Bajo Boquete, the houses of the coffee farms in Alto Boquete, and the Caldera river that snakes through a valley of three to four miles in length by one to two miles in width. To enter the region of Boquete, one must ascend the plain to an altitude of approximately 3500 feet above sea level, and then descend rapidly to the valley of the same Caldera river at an altitude of 3000 feet. (Cited in Henríquez, 1909: XLVII–III)[2]

The Río Caldera to which Morales refers is, in fact, just one of three major rivers that are channeled southward though the valley and the narrow *boquete* during the course of their short journeys to the Pacific. The Ríos Chiriquí and Cochea pass through the western edge of the valley, while the impressive Río Caldera is born out of no less than nine tributaries, which coalesce in the northern half of the valley just above the present-day *corregimiento*, or neighborhood, of Bajo Boquete which is by far the most urbanized of the six *corregimientos* which comprise the district.

With regard to the climate of Boquete, the average temperatures and annual amounts of precipitation vary significantly between the district's

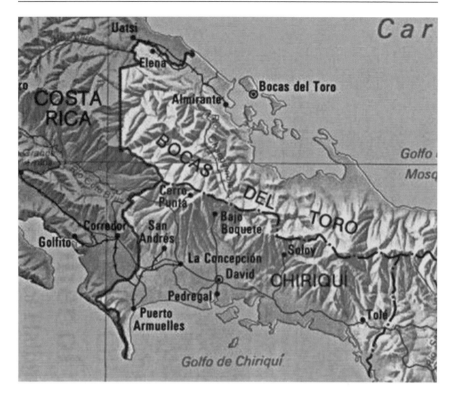

Figure 3.1   Relief map of western Panamá (courtesy of The University of Texas Libraries)

lower and higher elevations. Typically, the lower elevation areas experience significantly warmer temperatures than do the higher elevations. This, in addition to standard variations in precipitation, wind and cloud cover, provide for a number of microclimates, whose differences are readily appreciable during intra-district travel on any given day. Anecdotal evidence in support of these microclimates were present on a daily basis during my fieldwork in Boquete. Often the daytime weather in the basin would be sunny with calm winds and temperatures in the mid-twenties Celsius while the weather in the higher elevations would be cloudy and windy with light precipitation and temperatures in the upper teens.

The general climate, however, for Boquete and for the entire Pacific western quadrant of the isthmus is characterized by a pronounced dry season, or *verano*, which occurs during the first third of the calendar year

(Gordon, 1957). During the remainder of the year, Boquete receives abundant rainfall, which peaks during the months of August through November, and averages 3450 millimeters, or 136 inches, of precipitation annually (Sánchez, 2004.). During the *verano* season, daytime temperatures in the basin can reach the mid- to upper-twenties Celsius, while for the remainder of the year daytime temperatures range between the upper teens and mid-twenties Celsius. Regardless of these slight variations, the climate in Boquete is exceedingly comfortable. Only in the rarest of instances does the climate become uncomfortably hot or cold, and essentially, the only weather-related hazards that threaten Boquete are occasional extreme variations in precipitation, which result in either drought or flooding. Not incidentally, Boquete has increasingly come to be promoted as the 'Valley of Eternal Spring'.

As this utopian epithet also connotes, Boquete's vegetation is luxuriant and verdant year-round (Figure 3.2). In his field notes on the Chiriquí

Figure 3.2   View of the interior 'hidden' valley and surrounding slopes of Bajo Boquete, as seen from the southern rim of the basin (photo by author, 2005)

province, UC Berkeley geographer B.L. Gordon notes that, 'the vegetation of the Atlantic or Caribbean slope and the uppermost Pacific slope is dense forest; the lower part of the Pacific slope is a savanna' (1957: 7). This savanna to which Gordon refers is located between Davíd and Boquete, on the El Francés llano. To the north of this llano, in Boquete, the higher elevation slopes of the district are predominantly forested with several varieties of evergreen pine and cedar, many exceeding 40 feet in height. At lower elevations closer to the valley's rivers these evergreens give way to a mixture of oak, guayacán, acacia mangium, teak and a variety of palm trees (Henríquez, 1909). The arboreal landscape is complemented by a host of lush grasses, scrub trees and flora, most notably an exceptional variety of orchids native to the area. As a lasting legacy of the extravasative history of the now-dormant Volcán Barú, Gordon observes that, 'the soils on the … south slopes of [Barú] are largely derived from ash or lava, recently deposited [and] they are the most fertile in Panama' (1957: 6). The fertility of this highland valley and surrounding mountain slopes are immediately evident in the thick, luscious and flourishing natural vegetation coloring the entire district in multitudinous shades of green.

Historical Context

Pre-Columbian history

Although little is known about the pre-Columbian history of Boquete, what is for certain is that the area was home to a sizeable indigenous population that has since vanished from the area under mysterious circumstances. With regard to pre-Columbian life in Chiriquí, there appears to have been various tribes of the indigenous Chibcha group who occupied territory throughout the entire western isthmus. Some of these native groups have disappeared while others are still present in western Panamá today. In a monograph entitled *Chiriquí Culture*, Czech ethnographer Vàclav Solc tells of the first written accounts by Spanish explorers and missionaries describing the native peoples in the extreme western isthmus:

> in 1606, the missionary Melchior Hernandez visited the province of Chiriquí and most probably also the whole surrounding area and found the region to be densely populated. He left behind a list of the name of ten tribes which lived here and spoke six different dialects: Cothos, Borisques, Dorasques, Utelaes, Bugabees, Zunes, Dolegas, Chagres, Zaribas, and the Dures. (1970: 8)

The indigenous group believed to have inhabited the valley and slopes inside *el boquete* during the 16th century were the Dorasques (also known as the Doraces or Dorasks). Despite Hernandez's observation of a territory densely populated by various indigenous groups, by the time of his visit the Dorasques' population in the highlands undoubtedly was either already in decline or on the precipice of a rapid slide towards decimation due to circumstances that are not entirely clear.

Despite the fact that the Dorasques' population declined *after* the arrival of Spanish colonialists, there is no written evidence on the part of the colonialists to explain why an ostensibly hearty population should disappear from the territory altogether. The lack of attention to the indigenous population decline in Chiriquí may be attributed to the fact that, as Solc explains, the colonialists' interest lay elsewhere:

> It is no longer possible today to give an exact explanation for this depopulation. It could not have been merely the contact with Europeans, because for a quite long time the entire region was free from the direct influence of the white man, yet the population died out in large numbers. As a result, the earliest historical sources do not reveal very much about the territory of present-day Chiriquí. The conquerors concentrated their attention chiefly on the regions rich in gold such as Mexico, Yucatan and the lands of the Incas. The territory of present-day Panama lay outside their sphere of interest. Consequently older discoveries fell into oblivion. What actually happened to the Indians in those days is hidden in obscurity. (1970: 9)

One interesting theory regarding the Dorasques' final years of decline is put forth by Morales, who bases his speculation on a famous interview conducted in the 1870s by a Chiriquí landowner with an elderly indigenous man, who was suspected by many to have been the last surviving member of the Dorasques. Almost a century ago, Morales hypothesized as follows:

> In Boquete today there is not one indigenous person. Was the aboriginal race exterminated by the Spanish conquistadors? Did they migrate to the most inaccessible regions of the cordillera? The most probable explanation is that the indigenous peoples, enslaved and persecuted by their conquerors, abandoned the plains in which the conquerors evidently had the superiority of arms and discipline, and migrated to the highlands, valleys, and narrow passes of Boquete and to the cordillera in search of strategic, well-protected positions. Surely there were attacks and battles fought between invaders and aborigines, until the latter, decimated already, confined themselves even deeper in the mountains. (Cited in Henríquez, 1909: LVI–II)[3]

Regardless of the circumstances of their settlement and subsequent decline in Boquete, evidence of their life – and death – in the district can be seen in the numerous discoveries of Dorasquen *guacas*, or tombs, unearthed along the district's mountainous slopes. These *guacas* comprise shallow graves, which often are laden with rich cultural artifacts such as intricate tools and gold jewelry, and sealed with granite slabs, arranged in symmetric lines or circles (Henríquez, 1909). Among other findings, evidence obtained from these *guacas* indicates that modern-day mestizo and Amerindian inhabitants in this highland region are *not* the modern-day descendants of the Dorasquen people buried in these graves (Solc, 1970). Today, the Dorasques are distantly, yet affectionately, remembered by Boqueteños as a fiercely independent people who enjoyed freedom from oppression in the remote, hidden valley of Boquete prior to their mysterious disappearance.

Modern history

Following the decline of the Dorasques in Boquete during the 16th century, the area largely lay untouched for the majority of the subsequent three centuries. Under the colonial rule of Nueva Granada[4], the ruling powers perceived Chiriquí's largely indigenous population and their lands to be of little value or significance. In fact, as historian David McCullough explains, most of Central America remained untouched by the hand of colonial influence until the mid-19th century:

> For three centuries the gold in the stream beds of the Sierra Nevada had gone undetected and for all the commotion over the Central American canals in the first half of the new world-shaking nineteenth century, Central America remained a backwater. No canals, no railroads were built. There was not a single wagon road anywhere across the entire Isthmus. But in January of 1848 a carpenter from New Jersey saw something shining at the bottom of a millrace in Coloma, California, and within a year Central America [emerged] from the shadows. (1977: 33)

In a most unlikely development that would ultimately set the stage for Panamá's global ascendancy as the western hemisphere's most trafficked maritime thoroughfare, the California gold rush, some 3000 miles distant, actually spurred the first instance of modern foreign development in Panamá. Shortly after gold was discovered in California, a small group of New York businessmen quickly saw in the narrow Central American isthmus a strategic and lucrative opportunity to create a far superior and efficient transportation route to California via transoceanic travel. In 1855, their Panama Railroad Company (PRC) completed a track, not far from the path of the present-day canal, which quickly assumed a critical transport link in the interoceanic migration of eastern American prospectors en route to California and, to a lesser extent, Alaska. Within the first 10 years of the PRC's operations in Panamá, over 400,000 prospectors were shuttled across the isthmus en route to American gold country (McCullough, 1977). While most continued on their journeys to the American West, some remained in Panamá, seeking out opportunities on the isthmus during that hopeful era of prospect and manifest destiny.

It was not incidental, then, that gold was discovered in Chiriquí in 1858, during the heyday of the PRC's operations in Panamá. Solc describes below how this discovery served to initiate new interest in the remote region:

> No deeper transformation came about until the middle of the 19th century, when gold was discovered in the Province of Chiriquí. ... All of a sudden the province became the centre of attention for a large number of adventurers. Gold was found in the graves of the extensive graveyards known as 'huacas'. There was plenty of it to be found in the graves. It is said that in one graveyard alone gold to the value of 50,000 [U.S.] dollars was discovered in a short period. Consequently entire regions were plundered. (1970: 9–10)

Based on a first-hand account by Morales, many of these *guacas* plundered during this time were located along the mountain slopes in Boquete (Henríquez, 1909). The notoriety of Boquete's *guacas* undoubtedly contributed to outsiders' discovery of Boquete's other valuable asset: its fertile and rich soils.

At this time in Panamá, with the PRC proving the efficiency of intercontinental travel via the isthmus, the interest of North American and Western European parties in a transoceanic canal through the isthmus sent a wave of scouts and surveyors to the region, all searching for the most favorable route across the narrow land barrier. Shortly thereafter – beginning in 1880 with the French initiative and lasting until eventual completion by the United States in 1914 – construction on the Panamá Canal attracted hundreds of thousands of immigrant workers to the isthmus, effectively establishing permanent social and economic links between Panamá and Europe, the United States and the Caribbean region (McCullough, 1977). Foreign development in western Panamá also occurred on another front towards the end of the 19th century when the United Fruit Company established the Chiriquí Land Company,[5] devoted to large-scale banana cultivation along the Caribbean coast in the province of Bocas del Toro, directly north of Chiriquí (Gordon, 1957). Thus, by the end of the 19th century, Panamá had become a focal point for a variety of foreign interests. The soon-to-be nation was in the process of quickly rising out of obscurity and into the international spotlight, as foreign development occurred on multiple fronts across the isthmus.

The origins of the modern settlement of Boquete began as the 19th century drew to a close. During this time the highland territory between Volcán Barú and Boquete were covetously claimed as a *latifundio*[6] by a provincial politician, Juan Manuel Lambert, who walled off the narrow opening of *el boquete* to keep squatters out and his livestock contained within the highland valley basin (Sánchez Pinzón, 2001; personal interview, 2005). During the last 15 years of that century, though, a small group of indigenous and mestizo *labriegos*, or peasants, illicitly migrated north to the valley inside *el boquete* from the village of Dolega, located to the south on the El Francés llano, midway between Davíd and Boquete. In *Boquete: rasgos de su historia*, Milagros Sánchez Pinzón's definitive monograph documenting the 'living history' of modern-day Boquete, she writes of these peasants from Dolega: 'Despite the strong opposition that they encountered, a few humble farmers settled here permanently and, little by little, they brought or formed their families' (2001: 1).[7] The dispute over their claims to the fertile valley eventually led one of the squatters to file a complaint in the Colombian courts, over 1100 kilometers to the east in Bogotá. In 1903, the peasants won the right to legally settle and farm in the fertile and accommodating highland valley.

However, even at the beginning of the 20th century, Boquete remained extremely isolated from the outside world, as travel to the highlands, much less to the western half of the isthmus, remained a very difficult and lengthy journey. Until the late 1930s, when the Ferrocarril Nacional de Chiriquí completed construction on a rail line from Davíd to Boquete, the only way in or out of the highland valley was via an ungraded, dirt trail linking the Chiriquí highlands to Davíd (Sánchez Pinzón, 2001). More distant travels originating outside of the province necessitated oceanic travel, as there were no roads connecting the western isthmus to the relatively populous canal corridor located between the urban gateway cities of Colón and Panamá (City), nearly 500 kilometers to the east.

Despite the relative isolation of Boquete, a number of foreign settlers were living and farming on the land by the time Boquete was incorporated as a formal district of Chiriquí in 1911. By this time, the isthmus had gained independence from Colombia and was firmly established as the Republic of Panamá.[8] Foreign workers, adventurers and prospectors – many of whom did not originally intend to settle permanently on the isthmus – came to Panamá during this era of foreign-led development and found themselves, drawn by a host of different circumstances, living in Boquete. Attracted by the uncommonly fertile land and the pleasant climate encountered in the highland valley, dozens of unmarried, foreign men of North American, European and Latin American descent resettled to Boquete at the turn of the century. Here, they started new lives and new families, by claiming land for house and farm, and by marrying local indigenous and mestiza women of the area.

The stories of these foreigners' settlement in Boquete are not unlike that of John Landau, a man of German origin who immigrated to the province of Bocas del Toro as a young man in the 1870s, with dreams of establishing a banana plantation. However, after a disastrous banana blight that brought his enterprise to financial ruin in the early 1890s, Landau sold his plantation to the Chiriquí Land Company in 1899, and headed south, crossing the Cordillera de Talamanca by foot to eventually settle in Boquete (Sánchez Pinzón, 2001; personal interviews, 2005). Over the course of his life in Boquete, Landau fathered 11 children by two local Dolegan women, established a successful coffee finca on the slopes of Boquete, and even led a successful campaign to link Davíd with the town of Chiriquí Grande via railway line, in order to facilitate commerce and agricultural cooperation for the benefit of both communities. Fondly remembered by Boqueteños as 'El Pionero', Landau died tragically in 1919, while attempting to survey a suitable railway route to connect Boquete with the district of Changuinola, in Bocas del Toro, so that agricultural ties between the districts could be established. In a lasting tribute to Landau, Sánchez Pinzón writes:

> The brave German adventurer gave his life during the pursuit of a dream. His efforts were not in vain. The generations that succeeded him have assumed the challenge that he left behind and, although it occurred over a half century later, the line of permanent communication between Chiriquí and Bocas del Toro has become a reality. (p. 131)[9]

Among Boquete's *pioneros extranjeros*, 'foreign pioneers' as they are so affectionately remembered in Sánchez Pinzón's monograph, there is also the story of Antonio Serracín, an Italian immigrant who arrived on the isthmus prior to the end of the 19th century as part of the massive workforce that the French imported for their canal construction endeavor. Like Landau, Serracín heard about the agricultural opportunities in Boquete and made the district his home following the failure of the French canal endeavor. Serracín married a mestiza woman from Boquete and, like Landau, fathered 11 children, all of whom remained in Boquete throughout their lives (Sánchez Pinzón, 2001; personal interviews, 2005).

Serracín made his livelihood from the cultivation of coffee on the numerous fincas he established over his lifetime in the district; not surprisingly, the descendents of Serracín still cultivate coffee on these very fincas today.

The stories of Landau and Serracín exemplify a generation affectionately remembered as Boquete's foreign pioneers, who established roots in Boquete through their labor and the meaningful social and familial bonds they formed over time. Similar to the pioneers and settlers that Relph describes coming to North America from Europe during the same century, these men 'were making a decisive break with the place they had been born and raised;' and by 'carv[ing] their own new home out of the bush [they] were in effect reestablishing their roots – they were making a place authentically through their own labour and through a commitment to a new way of life' (1976: 76). In cooperation with the native Chiriquianos who settled in Boquete during roughly the same time, a habitable district and a successful agricultural industry came to fruition in the highlands of Boquete. Out of this native–foreign coexistence arose in short order a cohesive community – unified in this place by virtue of mutual needs and aspirations – which grew to share a common language, a common livelihood working the land and even common bloodlines.

By the time Boquete was recognized as an official district in 1911, the population had risen to 1589 inhabitants, the overwhelming majority of whom were native to the surrounding areas of western Panamá (DEC, 2003). While the foreign settlers of Boquete certainly played a significant role in the establishment and subsequent development of the district, their absolute numbers were quite small. In fact, throughout the entire *province* in 1911, only 394 foreign-born inhabitants, or 0.6% of the total provincial population, were reported to be living in all of Chiriquí (Controloria General de la Republica, 1945). Over subsequent decades Boquete's population experienced relatively robust growth, as additional Panameños but few other foreigners settled in the district (Figure 3.3). By 1920, the total population of Boquete had increased to 2669. This figure would double twice within the subsequent five decades so that, by 1970, the population was nearing 10,000 residents. At the time of the last census in 2000, just prior to the incipient wave of residential tourism, the total population in Boquete stood just shy of 17,000 inhabitants (DEC, 2003).

As Sánchez Pinzón so eloquently comments in her monograph, the highland region's spectacular history of foreign and native influences assimilating together over time has produced a unique identity for its present-day inhabitants. In her introduction, she writes:

District of Boquete

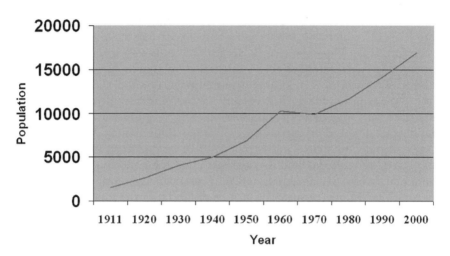

Figure 3.3   The total population of the district of Boquete since its formal incorporation in 1911 (Dirección de Estadística y Censo, 2003[10])

In the historical development of the districts of Chiriquí, the presence and the interaction of important figures, both native and foreign, have immeasurably blended together to sow in these lands the seeds of an identity that, over generations, has come into fruition. The particular spirit of each district, through whose roots flows the essence of the pioneers, [is akin to] bricks of a social edifice that today integrates the rich and diverse mosaic of this unique land.[11]

Indeed, the modern identity of the Boqueteño community is the present manifestation of past assimilation between native and foreign cultures and bloodlines. However, in the absence of replenishing foreign influences in Boquete throughout the subsequent decades of the 20th century, many remnants of this foreignness have either faded away or naturalized over time. In a place where its native inhabitants comprise a singular community, links to an outside world are provincial in scope, and few tangible artifacts remain to measurably link Boqueteños to their partial ancestries in faraway places. Often the only clue betraying Boqueteños' cosmopolitan roots are the idiosyncratic surnames they carry with them; surnames such as Taylor, MacIntyre, Watson and Higgins, which remain as vestigial links to the diverse pasts and distant lands out of which Boquete was born over a century prior.

Agricultural development

The impetus for the establishment of Boquete during the beginning of the 20th century derived from the incredibly mineral-rich soils found in the district, which are renowned as the most fertile in all of Panamá (Gordon, 1957). During incipient decades of Boquete's development, land ownership was established in such a way that a large number of Boqueteño families owned one or more fincas, or small farms, on which livestock was tended and a variety of crops were cultivated. Of the district's total area of 489.4 square kilometers, roughly one-quarter of the land was devoted to agriculture in 1946 (DEC, 2003; Ministerio de Agricultura, Comercio e Industrias, 1947[12]). By this time, the established pattern of agricultural land use was such that the 12,000 hectares of culti-vated land were divided up into 626 fincas, each averaging 19.5 hectares, or roughly 48 acres, in size. The system of land propriety in 1946, as it has remained more or less throughout subsequent decades, was such that the overwhelming majority (78%) of cultivated land was operated under direct ownership; only 17% farmed under usufruct agreements, and only 5% leased for cultivation by tenants (MACI, 1947). This all amounts to show that the industry of agriculture in Boquete is founded upon a rela-tively egalitarian system of land ownership. This pluralist system is composed of a multitudinous patchwork of small fincas, the majority of which are directly owned by landowners, each of whom may be seen as autonomous stakeholders in the political and economic arenas of Boquete.

While the focus of Boquete's agricultural industry has long centered on the production of coffee, a wide variety of fruits and vegetables are also grown in Boquete. At lower elevations under 3500 feet, a wide variety of produce such as beans, oranges, potatoes, cabbage, strawberries and blackberries are grown in the rich soils on the valley floor. At higher eleva-tions, along the mountainous slopes where the climate is significantly cooler and wetter, a wide variety of specialty coffees are cultivated.

Over the first half of the century, as modern transportation infrastruc-tures were developed both provincially and nationally, Boquete was elevated into the national market as a producer of fruits and vegetables for urban, domestic consumption and into international markets as a producer of specialty coffee for global consumption. By 1946, for example, over 300 fincas in Boquete were cultivating specialty coffee, contributing to a net annual harvest of over one million pounds of green coffee beans in the district (MACI, 1947).

Over subsequent decades the importance of agriculture, and espe-cially coffee, has only continued to grow in significance for the local economy, as well as for the socio-cultural identity of the Boqueteño community. As recently as the year 2000, roughly half of Boquete's economically active population derived its livelihood from a direct working relationship with the land.[13] In fact, the primary agricultural sector in Boquete employed more inhabitants in the district during the first year of the new millennium than the next eight largest economic categories *combined*.[14] When secondary sector industries that are indirectly dependent on agriculture – notably the business of processing and packing the coffee beans – are also included in this tally, the overwhelming predominance of agriculture in the economy of Boquete becomes exceedingly evident.

However as the agricultural industry, led by demand for Boquete's specialty coffee, has experienced continued growth over the generations since the district's founding, so too have related demands for cheap field labor to harvest the seasonal crops of coffee and produce. Over time, this niche has been filled by a migrant labor force of Ngobe Bugle, an acutely impoverished indigenous group native to the Caribbean regions to the north and east of Boquete (personal interview, 2005; Vakis & Lindert, 2000). Since the 1950s, makeshift and semi-permanent labor camps have been established on the periphery of the district, providing shelter for an ever-fluctuating population of Ngobe Bugle field hands and their families. While these indigenous workers ostensibly have established a profitable working relationship of interdependency with the local coffee growers, regrettably, chronic racial tensions plague the relationship between the Boqueteño community and the migrant Ngobe Bugle.

The Ngobe Bugle men, who as field laborers maintain a highly visible presence throughout the district, are popularly stigmatized by the Boqueteño community as an irresponsible and volatile social group prone to alcohol-fueled violence. Their commonly perceived behavior – as antisocial, unpredictable and potentially dangerous – is the basis for Boqueteños' open contempt for the Ngobe Bugle labor force, despite the community's reliance on them to sustain the agricultural industry (personal interviews, 2005). In this way, the Boqueteño community's regard for the Ngobe Bugle – holding a delicate balance between economic necessity and social distrust – is characteristic of countless communities' and even many advanced nations' ambivalence towards the imported, marginalized workforce living among them and laboring to sustain their economies. The spatial relegation of Ngobe Bugle tenements to the physical fringes of the district powerfully symbolizes the lamentable state of social affairs between these two groups in Boquete.

Current standard of living

Owing in great part to the quasi-egalitarian system of land ownership via which Boquete developed, Boqueteños today generally live by modest, yet comfortable, means relative to regional standards (Figure 3.4). Most Boqueteño households are part of a large and modest landowning middle class; the socioeconomic lower class having been inherited by the itinerant Ngobe Bugle, whose ever-fluctuating presence was measured at 18% of the total population in the most recent census from the year 2000 (DEC, 2003). The natural resource of exceptional soil fertility has ensured that the land consistently generates material and financial wealth for this large Boqueteño middle class. Thus, while the average Boqueteño household is not money-rich by any means, most are land- and resource-rich, and financially independent as well, generally owning their homes and farms outright. In strictly monetary terms, the median annual income in Boquete, at just over US$2000 in 2000, is one-third less than the national average of US$3250. However, this differential does not factor in the rural–urban imbalance between the Boqueteño population, 67% of whom live in rural areas, and the national population, 60% of whom live in areas classified as urban (DEC, 2003).

In a strictly local context, Boquete's residents enjoy a relatively decent standard of living. While Boquete lacks some of the most basic services (most notably the expansive district of 180 square miles lacked both ambulance and police vehicles as recently as 2005) residents nonetheless are provided with an adequate level of public services, including functioning public schools, medical clinics, and basic utilities and infrastructures. However, in another light, Boquete also has demonstrated high unemployment rates, as great as 15% in the year 2000; a rate that was roughly one and a half times higher than the national average (DEC, 2003).

Moving up to the larger regional and national contexts, Boquete is situated in a province and country that has, in many ways, yet to complete the process of modernization. As recently as 2000, over one-fifth of households in Chiriquí lacked electricity, almost as many lacked running water, and over 70% were in want of basic telephone service. This, in a country where almost one-tenth of the population was still illiterate and another tenth had yet to complete an education beyond the third grade at the dawn of the 21st century (DEC, 2003).

Thus, while Boquete's residents enjoy a relatively comfortable standard of living, in a broader context Boquete is situated in a region in which poverty, under-education, malnutrition and underdevelopment still very

Figure 3.4   The major intersection in Bajo Boquete, the most urbanized *corregimiento* in the district of Boquete (photo by author, 2005)

much exist. Underscoring this reality is a recent World Bank report, which found that the standard of living for indigenous peoples in Panamá is utterly abysmal: 83% live below the poverty level and one-half of their children are persistently malnourished (Vakis & Lindert, 2000). Significantly, this report found that out of all the indigenous groups in Panamá, the Ngobe Bugle of the western highlands was the most impoverished *and* the most malnourished group on the entire isthmus.

In a final context, to consider the socioeconomic status of residential tourists relative to the average Panamanian casts this analysis in a whole new light. In contrast to a per capita GDP of US$7,200 in Panamá during the year 2005, the per capita GDPs for the United States and Canada, the two largest sources of Boquete's residential tourist population, were US$41,800 and US$34,000, respectively (CIA World Factbook, 2005). This measure serves to provide a rough approximation of the incredible scale of economic disparity existing between native and foreign residents in Boquete. Residential tourists undeniably possess astonishing buying power in the local economy. From the local perspective, the growth of residential tourism is effectively creating a new class of super-rich in Boquete whose monthly spending budgets rival most local residents' *yearly* earnings. Quite possibly, residential tourism is not only creating a new socioeconomic class in Panamá, but further essentially spawning an emerging type of de facto citizen in Panamá; one based not on political status or civic participation, but rather on class status and consumer participation.

Origins of tourism

From the outsider's perspective, Boquete has long held meaning as a landscape of natural beauty and pastoral paradise for tourism-oriented visitors. Touristic interest in Boquete dates back to the early 20th century, when the United States' Isthmian Canal Commission (ICC) designated Boquete as an authorized vacation spot for its highly skilled, 'gold level' employees. Of this development, J.A. Henríquez, the Province of Chiriquí's Director General of Statistics, wrote in 1909:

> Recently, the growing interest ... [in] *El Boquete*, more from the foreigners than from the natives, has functioned to put the name of this Panamanian territory on the list of places recommended by the celebrity Doctor W.C. Gorgas, Director of the Office of Sanitation in the Zone, and U.S. Navy Coronel, so that the employees of the Isthmian Canal Commission spend their yearly vacations there. (p. 3)[15]

Upon returning from a paid-leave excursion to Boquete in 1908, canal engineer J.D. Kraus recounted for an ICC newspaper his 'day at paradisiacal Boquete' by recalling in sublime sensorial detail his initial approach into the American-endorsed vacation spot:

> ...[we] begin the gradual ascent towards the mountain range and the Boquete, now only about 12 miles away. The dew still glistens on the deep green foliage of shrubs and trees, happy birds are warbling their morning's song, here and there cattle and horses are contentedly grazing near the side of the road, and scantily clad children run out of huts and stare at us with their big black eyes, while we breathe the cool aromatic atmosphere of the bright morning with a delight to which we have long been strangers. (Cited in Henríquez, 1909: CXVII)

As such, Boquete came to be experienced in a unique and new way – from the perspective of the tourist – during the height of the United States' great dig across the isthmus. According to all evidence, the level of tourism in Boquete during the first decades of the 20th century was small,

yet significant enough to sustain two hotels which together could accommodate up to 20 visitors (Henríquez, 1909). For several decades at the
beginning of the 20th century, Boquete was well-known among the ICC
elite as a place for wilderness expeditions, such as hunting and fishing
and, alternatively, as an ideal destination for a rejuvenating retreat. In fact,
several written accounts by ICC employees imbue Boquete and its environment with spiritual healing qualities and refer to this place as a kind of
sanatorium (Henríquez, 1909).

However, upon completion of the canal, foreign interest in Boquete
altogether appears to stagnate and eventually declines beginning in the
1940s, persisting throughout much of the remainder of the century.
Under the political and economic turmoil of the military regimes in the
1970s and 1980s, geographically remote districts such as Boquete were
frequently deprived basic funding and services by an inefficient and
corrupt central government in Panamá City. Judging from the way
Boqueteños describe this era, Boquete was a wholly different place from
the prosperous and idyllic image described by the ICC sojourner in 1908.
One current resident describes conditions in Boquete just after the fall of
Noriega in 1989, as follows:

> [Boquete] was very, very, very depressed right after Noriega. There
> was absolutely no help for the coffee community. It was very, very
> impoverished. ... Seeing the level of poverty at that time in the area
> was a big shock. And it stayed that way ... extreme poverty ... broken
> down trucks in town. Everyone [was] looking for work, trying to find
> a job, but [there were] no jobs, really, here in Boquete.

During these years it is apparent that Boquete receded into neglected
isolation. However, as the 20th century drew to a close, Boquete was on
the verge of a new chapter in its history: the emergence of residential
tourism.

The Dawn of Residential Tourism

As Panamá emerged in the 1990s from the long shadows of de facto
military rule, the central government enacted a package of neoliberal
economic incentives which, as part of a larger effort to channel foreign
investment into the country, sought to attract relatively affluent foreign
residents, particularly retirees. The paramount incentives of this package,
which still exists in almost its original form, include a 20-year residential
property tax exemption and a lifetime tax exemption on all foreign-earned
income for all financially-independent foreigners who move to Panamá

(Figure 3.5). In addition, for foreign retirees, the *turista pensionado* visa allows individuals with a minimum income of US$500 per month – US$600 per month for couples – to take advantage of nationally mandated pensioner discounts on a variety of consumer products and services throughout the country.[16]

This strategy to generate economic investment and development by attracting foreign residents was largely modeled upon neighboring Costa Rica's highly successful program offering similar incentives, which had been in place since the late 1970s. The timing, however, was critical. Just as Panamá was emerging from relative isolation, rolling out the welcome mat to foreign residents and enacting this incentives package, Costa Rica was in the opposite process of scaling back its tax incentives to foreign residents in response to foreign residential oversaturation, social enclavism and a general souring of native – foreign residential relations, all of which were beginning to bear bitter socio-political fruits.

Figure 3.5   Real estate banner in Boquete promotes tax exempt status to foreign residential tourists (photo by author, 2005)

It was within these regional and political contexts that the exploration stage of residential tourism emerged in Boquete during the mid-1990s. In the decade since residential tourism's nascence, its development has advanced through three distinct phases, each of which generally correlate with the respective stages of development in Butler's (1980) theoretical model for resort destinations' cycle of evolution, which was briefly discussed in Chapter 1. This first phase of residential tourism's development in Boquete, the exploration stage, occurred roughly between 1994 and 1999, during which time approximately 25 foreign residents, whom collectively may be considered as the first wave of residential tourists, migrated to the district. During the exploration stage, as Butler characterizes it, a small group of 'explorer' tourists become attracted to the destination area due to its 'unique or considerably different natural and cultural features' (1980: 7). There are few, if any, tourist-oriented services or amenities available to accommodate these new visitors, so these 'explorers' must use local services and amenities; therefore, their interaction with local residents tends to be significant. And, indeed, Butler's exploration stage does well to describe residential tourism's origins in Boquete. The first wave of residential tourists generally purchased land directly from the landowners themselves and lived among local residents, interspersed among working fincas along the elevated mountain slopes.

However, coincidentally and importantly, this first wave of residential tourists arrived at an extremely critical time in Boquete's history; a period during which an economic crisis in the international coffee markets were creating ripples of extreme hardship that hit local growers and landowners first, but quickly permeated the entire socioeconomic chain in Boquete. By all accounts, this hardship that the local community was enduring at the time of the arrival of residential tourism was one of the most trying periods in the history of Boquete. In this context, as native residents vividly recall, residential tourism appeared as a divine economic savior, which offered suffering landowners the opportunity to liquidate their burdensome fincas, which were bleeding them into financial ruin, for precious, hard cash. As such, many of the pioneering residential tourists of this first wave were able to purchase coffee fincas at higher elevations from struggling coffee growers for a price that, in hindsight, would come to be seen as a steal: less than US$3 per square meter. Taking the global coffee crisis and the economic differentials between buyer and seller into consideration, these land deals were viewed as mutually beneficial at the time: desperate farmers received immediate economic relief in the form of hard currency, while residential tourists were able to purchase 'prime' properties in Boquete at a greatly deflated price.

The second phase of residential tourist development in Boquete occurred roughly between 2000 and 2003. In Butler's model this second development phase, the involvement stage, is characterized by an increase in the number of visitors, the creation of the first consumer-oriented services and amenities catering to tourists, and the emergence of promotional advertising to attract outsiders to this destination. Once again, this stage of Butler's model translates well to adequately characterize this period of residential tourism development in Boquete. During this involvement stage, the population of residential tourists living in the district more than doubled in size as foreign real estate developers and brokers, as well as the international media, began to discover and promote Boquete as an ideal residential tourist destination. In 2001, for instance, phase one of Valle Escondido – the district's first master planned and gated community, with a restaurant, retail shops and a golf course – was completed and heavily marketed internationally as a sophisticated alternative to the overdeveloped, mass retirement destinations of Florida, Mexico and Costa Rica (Figure 3.6). Many Boqueteños retrospectively point to the creation of Valle Escondido as the beginning, in earnest, of the residential tourist boom in Boquete. With an air of fateful recollection, one local business owner told me about the day representatives from *International Living*, an English language expatriate newsletter, visited Boquete to meet with community leaders:

> I remember in 2000, I went to the first meeting [when] *International Living* came to Boquete, and the owner of Valle Escondido, he was in that meeting. And that night I remember, I told myself, [the owner of Valle Escondido] is going to be developing Boquete; the way he was talking to these people, the way he was explaining what Boquete offers. And it happened. So I think that when he start[ed] Valle Escondido in 2001, he also made a strong relationship with *International Living* and then we had that advertise[ment] that [said] Boquete is the fourth place [of best places to retire], and I think he did a lot … to develop Boquete.

Shortly after the groundbreaking promotion of Boquete as a first-class retirement destination in this publication, other international media outlets, including the *Los Angeles Times*, *Fortune* magazine, the *Wall Street Journal* and the AARP's *Maturity* magazine, followed suit, promoting Boquete as one of the world's premier retirement destinations to a host of prospective residential tourists worldwide.

During this involvement stage of residential tourism's expansion, we see the origination of two important developments which, in retrospect,

Figure 3.6 'Community center' space in Valle Escondido, Boquete's first gated, master-planned residential community, which opened in 2001 (photo by author, 2005)

have proved to be critical to the identity and continuing evolution of residential tourism in Boquete. The first concerns the seeds of escalating commodification of land in the district, as non-residential real estate developers and brokers began to speculate upon and invest in land as real estate properties. This development had the effect of imposing a speculative, monetary value on land in Boquete that immediately began to compete with traditional values for the land as a productive, sustainable and familial wealth. The second important development to originate during this stage is the emergence of a concerted effort by outsiders, most notably by outsiders seeking to profit financially from the development of Boquete, to promote for mass appeal an image of Boquete as an 'idyllic', 'exclusive', 'premier' and 'first-class' destination for residential tourists. While these promoters may not have been the original creators of this particular representation of Boquete, they can be credited with packaging and promoting this ideological perspective for mass consumption.

In Butler's model, the origins of the third phase, the development stage, are marked by the arrival of a long and transformative era of mass tourist development. In 2003, a distinct stage of mass residential tourist development began in Boquete. Since then, the population of residential tourists has boomed to over 500 residents and construction on no less than eight additional master-planned, gated residential communities and several golf courses has commenced in the district (Figure 3.7). During the initial years of this development stage since 2003, Boquete has greatly accelerated its transition from an insider-oriented agricultural community into an internationally marketed residential tourist destination. With over 2000 residential building permits currently in circulation and up to 700 additional lots and homes being created in subdivided residential communities under development, there is strong evidence to support the widespread belief that the residential tourism population in Boquete may feasibly reach as many as 5000 inhabitants within the next decade. Similar growth projections are cited in a report recently produced by a private committee of Panamanian economists and developers exploring the limits of residential tourism in Boquete. The group estimated that there were currently between 200 and 300 residential tourist households in the district (Compite Panamá, 2005). However, by the year 2012, the group projects a total of 1743 residential tourist households in Boquete. At just two residents per household, this projection would imply a residential tourist population of just under 3500 inhabitants; a 600% increase over the residential tourist population, as of 2005.

To accommodate this foreign growth, a variety of new residential tourist-oriented amenities and services has also emerged within the past three to five years. These include a 24-hour grocery store; a gourmet, international food market, which proudly stocks hard to find specialty items from the US and Europe; a handful of Spanish language schools and translation services; local branches of four Panamanian banking institutions; an international shipping service, which specializes in importing residential tourists' worldly possessions; and no less than a dozen new real estate firms and restaurants, all of which cater almost exclusively to the elite, English-speaking class of residential tourists.

In contrast to earlier waves of residential tourists, the third wave arriving during this present stage of mass development increasingly is purchasing or constructing homes on smaller, subdivided residential lots in segregated residential enclaves. Whereas the former waves were able to purchase land directly from local landowners and coreside with native residents, for the third wave of newly arriving residential tourists virtually all property available on the market is offered exclusively through real estate firms, which have assumed a highly lucrative middleman role between local landowners

Figure 3.7 Scale model of Cielo Paraiso, one of no less than eight gated, master-planned communities currently being developed in Boquete (photo by author, 2005)

and residential tourists. The introduction of real estate brokers, including both planned community developers and independent real estate agents, undoubtedly has contributed to the sharp increase in land prices, which have risen 500% on average in less than ten years. For example, properties for which the going rate was under US$5 per square meter in the late 1990s are now selling for as much as US$35 per square meter. Much of the current production of real estate in Boquete is created by foreign real estate developers who buy fincas from Boqueteño landowners at 'wholesale' prices, then subdivide them into smaller residential lots, before 'flipping' them to residential tourists at a greatly inflated 'retail' price. As a result of this free market practice of mass land consolidation and subdivision, the settlement pattern of residential tourism has become increasingly segregated into foreign-owned and -occupied residential enclaves, whose entrances are often gated and staffed with security guards. In the following two chapters, we shall explore, in part, the greater implications of this emerging, mass residential tourist settlement trend in Boquete.

Conclusion

Throughout its five centuries of documented history, visitors and inhabitants have been drawn to the special environment of Boquete for a variety of reasons. In one form or another, all of these groups have sought to prosper from the land and its natural resources. The Dorasques of the 16th century sought isolated refuge; the native and foreign pioneers of the late 19th century sought fertile land on which to farm and homesteads in which to start their families; the ICC tourists of the early 20th century sought wild adventure and, alternatively, the healing and rejuvenating powers of the atmosphere; and, most recently, the residential tourists of the 21st century seek in Boquete a relatively low cost of living, an exceptional climate and stimulating experiences of exotica.

The examination of Boquete's history demonstrates that change is, indeed, a part of its identity. In contrast to casual assumptions that might otherwise be inferred, the existence of foreign settlers and the presence of a tourist identity in Boquete are not novel to the present era of residential tourism. Neither is the idea of newcomers encroaching upon established occupants an entirely new phenomenon in Boquete. The pioneers of the 19th century squatted on another man's land, illegally at first, in order to establish the present settlement of Boquete. Now, over 100 years later, another group of newcomers has arrived to make Boquete their home and to use the land to achieve their own ends. In many ways what is happening in Boquete today with the development of residential tourism is nothing new.

However, at the same time, residential tourism is a phenomenon entirely unknown to Boquete. While tourists previously visited Boquete and pursued lifestyles of leisure and consumption here, their visits were temporary and their impacts were transitory. While foreign settlers have previously made Boquete home, their lives here were productive, and they fully assimilated with the native community. Residential tourism is different. Already, the place-changing scale of land modification and real estate development, the incredible inflation of land values and the creation of a new socioeconomic class of residents are all evident indications that Boquete is rapidly entering into a new and unprecedented era in its history which is characterized by the impressive growth and development of residential tourism.

Ultimately, however, while residential tourism is in the early stages of development, many futures are possible. What remains to be seen is how residential tourism will affect the primary industry of agriculture, which has served as the bedrock of this community's livelihood and collective identity for the past four generations. In the long run will agriculture and residential tourism evolve into a symbiosis or will they compete for the future identity of Boquete? Perhaps the biggest unknown relates to how this present generation of foreigners will ultimately interact with the established native community. Will they assimilate to create a unified and diverse Boqueteño community, as did the former generation of foreign settlers? Or will their socioeconomic and lifestyle differences make meaningful assimilation improbable? Many questions remain as we move forward to explore Boquete at this momentous crossroads, as an era of mass residential tourist development dawns in the district.

Notes

1. The length of the isthmus, on which Panamá is located, is longitudinally oriented roughly along an east–west axis. As such, in the relational context of the broader region, Panamá is situated with the Caribbean–Atlantic to the north, Colombia to the east, the Pacific to the south and Costa Rica to the west.

2. 'La entrada de esa región se halla á treinta millas de Davíd y el camino es un plano inclinado que el viajero asciende sin advertirlo, hasta una altura de tres mil quinientos á cuatro mil píes. Es tan suave la subida que solo cree uno haberla realizado cuando vuelve los ojos hacia atrás y ve á distancia el océano y las islas próximo á la costa adyacentes. … A corta distancia de la parte más estrecha, la llanura se ensancha nuevamente para terminar, luego, cortada á pico por un despeñadero abrupto desde el cual se ven, abajo, el poblado del Bajo Boquete, las casas de las fincas de café del Alto Boquete, y el río Caldera que serpentea por un valle de tres ó cuatro millas de largo por una ó dos de ancho. Para entrar á la región del Boquete, es preciso, pues, ascender por la llanura hasta una altura aproximada de tres mil quinientos pies sobre el nivel

del mar, y luego descender rápidamente á buscar el valle del mismo río Caldera á una altura de tres mil.'

3. 'En el Boquete no hay ahora ni un solo indígena. ¿Fue exterminada la raza aborigen por los conquistadores españoles? ¿Emigró ésta para las regiones inaccesibles de la cordillera? Lo probable es que los indígenas, esclavizados y perseguidos por los conquistadores, abandonaran las llanuras en donde éstos tenían evidente superioridad por sus armas y disciplina, y emigraran a las alturas, valles y desfiladeros del Boquete y de la cordillera en busca de posiciones estratégicas bien protegidas. Seguramente hubo ataques y luchas reñidas entre invasores y aborígenes, hasta que éstos, diezmados ya, se internaron más aún en las montañas.'

4. Spanish-controlled viceroyalty governing over northern South America and Panamá from 1717 until 1819, and later, for a brief period, the name for the republic comprising present-day Colombia and Panamá.

5. Incidentally, the establishment of the Chiriquí Land Co. came about as a result of extensive surveying and infrastructural development conducted in the area during the 1850s, under the joint authorization of the Colombian, Costa Rican and United States governments. The latter government, under the direction of President Lincoln, had considered Chiriquí as a possible site for slave colonization prior to the American Civil War, as a possible solution to defuse escalating regional tensions between the Union and Confederacy (see Osorio, 1988).

6. A large, private estate.

7. 'A pesar de la fuerte oposición que encontraron, algunos de los humildes agricultores se asentaron permanentemente y, poco a poco, trajeron o formaron sus familias.'

8. Incidentally, Panamá unquestionably owes its independence to intervening actions by the US government, which viewed the Colombian government as standing in the way of the United States' resolute intention to complete and control the isthmian canal (see McCullough, 1977; Robinson, 1907).

9. 'El valeroso aventurero alemán había entregado su vida en la consecución de un sueño. Su esfuerzo no fue en vano. Las generaciones que le sucedieron asumieron el reto que dejó y, aunque transcurrió más de medio siglo, la vía de comunicación permanente entre Chiriquí y Bocas del Toro se convirtió en realidad.'

10. Henceforth cited as DEC, 2003.

11. 'En el proceso de desarrollo histórico de los distritos chiriquianos, la presencia y la interacción de personajes, tanto nativos como extranjeros, se mezcla indefiniblemente para sembrar en estas tierras las semillas de una identidad que, generacionalmente, se ha venido desarrollando. El espíritu particularista de cada distrito, por cuyas raíces fluye la savia de los pioneros, se ha convertido en ladrillos del edificio social que hoy integra el rico y matizado mosaico de la idiosincrasia de esta tierra.'

12. Henceforth cited as MACI, 1947.

13. Over 43% of the total economically active population (55% of total economically active males) in Boquete was employed in the primary sector industries of agriculture, livestock and forestry during the year 2000 (DEC, 2003).

14. Measured by the number of individuals who derive their livelihood from each category, the next eight largest economic categories after agriculture are: retail commerce, construction, manufacturing, domestic service, transportation,

storage and communication, public administration, education and hotel and restaurant (DEC, 2003).

15. 'No hace mucho, el interés creciente ... [en] El Boquete – más á los extraños que á los criollos – ha hecho colocar el nombre de ese territorio panameño en la lista de los lugares recomendados por el célebre Doctor W.C. Gorgas, Jefe de la Oficina de Sanidad en la Zona, y Coronel de la Armada de los Estados Unidos, para que los empleados de la Isthmian Canal Commission pasen allá sus vacaciones anuales.'

16. Pensioner discounts include: 25% off restaurant meals, 30% off public transportation, 15% off medical bills, 10% off prescriptions, 25% off domestic airfare and 50% off entertainment.

Chapter 4

Longing for Landscape: Assessing Residential Tourists' Experiences of Boquete

Introduction

The fundamental focus of this chapter concerns an effort to weave together a variety of sources and voices in order to illuminate the prevailing ways that residential tourists experience their place of residence in Boquete. Despite subtle variations in the social and economic composition of the residential tourist cohort in Boquete, residential tourists' intentions for living in this place are relatively homogeneous. Indeed, residential tourists share quite similar experiences of this place because they also share similar motivations for living here and, collectively, they socially negotiate and construct a shared residential tourist identity and community here in Boquete. In this chapter I argue that residential tourists fundamentally experience Boquete not as a place, but rather as a landscape from which they are alienated in a number of ways. The underlying implication of this experience is that the meaning residential tourists assign to their immediate surroundings – both human and physical – is derived not from direct engagement but rather from a passive, disaffected perception of their surroundings from a distance. Whereas meaning derived from experiences of direct engagement with the surrounding world is created through processes of collective interaction, sharing and negotiation, meaning derived from experiences of indirect engagement with the surrounding world is created through the passive and individualized processes of selective vision and the projection of personal ideals and desired meaning onto objects in sight. As such, by fundamentally experiencing Boquete as landscape, residential tourists' experiences of and meanings for their surrounding world are more informed by personal ideals and remote perception than by shared experience and collective meaning derived from active engagement.

In proceeding towards this conclusion, this chapter is divided into two main sections. In the first section, I construct what I term the promotional grand image of Boquete. The framework for this section is modeled after Buller and Hoggart's (1994) analytic method, in which the authors evaluate how British expatriates' residential experiences of rural France compare to promotional images of expatriate life in this region, as advertised in the

British media. Using their work as a methodological model, I undertake a critical analysis of place-based real estate advertisements which aim to attract residential tourists to Boquete. From this analysis I identity four main promotional images, or tropes, of Boquete, the sum of which comprise what I term the promotional grand image of Boquete.

In the second half of this chapter, I employ this promotional grand image of Boquete as a comparative framework for examining how residential tourists articulate their own personal experiences of Boquete. Towards the conclusion of this chapter, I briefly explore how the formation and growth of a distinct residential tourist community, which is socially isolated from its native counterpart, serves to facilitate and reinforce this group's predominant experience of Boquete as landscape.

Promotional Grand Image

Place-based advertising

In physical space, Boquete has quickly evolved into a residential tourist 'theatre of consumption' (Leiss *et al.*, 1986), where real estate commodities are being (re)produced, subdivided, marketed, sold and consumed with increasing prevalence and conspicuity. Today, one cannot walk through Bajo Boquete without confronting an arsenal of advertising signs and images pitching such messages as: 'Land For Sale', 'Own Boquete', 'Farms, Lots, Homes For Sale' (Figure 4.1). The omnipresence of real estate advertisements – all in English and all clearly marketed towards the residential tourist class – which are scattered throughout the district all serve as visible reminders that Boquete has become a bona fide marketplace for residential tourist consumption. However, the promotion of place consumption visible in the physical spaces of Boquete pales in comparison to the advertising blitzkrieg taking place in the virtual spaces of Boquete on the Internet. In this virtual world, Boquete is, first and foremost, represented not as a living place, but rather as an ambiguously generic consumer's paradise where audacious residential tourist dreams and fantasies are manufactured and commodified. The paltry number of purely informational websites about Boquete has been relegated to the bowels of Internet search engine queues, buried under pages and pages of links to flashy real estate promotional websites, which grow in number by the month. Place promotion, which geographer Velvet Nelson (2005: 131) defines as 'the deliberate use of publicity and marketing for the purpose of communicating selective and specific images of a place to a target audience,' is certainly an active and influential force shaping residential tourists' initial perceptions of Boquete; these are perceptions that form in the mind long before new residents ever set foot in the place they intend to call home.

Figure 4.1   One of several signs in the commercial center of Bajo Boquete which market real estate to residential tourists (photo by author, 2005)

Fundamentally, media, through which advertising messages are communicated 'help shape and set the parameters of discussion and understanding' regarding a particular issue, Anders Hansen contends (2002: 500). To be effective, place promotion must successfully reflect its targeted audience's intentions and desires for that place. As such, it is an adequate starting point to construct a theoretical socio-cultural model regarding how residential tourists might experience Boquete. In support of this idea, McHugh, in his analysis of retirement community promotional advertising in the United States, argues that place images are 'mold and mirror of deeply embedded ... attitudes and societal values' (2000: 103). Similarly, in their analysis of residential place experiences in Bedford, Connecticut, Duncan and Duncan insist that 'advertising spins narratives that relate an object for sale to a whole constellation of places, practices, and other objects. In order to be efficacious, these narratives draw upon culturally ingrained symbolic systems that *resonate* with the consumer' (2004: 51, emphasis added). In other words, successful advertising appropriates valid, socially held values about certain consumer products, and creatively reflects these values back to the intended audience of consumers, in order to relate the products being sold to a larger constellation of identifiable social values and desires. Ultimately, in striving to make this connection, place-based advertising is about crafting a certain image and character of 'a place, a way of life, and a place-based identity' (Duncan & Duncan, 2004: 49) that are highly appealing to outsiders (Burgess, 1982; Perkins, 1989).

As residential tourism has become firmly established in Boquete during the past five years, a clear and coherent rhetoric of imagery themes, or tropes, has emerged within place promotional advertisements. These tropes, I argue, serve to reflect, inform and normalize among residential tourists a collective experience of Boquete as an aesthetic and consumable landscape. The tropes function to idealize certain features of Boquete, while wholly obscuring other very real aspects of Boquete as an everyday place and community.

Before we examine the images of place promotion encountered in the advertising of Boquete as an ideal destination for residential tourism, it is important to understand who are the producers of Boquete's promotional advertisements and what is the context of the advertisements' production. As foreign interest in residential tourism in Boquete has exponentially grown over the past three to five years, so too has the level of sophistication in developing, promoting and selling real estate within the district. As described in the previous chapter, the majority of real estate brokers and developers currently conducting business in Boquete are foreigners, often from the same countries of origin as the residential tourists to whom they are marketing their real estate commodities. Consequently, the place promotion of Boquete occurring at present is overwhelmingly being produced by outsiders for consumption by outsiders.

Because the producers of place promotion share a similar socio-cultural identity with their directed audience, they arguably are best attuned to the subtleties of desire that motivate residential tourists to seek residence in Boquete. Buller and Hoggart contend that, for prospective expatriates, 'buying a home overseas, especially for those with meagre personal knowledge of the country and locality involved, and particularly when changing a primary residence, is a big step. To make this move, buyers have to be convinced that they will find the "dream" they are in search of' (1994: 100). The purpose of these place-based advertisements, then, is to fulfill the exact desires of prospective residential tourists and convince them that their residential tourist dreams may be attained in Boquete. In addition, these promotional advertisements must assure prospective residential tourists that investing their life savings into this rather unconventional endeavor is a rational and economically sound decision.

The following analysis of place-based advertising in Boquete is based on a sample of real estate promotional images and texts which I encountered on Internet websites, in print media and in the physical spaces of Boquete. Of these sources: seven are advertisements for master-planned residential communities; four are advertisements for the services and properties of residential real estate agencies; and three are non-specific, yet commercially motivated, 'move to Boquete' themed lifestyle advertisements. From this analysis, I present below the four primary promotional tropes, or themes, which collectively capture the essence of how Boquete is packaged and marketed as an ideal residential tourist destination to prospective residential tourists.

Trope of the natural ideal

The most fundamental and salient theme evident in the place-based advertisements of Boquete as an ideal destination for residential tourism is the trope of the natural ideal. This trope appeals to prospective residential tourists by promising an intimate relationship with a landscape that is truly natural and unspoiled; one that is not available in their countries of origin. The trope of the natural ideal evokes an implicit contrast to the chaotic landscapes of urban disorder from which these prospective residential tourists seek to escape. For instance, one lifestyle advertisement, which promotes residential tourism in Boquete, tells its readers, 'there is something in even the most urbanized soul which yearns for *reunion with nature*' (emphasis added). Evoking subtle reference to man's origins in the Garden of Eden and his subsequent expulsion into dystopia, the advertisement sells Boquete to the developed world's urbanites as a fresh setting for man's rightful return to a harmonious and superior 'nature'.

Adding a utopian dimension to this trope of the natural ideal, another real estate advertisement urges readers to, 'discover Panama's Secret Shangri-La.' Guiding prospective buyers through an imaginary tour of Boquete en route to their master-planned, gated residential community, the advertisement continues:

> You take a ten minute walk from the nearby picture perfect riverside town … and you pass through a narrow passage and beyond you'll gasp with amazement as you enter a real secret Shangri-La … with it's [sic] own micro-climate … where spring reigns eternal.

Evoking the image of a landscape of paradise, this promotional narrative offers potential residential tourists the real-life opportunity to live in an environment of exotic nature that ostensibly possesses *unreal* beauty.

The most efficient shorthand for conveying this trope of the natural ideal in Boquete's promotional advertisements is through use of the keyword 'paradise', which is the second most prevalent keyword utilized in promotional literature surveyed for this analysis. The only keywords appearing with greater frequency in these advertisements were the words 'natural' and 'nature'. In several of the advertisements, one finds references to Boquete as a 'secret' or 'undiscovered' paradise, intended to convey not only a scene of perfect 'nature', but further one which the residential tourist may privately enjoy without having to share it with others. In fact, therein lays the allure of the trope of the natural ideal: it is the idea that one may own a piece of this paradise for a price. This trope effectively commodifies not just land in Boquete; more importantly it commodifies an image of utopian landscape and situates this fantastic image in Boquete. This trope is epitomized by one real estate firm's advertisement in Boquete's bilingual newspaper. The headline reads: 'For sale … a slice of paradise' (Figure 4.2). Below the bold tagline there appears, as the visualized objectification of this 'paradise', a photograph of a verdant expanse of the highland basin in Boquete.

Similar to this photograph, the promotional imagery of this trope paints for prospective residential tourists an alluring vista of natural paradise through which they may escape their blighted and imperfect spatial realities of urbanity and overdevelopment. This alluring landscape of Boquete is

Figure 4.2   Real estate company advertisement which appeared in the May 2005 edition of the *Bajareque Times*, Boquete's bilingual monthly newspaper

painted in the broadest, most abstract strokes so that the emptied-out natural setting may be adaptable to the highly individualized contexts of fantasy and escapism that each prospective residential tourist brings to this Edenic vista of imagination. The imagery of this trope, however, is built largely upon a murky foundation of absence: the absent, negative image of civilization from which this verdant fantasy beckons us to retreat, and of the mundane, everyday contexts of Boquete as a real place and living community.

Trope of the authentic village

Closely related to the trope of the natural ideal in Boquete's real estate promotional advertising is the trope of the authentic village. This trope builds on the image of the natural ideal by offering prospective residential tourists the opportunity to live in a quaint, 'authentic' village, in which its humble and contented inhabitants live simply off the land. The promotional imagery characterized by this trope also relates to Tuan's (1977) and Porteous's (1996) notions of middle landscape because it situates this 'authentic village' of Boquete in an imagined, intermediate space in between the extremes of 'nature' and 'civilization' which, as mentioned in in Chapter 2, is spatial fodder for the fanciful creation of idealistic landscape imagery. Similar to Duncan and Duncan's idea of the 'invented village', the crafted images classified under this trope evoke feelings of nostalgia for 'simpler, quieter, more wholesome places that have an air of historical authenticity and an aura of uniqueness about them' (2004: 5). In contrast to the exotic undertones presented in the previous trope, the trope of the authentic village seeks to connote comfort, security and knowable community, lest the thought of a total escape to Edenic 'nature' seems *too* extreme for some prospective residential tourists.

In this way, one online advertisement for a master-planned community in Boquete offers prospective residential tourists the 'special characteristic of a private village … to provide a safe place for your pleasure.' At this residential development, the promotional narrative continues, 'you will enjoy a quiet environment surrounded by a country side view of mountains,' and experience 'an ecological and tourist feeling with the best climate and security.' In this image, the 'authentic village' is associated with comfort and protection, while still being close to nature.

In another advertisement for a gated development of residential properties, prospective residential tourists are offered, in large bold type, the opportunity to 'own a share of a working coffee plantation, tastefully woven among the exquisite custom homes.' Evoking nostalgia for an imagined community of yeoman farmers (albeit with custom homes), the promotion sells Jeffersonian idealism to those seeking an imagined return to a simpler and better time of quaint, rustic village living. Of course, residents here surely will not owe any real obligations to this 'working plantation' surrounding their homes. They will not lose sleep over the liabilities of blight and insect infestation which notoriously prey on coffee plants, nor will they suffer from long days of hard labor required to cultivate and harvest the crop. Rather, this 'working plantation' will serve as a backdrop, a visual amenity, for residential tourist life in this real estate development. The scene will be available to enjoy when it is convenient and ignore when it is not. It will remain in the background available to reinvigorate, as needed, the romantic fantasy of life in an authentic village.

Encountering place-based imagery similar to this trope in his research, McHugh comments that: 'Escape is central in utopian thought … the great founding myth of America, a cultural motif that has been expressed throughout American history as a heightened propensity to migrate to greener pastures wherever they are deemed to be' (2003: 173). The desire to escape the chaos of modernity finds refuge in the image of the 'authentic village', which evokes at once nostalgia for an imagined place and time of social harmony, Arcadian simplicity and aesthetic beauty. Like this, one advertisement promises its readers that, upon entering their master-planned community in Boquete, 'you feel as though you're step-ping back in time.' Meanwhile, another general residential tourist lifestyle advertisement evokes nostalgia for simpler times more explicitly:

> Why do people come to Boquete? It's still outrageously affordable. There's a feeling of freedom and security, something like being in the U.S. in the 1950s. The countryside is beautiful. The town is quaint – something like the ones in the old cowboy and Indian films.

Blending anachronistic images of two distinct and highly idealized American eras, this advertisement evokes nostalgia not only for the inno-cent childhood years of the baby boomer generation, but also for an earlier frontier era reminiscent of adventure, opportunity and optimism.

Overall, like the preceding trope, the promotional imagery character-ized by the trope of the authentic village seeks to play off prospective resi-dential tourists' desire to escape the disorders of urbanity and modernity. Building on the imagery established through the trope of the natural ideal, the imagery of the authentic village offers residential tourists retreat to a simpler time and place, where exotic nature and adventure lay just beyond the (oft-gated) comforts of the small, community village. What is conveyed via images of the authentic village is a heavy dose of fantasy regarding what community life is like in Boquete. Notably absent from these promotional appeals are any meaningful references to or specific representations of the actual, living community that has existed in Boquete for more than a century.

Trope of exclusive distinction

The third trope, that of exclusive distinction, is an explicit attempt by promoters to define and link as compatible the 'sophisticated' identities of residence and resident. With the promotional imagery characterized by this trope, advertisers appeal directly to prospective residential tourists' tastes, packaging Boquete as an exclusive and distinguished destination capable of satisfying their discerning palates. For example, the most promi-nent master-planned community in Boquete, Valle Escondido, introduces prospective residents to the gated estate on their website as follows:

> At a time when all of the great travel locations in the Americas are beginning to resemble each other, and where every once beautiful land-scape is being increasingly dotted with generic tourist resort construc-tion, it seems like it's harder than ever to just find a clean, unspoiled, quiet, soul-cleansing spot to unwind, relax and get away from it all. As the maddening crowds flock to Cabot [sic] and Cancun, and the spring

break legions cram into nightclubs and bars across Mexico and Florida, where does a person go when all they want is peace and quiet, sun and serenity? They go to Valle Escondido, in beautiful Boquete, Panama.

Conveyed in this advertisement is the notion that Boquete is not the typical tourist landscape of overdevelopment and inauthenticity. Employing the place names of four mass tourist and retirement destinations as dissociative symbols, this advertisement pitches Boquete as an alternative, off the beaten path destination for the discriminating and worldly residential tourist.

This trope of exclusive distinction similarly is evoked in the place description for an up-and-coming residential tourist resort community, which currently is being developed in the district by Canadian developers. A print advertisement for the development, whose slogan not incidentally is 'far from the ordinary', opens with the following invitation:

There are certain people who know that there is more to life if you actively seek it; who have an adventurous spirit that longs to discover and investigate uncharted territory. If you are one of these people, we invite you to explore Cielo Paraiso [Heaven Paradise] and uncover the mystique of this exclusive resort community in Boquete, Panama.

With a subtle hint of magical realism, this image of Boquete brings to mind a landscape so exotic that it exists outside the domain of mapped territory (Figure 4.3). This particular advertisement, as well as the trope of exclusive distinction it exemplifies, implicitly appeals to residential tourists' desire to live among a small, exclusive group of worldly and sophisticated residential tourists who demand experiences that are far richer and less mediated than those available at overdeveloped mass tourist and retirement destinations.

This trope of exclusive distinction is further conveyed in a newspaper advertisement for Own Boquete, a residential real estate firm. The bold heading of the advertisement declares: 'Some people live looking at the mountain. Some people live near the mountain, but only a few live on the mountain. Come visit us and see what the good life is all about.' Like the previous promotional narrative, this advertisement seeks to complementarily relate the identities of destination and residential tourist, and distinguish both from the run-of-the-mill mass residential tourist destinations and personalities, so that the identities of both become established as tastefully exclusive. Through the promotional imagery of this third trope, Boquete becomes imagined as 'a privileged and unique place in the world,' for an exceptional class of residential tourist, as yet another real estate advertisement claims.

CIELO PARAISO
BOQUETE • PANAMA

There are certain people who know that there is more to life if you actively seek it; who have an adventurous spirit that longs to discover and investigate uncharted territory. If you are one of these people, we invite you to explore Cielo Paraiso and uncover the mystique of this exclusive resort community in Boquete, Panama. • Cielo Paraiso offers resort style living at its best. Estate homesites with views to the spectacular Baru Volcano, the jagged peaks of the Talamanca Mountains, the Pacific Ocean and islands and the towering Jaramillo Mountain to the north are available within this private gated community. Relax and enjoy the sunset and the moonrise at the Clubhouse or simply stay home and enjoy your custom designed and built home.

PRIVATE 18-HOLE CHAMPIONSHIP GOLF COURSE DESIGNED BY J. MICHAEL POELLOT
FULL SERVICE CLUBHOUSE INCLUDING TENNIS, SQUASH, POOL, SPA & FITNESS CENTER
PLANNED OPENING FOR THE GOLF COURSE AND CLUBHOUSE IS EARLY 2007.
PRE-SALE RESERVATIONS FOR ESTATE RESIDENCES ARE NOW BEING ACCEPTED.

Phone: (507) 720.2431 • Fax: (507) 720.2432 • e-mail: sales@cieloparaiso.com

Figure 4.3   Promotional advertisement for an 'exclusive resort community,' which appeared in an English-language Panamá travel magazine in 2005

Trope of landscape prospecting

The fourth imagery trope presented in the place promotion of Boquete to residential tourists is that of landscape prospecting. While this theme has much to do with touting real estate in Boquete as an incredible financial investment, it also seeks to impress upon the prospective residential tourist an urgency to act now in order to experience the quaintness of Boquete before impending growth and development irrevocably degrade the landscape. In this sense the trope evokes two distinct, yet related, images of what Boquete's identity will be like in the future, in order to motivate real estate sales in the present. Taken as a whole, the trope implies the following: come invest in an authentic residential tourist experience in Boquete now, while at the same time, investing for financial gains in the future.

The first half of this trope can be seen in the following excerpt from an online real estate promotional advertisement: 'Have you ever been to a place where you met someone who told you, "yeah, it's nice now ... but you should have seen it 10 years ago"? That's what we think you'll be saying about Panama not so many years from now.' A similar online advertisement declares that, 'you can be one of the original pioneers in what is poised to be this decade's next great retirement destination. But you'll have to act quick because the secret's out!' These promotional appeals go the furthest to quantify the desirable amenities of Boquete as limited commodities ripe for consumption by residential tourists. They effectively function to flatten the complex, experiential depth of Boquete, as a living, dynamic place, in order to present the clear and simple image of Boquete as an emerging marketplace for residential tourism. Through this imagery of landscape prospecting, Boquete becomes represented as an unaffecting, inorganic commodity or resource to be tapped, exploited and disposed of upon depletion.

Boquete is also promoted as a landscape of real estate investment to pragmatic and/or opportunistic residential tourists seeking a sound and/or lucrative financial investment. One lifestyle promoter exalts the financial sensibility of residential tourism in Panamá as follows:

> Panama is truly one of the best, if not the best residency deal in the world today. For the price the benefits are incomparable. Not to mention the extraordinary opportunity to be a pioneer in this decade's great retirement haven. We expect property prices to continue their rapid climb here as they did in Costa Rica when they introduced their famed Pensionado Program. It is a great chance to get in on the ground floor at an incredibly low price on what we believe to be the number one retirement haven of the decade.

Through the trope of landscape prospecting, Boquete and Panamá in general are marketed as inanimate commodities rather than organic, mutable places with rich histories, unique ways of life and, most importantly, real communities of people going about the daily business of living, dying, working, interacting, prospering and struggling. Instead, these dynamic places are presented in the image of exploitable commodities to be bought and sold for profitable gain, much like those traded and speculated upon in the financial markets.

Along the same lines as this 'act now' investment appeal is the following narrative from an online advertisement pitching the services of a local real estate firm. It seductively predicts that 'if you missed out on double digit returns on such locations the likes of San Miguel Allende, Lake Chapala, Cabo San Lucas, Aspen, Vail and others, you may have one more chance. Boquete will likely follow suit.' By analogously associating Boquete with a class of socially regarded first-class tourist and retirement destinations, this enticing image seeks to place a speculative value on the commodities of real estate property and landscape amenities in Boquete.

Discussion

Ultimately through these four tropes, the place promoters who seek to market Boquete as an ideal destination for residential tourism effectively *frame the setting* for residential tourists' initial encounters with Boquete. The aggregate imagery of these four tropes results in what I term the promotional grand image of Boquete as an idealized landscape for residential tourism. The promotional grand image is an elaborate and imaginative *parergon*, or 'by-work', which awaits the heroic action, the prospective residential tourist, to inhabit and orient the setting (Andrews, 1999). In this sense, it represents an inviting, vacant landscape of illusory paradise beckoning the prospective residential tourist to 'insert oneself here'. This landscape represented through the promotional grand image is coherent, simple and benign; a landscape that is at once utopian in nature, a rural idyll, an exclusive and authentic experience, and a capitalistic commodity to be bought, sold and speculated upon.

In essence, the promotional grand image of Boquete offers prospective residential tourists a manufactured and illusory landscape, not a real place. The promotional grand image evokes Cosgrove's idea of landscape as a way of seeing that 'distances us from the world in critical ways, defining a particular relationship with nature and those who appear in nature and offers us the illusion of a world in which we may participate subjectively by entering the picture frame along the perspective axis'

(1984: 55). It encourages prospective residential tourists to project their own romantic fantasies of paradise, exclusivity, sublime 'nature' and simple village living onto the fabricated canvas of landscape, which obscures the mundane and imperfect, yet real and dynamic, qualities of Boquete as a place and community. It invites these outsiders to look with self-serving eyes upon the whole of Boquete and its many parcels of land through aesthetic and financial lenses of perception.

This grand image promotes the experience of Boquete as an idyllic landscape of residential tourism by reducing the complexities of place into commodity fetishism for visual and real estate consumption. The result is that Boquete becomes presented as a 'world apart': an illusory world of consumption alienated from the contexts of its production (Mitchell, 1996; Sack, 1992). The images of Boquete presented in these advertisements are given no contextual basis for grounding them in time and place; rather they are presented as floating, unfettered illusions of a manufactured paradise free of makers or history.

What is notably absent from this promotional grand image is any reference to Boquete as a dynamic, meaningful place with value that transcends these aesthetic and financial preoccupations. These very real qualities of Boquete that have been omitted from the promotional grand image are collectively what McHugh (2003) terms the 'absent image'. While the promotional grand image is neat and tidy, the 'absent image' existing beneath the promotional image's facade is too dynamic and imperfect to be represented visually. It comprises all of the tangible and intangible elements of Boquete, as a place and community, which are obscured by the curtain of the promotional grand image of Boquete as landscape.

In its totality, this promotional image functions to create a residential tourist landscape through many approaches: by 'restoring nature to her pristine condition,' (Meinig, 1979); by erasing the social, cultural, historical and political realities of place in order to create illusions of order, simplicity and coherence; by offering residential tourists a consumer's paradise; and, in general, by representing Boquete as a bare, aesthetic canvas onto which residential tourists may project their personal fantasies, ideals and desires. Importantly, though, the promotional grand image of Boquete and the landscape of residential tourist paradise it represents are just as much sustained by what is absent as they are by what is (re)present(ed). This is because the images of Edenic paradise, authentic village life, exclusive living and joyful consumption rely on illusion and a measured estrangement from the everyday, real contexts of Boquete as a dynamic, organic place in order to sustain the precariously contrived image of this grand landscape.

Having established and explored the promotional grand image of Boquete, we must now assess this representation's credibility. In other words, to what extent does this commercially driven representation of Boquete correspond with established residential tourists' actual perceptions of Boquete? After all, it is quite feasible to imagine how this grand image might appear as a fantastic and contrived sales gimmick to the experienced residential tourist living in Boquete. On the other hand, the allure of willful seduction and the desire to see Boquete as the idyllic residential tourist paradise of one's dreams should not be underestimated. Indeed, upon exploring residents' perceptions of their surroundings in the exclusive community of Bedford, Connecticut, Duncan and Duncan comment that these residents 'sense a knowingness about the imagery that [they] realize is an illusion and yet is deeply pleasurable in its association nevertheless. One could say that there is a kind of cultivated fantasy, a belief that one wishes to retain in the face of contradictory evidence, not unlike an older child's belief in Santa Claus' (2004: 51).

Regardless of how closely residential tourists' actual experiences of Boquete ultimately correlate with the promotional grand image, this projected and highly publicized representation of Boquete nonetheless provides an excellent conceptual basis for examining how outsiders see Boquete and why this place has acquired special, international status as an 'ideal' residential tourist destination in recent years. However, there is good reason to suspect that the promotional grand image does indeed play a significant role in shaping residential tourists' enduring perceptions of Boquete. In fact, McHugh argues that one's first impressions of a place 'tend to remain as residue, shaping long-lasting views about a place as a discovered home' (2003: 167). In this regard the promotional grand image may very well serve as both 'mold' and 'mirror' (McHugh, 2000) of residential tourists' ideological perceptions of Boquete; reflecting as well as informing the shape of their experiences in this new place of home.

Individual Articulations of Place Experience

Given that the promotional grand image's dominant theme concerns the natural environment of Boquete, it is not surprising that residential tourist informants emphasized their personal encounters with 'nature' in Boquete while articulating their residential experiences during interviews. Significantly, many of the same pristine and surreal aesthetic qualities ascribed to Boquete's environment in the trope of the natural ideal are readily apparent in residential tourists' own articulations of their experiences of Boquete. Take for example the sentiments of Charles and Melinda,[1] a residential tourist couple, originally from the northeastern United States, who had lived in the district for five years at the time of our interview at their home in the *corregimiento* of Alto Boquete. Responding to the question of why the couple chose to move to Boquete, Melinda immediately told me: 'One thing that hit us the first time we came [to Boquete] – and it just endures – is the beauty of the nature: the plants, the flowers.' She continued speaking of the natural surroundings, exclaiming that, 'every day there is some encounter with nature [that is] unexpected … the view of the clouds every day is different. It's just an amazing area.' Hearing about Melinda's experiences, I was struck by the intensity with which she invoked and objectified 'nature' as if it were some benevolent visitor with whom her path crossed on a daily basis. Towards this 'nature', she unquestionably expressed great reverence; however, at the same time, she conceived it as an entity apart, something that could be selectively channeled when the desire for its inspiration arose.

This experience of 'nature' as a discrete, majestic entity to be encountered and admired is reminiscent of J.B. Jackson's (1997) commentary regarding the 'Amateur Thoreaus' who, according to Jackson, 'proclaim that nature is something outside of us, something green which we can perhaps enjoy as a spectacle … but which is only distantly related to us' (p. 339). Melinda's attitude towards 'nature', which exemplifies the prevailing sentiments of many residential tourists in Boquete, indeed subtly implies a certain distance and detachment between herself and 'nature'. Equally notable in her remarks is the primacy of visual perception and aesthetic evaluation to her experience of the natural world around her.

The incredibly high aesthetic value that residential tourists ascribe to their natural surroundings in Boquete is so intense and profound it often borders on appreciating it as a sacred entity. This is epitomized, perhaps in the extreme, by the sentiments of Walter, an unmarried and retired residential tourist from the southern United States who, at the time of our interview, had been living in Boquete for three years. For the occasion of our interview, Walter invited me up to his state of the art residence, which had just been completed atop an elevated vista surrounded on all sides by coffee fincas. This layout created the appearance of a luxuriously inhabited residential island rising out of a sea of waxy, green coffee bushes.

In recounting his first visit to Boquete years before, Walter said: 'the feeling I had when I first saw [Boquete] was that this is a place that is enchanted.' Unprompted, Walter continued to describe his initial discovery of a sublime 'nature' in Boquete, literally referring to the experience as a 'spiritual awakening':

After several hours [of touring Boquete], I literally got to where my
front door is … and I had a religious experience. I wasn't levitating or
anything like that, but I saw the view of the valley and I don't know if
I found Boquete or Boquete found me, but I knew *instantly* that this
place was special. … It was the land, the view and the peacefulness.

It is a very *magical* area. I have a view out of any window, any door.
Turn around and there's Volcán Barú [*pointing out a window to the
north*]; there's the valley [*pointing west*]. And, you can't see the blue of
the water [*pointing south*], but I'm looking at the ocean from here,
sitting in my chair. … And that's not with binoculars or a telescope.
Where else can you do that? I look out the front [of the house] and I've
got [the neighborhood of] Jaramillo and the clouds, the mist that's
very natural. So, I knew it was special and … I knew instantly that this
was where I was going to retire. [I] canceled the plans in Costa Rica,
and [I] began the process of living here.

Hearing Walter describe the panoramic view of the surrounding landscape from his wrap-around, floor-to-ceiling windows, one could just as
easily imagine him describing the scenes in a series of framed landscape
paintings. Like Melinda's encounters with nature, in Walter's experiences
visual perception plays a principal role in his relationship with the
surrounding world; a world which is fundamentally valued for its
aesthetic – and perceived spiritual – qualities. From hearing Walter
describe his surroundings, one does not get the sense that his knowledge
of these surroundings is based on direct engagement and interaction. On
the contrary, by referring to this natural landscape as 'spiritual,' 'sacred,'
and 'magical,' there, indeed, appears to be an element of willful detachment, and a conscious effort to see the surrounding world in a highly
idealized manner from atop his residential perch.

Certainly, Walter's experience of his surroundings is what Relph (1976)
would consider to be motivated by 'authentic' and sincere intentions.
However, while this residential tourist has imbued his surroundings with
profound meaning, this meaning is wholly *personal* and, therefore, disconnected from the larger network of social meanings for these surroundings
as places of labor, struggle, home, community and so forth. This experience
of Boquete as a majestic, natural landscape, and the spiritual and benevolent significance attributed to it, fundamentally neglects to consider how
others, such as the workers who must toil daily in the fields of labor
surrounding his residence (and, in fact, were present in these fields during
our interview), might experience this environment differently and, therefore, find wholly dissimilar meaning for this space (Figure 4.4).

Figure 4.4   In the background, a residential castle recently constructed by a foreign residential tourist couple. In the foreground, a coffee finca with Ngobe Bugle laborers preparing the fields for the upcoming harvest (photo by author, 2005)

Residential tourists' detached, individualistic experiences of their surroundings in Boquete, as illustrated by Walter's narrative description, are not due to these individuals' egregious disregard for alternative experiences of and meanings for Boquete; the point, quite simply, is that a passive and selective engagement with their external environment, both natural and human, fails to provide them with a more complete, socially negotiated understanding of Boquete as a complex, multidimensional place. Their dissociated condition affords them only a highly personalized, two-dimensional image of Boquete. Fundamentally lacking is the third dimension of depth inherent to place: shared experience and collective, negotiated meaning.

This way of seeing Boquete as landscape is further reflected in residential tourists' experiences of the Boqueteño community. Similar to the correlation between the trope of the natural ideal and residential tourists' experiences of 'nature' in Boquete, residential tourists' actual experiences of the Boqueteño community closely correspond to the trope of the authentic village encountered in the place-based advertisements promoting Boquete as a destination for residential tourism.

Consider the experiences of Mark and Linda, a married residential tourist couple, originally from the Midwestern United States, who had been living in the district for 10 months at the time of our interview. The gregarious couple, in their mid-50s, were renting a small farmhouse on the edge of the district, approximately 10 kilometers outside Bajo Boquete. They excitedly told me about their plans to open a small bed and breakfast in Caldera, a rural *corregimiento* on the outskirts of the district, far away from the nucleus of residential tourism settlement and development focused around Bajo Boquete.

Freely speaking about the decision to locate their bed and breakfast and future place of residence in the neighborhood of Caldera, Mark explained:

> I think [Bajo] Boquete is not that attractive of a downtown. ... They had a lot of old buildings and stuff, and instead of doing anything to fix them up and give some historical kind of feeling to the town, like you're in a little Swiss Alp town [be]cause that's what it'd be. It's sort of like a Swiss Alp town; you come down in and it's like what you see in the Switzerland area, only it's a conglomeration of not very good modern architecture, not very good historical architecture, [and] some really little nice things. It's mishmash, so it's Los Angeles-alpine reduced down to three thousand people ... in a static valley.
>
> Come over to Caldera and you have a total sense of a gorgeous little town. ... The houses are spaced *way* far apart and the mountain views are just gorgeous and *not static* because there's always continually clouds hiding [the mountains] and revealing them, and hiding them and revealing them. Many times I've been [in Caldera] in the evenings and – it isn't really a town square like in Mexico where people come out at night and hang around – but people come out and promenade ... In the late afternoons, I've seen women with their umbrellas, for shade, walking down the street, and I go, God, that's a Monet painting. (emphases in original)

In Mark's comparison of the two neighborhoods what is immediately evident is that all of his surroundings – from the buildings, to the mountains, to the inhabitants of Caldera – are scrutinized not for their functional identities or values, but rather for their aesthetic values, as merited by his personal tastes. What his statements – most particularly those regarding Bajo Boquete – reveal is a tremendous lack of understanding and appreciation for the way that Boquete has organically evolved over time to become a meaningful place of home, work and community to its residents. What trumps an awareness of or sensitivity towards the greater functional and social significances of these physical forms and spaces is Mark's preoccupation with their superficial and highly-personal significance as aesthetic forms. His perceptions are guided by his intense and highly personal yearnings to have the facade of Boquete beautified so that it may become more visually attractive.

While elements of visual objectification and appropriation are close to the surface of his impressions, what also lies embedded in his observations of Bajo Boquete is the veiled political and ideological belief that someone should take physical control to remake and, in the process, beautify the physical forms and spaces of this place. At the heart of this ideological belief there is an emphasis of his personal values over the socially negotiated collective values of the community, and a possessive and consumer-oriented mentality which prizes landscape appreciation and aesthetic tastes over notions of the public good and of place as an organic – if visually untidy – field of care. This instance of social nescience, manifest in the egocentric experience of place as aesthetic landscape, is symptomatic of the more general condition of social alienation which isolates residential tourists from the greater native community. While residential tourists do not purposely intend to be insensitive to the notions of place and community, they nonetheless lack a cultivated sense of true awareness that their surroundings signify much more than what is revealed in their form and appearance.

Interestingly, though, Mark's aesthetic evaluation of his immediate environment does not end with the natural and built environments of Boquete, but rather extends even to the human environment. Again, Mark's tendency to assign meaning to native residents solely based on their appearance betrays a profound alienation and experiential distance isolating him from their true identities as complex and dynamic individuals. Just as residential tourists are detached from meaningfully experiencing and engaging with place, so too do they live, despite intimate physical proximity, quite experientially detached from the soul of the Boqueteño community. Much of this social disaffection results from the simple fact that they are not subject to the socializing imperatives of work and civic participation, since they are mostly retired and are afforded only residential status, not citizenship. Their social participation in the local community is further hindered by the significant language barrier isolating English-tongued residential tourists from the Spanish-speaking community at large. These secluding social conditions foster and, indeed, encourage an experience of the Boqueteño community as landscape. Accordingly, the community is reduced in dimensionality to the scene of a quaint village, with its visually distant inhabitants appearing on the landscape as static images, stripped of their individuality and depth. From the perspective of the socially alienated residential tourist, the mere visual appropriation of the surrounding world and its human inhabitants are similar to viewing a work of landscape art, just as Mark relates above.

Residential tourists dearly wish to *see* this community as benevolent and contented, and its daily activities as harmonious and humbly simple, in order to validate their illusions of Boquete as a landscape of residential tourist paradise. This tendency to view community life in Boquete as genuine, prosperous and thoroughly benevolent closely correlates with the trope of the authentic village. In the absence of real, experiential knowledge about the native community, residential tourists create an imagined reality, or willful image, to mediate the void.

After having heard about Boquete on a television program on the cable television network MSNBC, Susan, a retired school teacher from California, moved to Boquete with her husband in 2004. At the time of our interview, the couple were renting a Mediterranean-style villa in the prominent residential development of Valle Escondido, where a great number of foreign residential tourists also live. Despite being happy with her new life in Boquete, Susan expressed a desire to move beyond the walls of Valle Escondido, which she perceived as being not only an enclave of social isolationism, but also a social stigma from the perspective of the native community. In fact, during our interview, Susan told me she had recently removed the 'VE' decal from her automobile, which allows residents to expediently bypass the scrutiny of guards stationed at the gated entrance, because she was embarrassed of this 'scarlet letter' which identified her as a resident of this exclusive community to the Boqueteño community at large.

Like so many other informants, Susan compared living in Boquete to the nostalgic era of her childhood. 'This is like living back in the fifties; it's such a laid-back lifestyle,' she told me. In recalling her how her impressions of the community had changed since she first arrived, Susan related the following:

> The town [of Boquete] itself, initially I was like, oh wow, this really is a little Central American town. But then after we established ourselves living here, it's our home. Boquete is just this charming, wonderful, laid-back community. The Panamanian people are as sincere and nice as any people you would ever want to meet. We've never had so many people smile at us.

We walk a lot more places than we did in the States. We don't use our car nearly as much. In fact, the first six weeks we were here, we didn't even have a car. We just walked to town, got our groceries; walked to town, went to the restaurant; walked to town, looked in the little stores; sat in the park and watched the local people. ... There's always some little [activity] in town going on that you can just go in and just watch.

This is really a family-devoted culture. We watch the Indians who walk in from the hills every morning to bring their children to school and then walk them home miles after school is over. Everybody is *so happy* that it rubs off on you. (emphasis in original)

Like most residential tourist informants, Susan expresses profound respect and admiration for the native community. However, her experiences also evince the ideology of sight, separation and distance that characterize most residential tourists' relationship with the community. The primacy of visual perception in forming her impressions of the native community is undeniably present in her repeated use of the verb 'watch'. Notably absent are any references to an active engagement with the people and social activities taking place around her. She essentially casts herself as a passive observer of the lives and scenes which pass through her field of vision. Solely based on her observations of the Ngobe Bugle parents walking their children to school, Susan understands them to be 'happy' people. Similar to Walter's experiences of 'spiritual' nature above, this imputing of meaning onto the landscape and figures in the landscape represents a type of ordering and control over the natural and human subjects so that the scene may be experienced as harmonious, just and good. Indeed, Raymond Williams contends that the experiential distance separating observer from observable object is 'mediated by a projection of personal feeling' which creates a 'subjectively particularised and objectively generalised' significance for the latter (1973: 134).

However, this visually acquired 'knowledge', and the meaning created from it, is incomplete, at best, and often downright deceiving. For example, Susan's perception of the Ngobe Bugle neglects to take into account the acute poverty and racial discrimination with which this local indigenous population is afflicted, as discussed in the previous chapter. This difference between observation and reality ultimately relates back to Berger's conclusions about landscape: 'Landscapes can be deceptive. Sometimes a landscape seems to be less a setting for the life of its inhabitants than a curtain behind which their struggles, achievements and accidents take place'. (1977: 13, 15; as cited in Cosgrove, 1984)

Residential tourists in Boquete desire two experiential ideals: they desire to experience Boquete as an aesthetic landscape of residential tourist paradise; yet they also desire a modicum of fellowship with and belonging to the greater Boqueteño community so that the former experiences feel meaningful and authentic. As a result of this strange psychological brew of desires, residential tourists are apt to selectively nurture small kernels of empirical observation or trivial gestures of community that will bolster their elaborate fantasies regarding both their lives and their surroundings in Boquete. From these small kernels of truth, residential tourists extrapolate to create a larger entity of imagined meaning in order to legitimize as authentic their ideals of social harmony and bondedness with community.

For instance, later in my interview with Charles and Melinda, Charles told me about his relationship with the native Boqueteño community during the first years of the couple's residence in Boquete:

> It was wonderful … I could walk down town and stick my head into a coffee shop and there'd be Indians and Panamanians in there. I'd go in and sit at a table, but because it's me, next thing I know I'd start a conversation and I'm one of the gang, you know? I drive down town and my arm gets sore from waving at everybody [*laughs*].

However, before Charles could finish laughing, Melinda quickly added with playful enthusiasm:

> And he walks down the street and touches everybody [and] he calls them 'amigo, amigo'. … And he's always saying 'sí, sí, sí', and I told him, stop saying sí … because you don't know what you're saying yes to [*both laughing*]!

Abruptly, however, a serious look appeared on Charles' face and he admitted to me: 'My Spanish is marginal.'

As our conversation progressed, it gradually became apparent that Charles's claim of being 'one of the gang' among the local community could not be possible, given that Charles lacked the minimum language proficiency necessary to engage in meaningful conversation with native Boqueteños. This language deficiency is surprisingly common among the residential tourists that I interviewed and is, I strongly suspect, representative of the residential tourist population at large in Boquete. This deficiency is a significant communication barrier which stands in the way of meaningful interaction and, by extension, the social and intercultural exchange of ideas, experiences, perspectives and values that are critical if residential tourists are to acquire a meaningful understanding of Boquete as a place and community. This communication divide fosters a landscape view by reducing the complex phenomena of place and community into simple gestures, trivial observations, and static images and objects, about which their significances are ambiguous, illusory and freely open to the perceiver's desired interpretation. Despite what was earlier revealed about his inability to meaningfully interact with the greater Boqueteño community, Charles later told me:

> You fall into the whole community – you know you go into the stores and they know you. I came to in a small town in New England and that's the way it was: our family business was the hardware store. And so, consequently, I knew everybody in town and they knew me. … And that's the way it is here. So we feel that we have a wonderful relationship with almost everyone in town.

As outsiders who are not familiar with collectively negotiated experiences and meanings of place, residential tourists rely primarily on their own ideals and intentions for living in Boquete to guide them through the process of constructing meaning *in situ*. As the tropes of the natural ideal and the authentic village have demonstrated, and as residential tourists' perceptions and experiences have confirmed, Boquete is primarily experienced by these outsiders as an imagined landscape of natural paradise and social utopia. It is a canvas onto which residential tourists project their ideals and intentions for their residential tourist lives in this place. Any signs, scenes or objects observed *in situ* which help to reinforce and corroborate this desired image of Boquete are immediately appropriated and assigned meaningful values. Any aspects of Boquete which do not conform to this assembled illusion of Boquete are selectively discarded, overlooked or remain unseen.

However, the fundamental value which residential tourists attribute to their experiences of Boquete only truly becomes evident when the forces of growth and development are brought into consideration. One of the most unexpected findings to come out of my interviews with residential tourist informants was the highly consistent feelings of animosity that these individuals privately expressed towards prospective and newly arriving residential tourists. This sentiment towards residential tourist newcomers plainly exposes established residential tourists' fundamental motivations for living in Boquete.

Simply put, these inbound residential tourists – and the wave of mass residential tourist development and institutionalization on which they are arriving – represent a clear and grave threat to the fragile, carefully contrived image of Boquete as a landscape of residential tourist paradise. Specifically, additional residential tourist growth and development threaten to shatter the images of the natural ideal and the authentic village, as well as the illusion of exclusive distinction, by turning Boquete into a destination for mass residential tourism. These transformative changes are certain to disrupt established residential tourists' fragile image of exclusive distinction, the delicate ideological fulcrum upon which they have balanced their aesthetic illusions of pristine nature and the rural village, on the one side, with their social illusions of genuine community solidarity and belonging, on the other.

Oddly enough, the more visible the promotional grand image of Boquete becomes – prompting newer waves of residential tourism development and settlement – the more it destroys the very ideals, illusions and imagery on which it is founded and which it seeks to promote. With these new pressures it begins to be crushed by the weight of too many prospectors seeking to profit from the landscape, whether experientially or financially.

In responding to the perceived threat that these newcomers pose to the idealized natural and social landscape of Boquete, Walter wryly told me towards the end of our interview:

> I jokingly say that I'm going to go out to the sign that says 'Bienvenidos a Boquete' and I'm going to put another sign under it that says 'Boquete's full, now go home'. I'm part of the problem, I know that. But now that I've got my piece of heaven, screw everybody else [*laughs*].

Despite his overt sarcasm, in response to my next question – regarding what advice he would have for retirees considering moving to Boquete – Walter soberly responded, with any pretext of jocularity now vacant from his face and tone: 'Bluntly speaking, don't come. That's my answer.'

Inevitably, when I would broach the subject of residential tourist growth and development with informants towards the conclusion of the scripted portion of the interviews, they invariably became gravely serious and visibly concerned, revealing a new dimension to their personas. As such, when I asked Charles and Melinda about their sentiments regarding this issue, Charles immediately replied without pretense: 'I hate it. I can't stand it. That's why you see the "For Sale" sign in my front yard.' Indeed, the couple revealed to me that they had decided to move further away from Bajo Boquete in order to escape the successive waves of residential tourist growth and development which, over the past three years, had begun to encroach upon the undeveloped forest that once buffered their property, and which had become for them, painfully visible on the surrounding landscape. Melinda described the stimulus for their decision to relocate as follows:

> When we first came here and we bought this piece of property we were the only [foreigners] here. We had a small group of indigenous Indians that lived on the other side of the ravine, but that was *all* that was here; and so no [visible] lights, no nothing. There was an old little road down there and a little road up there, and we just thought [we would have] ten years of tranquilo, just being by ourselves, but it didn't happen because a few years later – one year later – that's when the floodgates opened. (emphasis in original)

In essence, subsequent residential tourism growth and development is ruining their romanticized image of Boquete as a utopian landscape, littering the scene with visible evidence that contradicts the natural, authentic and exclusive ideals they have carefully constructed for their surroundings. The couple essentially implied that, as the amenity of landscape begins to degrade in Boquete, they now are willing to go so far as to relocate their residence to another part of Panamá in order to reclaim this highly prized landscape of residential tourist paradise.

To be fair, though, established residential tourists' animosity towards subsequent residential tourist growth and development in Boquete is not entirely motivated by self-serving interests. In fact, many residential tourist informants demonstrated genuine, altruistic concerns, on behalf of the native community, towards the previously unknown phenomena of greed, land prospecting and residential displacement that mass residential tourist growth and development have ushered into Boquete.

This altruistic concern is exemplified by the sentiments of Douglas and Carolyn, a 'first wave' residential tourist couple of Canadian origin who, at the time of our interview, had lived in the district for almost eight years. Self-proclaimed free spirits, the sixty-something couple first 'discovered' Boquete in 1995, during an extended excursion through Central America in their van following their burn-out from professional careers in British Columbia. Douglas told me that although Boquete has been greatly 'dressed up' since their first visit (at which time, Douglas reported, Boquete was 'slightly shabby,' 'blue collar,' and 'easy to be in'), he expressed that Boquete 'still feels real.'

Douglas and Carolyn spoke with me at length about their concerns for the real estate frenzy that has permeated Boquete within the past three years, inflating land prices by as much as 500%. Describing the escalating commodification of Boquete, Douglas declared:

> Many times we look at it these days as almost an epidemic of greed. It's like a virus that came in and took hold; it affects everybody and it changes people's senses. So instead of looking at [Boquete] for quality

of life, they look at it [for] quality of bank account enhancements. And that's too bad because that changes your perception.

A lot of [residential tourist newcomers] are coming for very different reasons than when we arrived here. We came here to make this our home, and a lot of those people who I've talked to, or seen around, or listened to – and you go out to a restaurant and listen to the conversations, well it's about 'well, I only paid [such] and [such] for this land' and 'I got it for this and I'm going to resell it and we'll split it up' and this kind of stuff. That's not home. You don't talk about your home that way.

Like Douglas and Carolyn, several other residential tourist informants expressed similar, charitable concerns for the perceived negative impacts that mass residential tourist growth and development were creating for the native community. (Oddly enough, though, despite informants' complicit role in creating these perceived negative impacts, informants always blamed *other* residential tourists – the newcomers – for tipping the scale of balance to engender these problems.) While their concerns about the impacts of residential tourist growth and development on the native community are commendable, they are also particularly noteworthy for this investigation because they demonstrate an implicit acknowledgment on the part of these residential tourists that a significant differential in place experience exists between native and foreign residents. This is an unspoken acknowledgment that there exists a special bond between insiders and place; a bond which they do not share, nor even fully understand, but nonetheless a bond, which these outsiders recognize as threatened, and towards which they are sympathetic.

Ultimately, though, the threat alone of anticipated residential tourist growth and development reveals the true value of Boquete to many established residential tourists, not as a meaningful and unique place of home, as many insist, but rather as a valued landscape of residential tourist amenities. As the new dynamic of growth and development becomes more and more a visible and tangible reality in Boquete, it is beginning to expose residential tourists' tenuous and unstable ties to their 'place of home'. Indeed, it appears as though Boquete serves more as an ideal *location* for the residential tourist lifestyle, and more of a suitable spatial context for the illusory landscape of natural paradise and social utopia, than as a meaningful *place* of home. Despite common declarations of Boquete being residential tourists' existential home, many indications point to the veiled truth that, for many established residential tourists, this 'home' in Boquete is in fact a conditional *thing* that they are willing to recreate elsewhere, if and when the facade of Boquete ceases to entertain their ideals and illusions of residential tourist paradise. Despite the noble concerns that Douglas expressed earlier in our interview, later, sitting in front of an oversized picture window in his living room over-looking Bajo Boquete from high above, Douglas admitted:

> What I'm worried about is losing that kind of greenness. If you do this Vail of Central America or this Aspen of Panama, what happens is that's a huge development pressure that goes on. I'm going to lose my view of what I came to Boquete for, which was this greenness and this lushness.

Like Charles and Melinda, Douglas told me that he and his wife were seriously contemplating relocating away from Boquete in response to the new and anticipated residential tourist growth and development which they perceive will ultimately destroy what they value most about Boquete: its landscape.

The ties binding residential tourists to Boquete are fragile to begin with, and they are liable to weaken even further as the pressures of growth and development continue to undermine the utopian ideals of Edenic 'nature' and social harmony that residential tourists see in its landscape. This is more or less what a native Boqueteña, who owns a modest boarding house in Bajo Boquete, predicted one afternoon during an informal conversation with me in her living room:

> I don't doubt that [many foreign residents] will leave because one thing that I see, if these people move to a country [where] they don't know the language, they don't know the people, they are only looking for a [certain] quality of life, and if they don't have that, well [*snaps her fingers and motions away*]. It's not like me. I own this property and it belongs to my family and I'm *tied* to what I have [and] I don't think they are.

Shortly after hearing this, I met with Frank and Angela, an elderly American residential tourist couple in their seventies who, at the time of our interview, had been living in Boquete for five years. Interestingly enough, during his professional career, Frank garnered international acclaim as a field photographer for one of the world's oldest and most prestigious nature magazines. Amazingly, following his decades of field assignments to virtually every corner of the world, he and his wife chose to make their retirement home in Boquete. I visited the couple at their resi-dence high on the upper slopes on a cool and misty morning, when the prominent *bajareque* clouds of thick mist had rolled over the northern rim of the highland basin, blanketing the valley below. I spoke with the couple for several hours on their porch, overlooking fog-laden Bajo Boquete far below, listening to stories about their lives and experiences here in Boquete during the past five years. Throughout the interview they made deliberate efforts to demonstrate to me how much this place meant to them as their home and how much they cherished their relationships in the Boqueteño community. Inevitably, though, our conversation drifted towards the topic of residential tourist growth and development. Perceptibly, the mood of the interview shifted into a somber state as Frank, now scowling, offered his thoughts on the topic:

> There are houses that are springing up everywhere and lots being subdivided everywhere. I heard a figure about so many *thousands* of lots having been subdivided and being available here, and I find that appalling.

> If it gets to the point that it's untenable for us, I think there are other parts of the world. We'll just move up to a little cabin in Alaska [*wife chuckles*] and buy a lot of firewood and get the thing well insulated.

After a morning-long visit with the couple, in which I had toured their house and met their part-time caretaker, a gracious Boqueteña woman, and listened to their stories from their years of residence here in Boquete, this essentially is what it all boiled down to for them. Abruptly contradicting their professed social bonds with the Boqueteño community and their stated commitment to Boquete as their meaningful home, Frank and Angela casually betrayed how, with such ease, they would be willing to give up everything they have created here in Boquete just as soon as residential tourist growth and development surpasses an arbitrary threshold of tolerance. Echoing the sentiments conveyed in the trope of landscape prospecting, the couple convey the attitude that, once the prime of the commodity of Boquete's aesthetic landscape is depleted, their main purpose for living here will have passed. Their residential tourist lifestyle of leisure and consumption they will gladly recreate elsewhere to a recreated landscape of natural paradise and social utopia.

Many residential tourist informants essentially reveal themselves as landscape nomads: individuals willing to recreate their home further along the frontier of development whenever the valued amenities of landscape in their present location begin to deteriorate under increasing pressures of growth and development. For the landscape nomad, the desire to live in a particular *place* is trumped by the desire to live among a particular *setting*, with a specific, highly desired landscape. Of course, in the greater context of this chapter, this theoretical idea ultimately raises more questions about residential tourism, Boquete, and the shape of their respective futures than it provides answers. I will further probe the exploratory ideas of landscape nomadism and a frontier of residential tourist development, as well as investigate several prospective scenarios regarding the future of residential tourism in Boquete, in the final chapter.

A Community Apart

Revisiting Burnett's (1975) rather cogent notion of 'local community', which was explored in Chapter 2, we are reminded that a discrete local community comprises a group of individuals who share a defined spatial context (such as a neighborhood or town), who participate in common activities (i.e. interaction and involvement) and who all share a sense of cohesive attitudes (i.e. identity and interests). While native and foreign residents of Boquete easily qualify as a unified local community under the first criterion, already it is becoming apparent that, in Boquete, residential tourism represents new social practices, behaviors and lifestyles; new cultural attitudes, perceptions and intentions; and a new and elite socio-economic class of inhabitants. In sum, residential tourism is a novel and distinctive social model that has taken root in Boquete, and which rivals the traditional social model under which inhabitants of this place have lived since its formation. The peregrine practitioners of this new social model have, in essence, formed their own local community around a distinct set of residential tourist activities and attitudes. In the creation and recreation of a distinct residential tourist community, the experience of Boquete as landscape not only is a defining attitude which *contributes* to the formation of this distinct community; also, it is a reinforced social *outcome* of this community. The experience of place as landscape, as an alienated condition, serves to isolate these practitioners from the larger community and, in return, their collective isolation from this larger community serves only to perpetuate their alienated condition of landscape experience.

Residential tourists' personal ideologies regarding Boquete as landscape become concretized and propagated through social interaction with other, like-minded residential tourists who possess similar lifestyle behaviors, cultural backgrounds and motivations for residing in Boquete. Individual residential tourists find little need to venture outside their insular social comfort zones, as the majority of their social needs are met within the social sphere of residential tourism. This pattern of social segregation functions to inhibit meaningful interaction and exchange with the larger, native community. Without these opportunities for meaningful interaction, residential tourists are prevented the chance to learn about the native community's experiences of and meanings for Boquete as a truly meaningful place.

Increasingly in Boquete, residential tourists' and native Boqueteños' social lives play out along two parallel paths of socialization where occasions for intersecting are becoming more infrequent as the model of residential tourism becomes more developed and institutionalized. These mostly exclusive paths of socialization are fractured along three primary factors: preferred tastes and traditions, language of use and cost of participation. Not incidentally, these factors of social distinction have each acquired symbolic social currency, serving to effectively communicate for which residential group any given social activity, organization or establishment is intended to serve.

The disparity in preferred tastes and traditions which exists between the native Boqueteño community and the residential tourist community has necessitated the creation of new services and social activities that specifically accommodate the accretion of the latter community. For example, in response to residential tourists' preference for gourmet food products and gastronomical comforts of home, a specialty grocery store opened its doors in Boquete in 2005, catering particularly to foreign tastes – and foreign wallets. Unlike the local supermarket in town, this specialty foods market stocks its shelves with American- and European-made products, as well as imported, gourmet food items such as Spanish goat cheese, Italian prosciutto, exotic truffles and fine wines from around the world. As a result, the quite social activity of grocery shopping has become segregated in Boquete, as many in the residential tourist community frequent the specialty market at one end of Bajo Boquete, while the majority of the native Boqueteño community shop in the local supermarket across town. On the surface, this new commercial establishment may appear as a benign and inconsequential accommodation whose impact is little more than to satisfy residential tourists' specific tastes for gourmet products and the comforts of home. However, imagine the greater social effects when this one example is replicated – as it currently is being done – throughout all patterns and contexts of socialization in Boquete. The experiential divide isolating two very different communities and their two very diverse ways of experiencing the very same spatial context is widening perceptibly.

Similarly, a number of newer restaurants whose advertisements and menus are printed in English, and whose entrées cost US$15, on average, effectively communicate through the symbols of language and cost that their social establishments are intended exclusively for the residential tourist community. In fact, their costs alone virtually guarantee that participation will be prohibitively expensive for the overwhelming majority of the Boqueteño community, who live in a different socio-economic reality. This is also the case for a number of highly publicized social activities, such as the

US$25-a-plate Thanksgiving, Christmas and New Year's Eve holiday galas hosted annually at the premier hotel in Boquete.

The symbolic barriers of preferred tastes and traditions, language of use and cost of participation are quite effective for fracturing the residents of Boquete into two distinct communities and for communicating to each the places where it does and does not belong. As the social model of residential tourism continues to be developed in Boquete, these visible markers of segregated socialization are becoming increasingly visible, branding all social establishments, activities and events with an identity, according to the perspective of each community, that is distinctly either *ours* or *theirs*. As the social and experiential divide broadens in Boquete, residents become increasingly isolated into two communities, each socialized to know their place in Boquete.

This pattern of social segregation is also the result of the coexistence of two groups whose lifestyles and daily motivations are wholly incongruent. While native Boqueteños arguably occupy the majority of their waking hours concerned with sustaining their livelihoods through work, residential tourists are left to occupy their days with activities of leisure and consumption. These groups' contrasting daily routines not only reduce the occasion for their meaningful interaction, they also further widen the already significant gap existing between the native and foreign experiences of Boquete. Without meaningful interaction across this divide, residential tourists are prevented the opportunity to acquire a meaningful understanding of Boquete as a multidimensional place and dynamic community, which is obscured by the aesthetic curtain of landscape. Whether it is through explicit landscape-oriented social activities, such as hiking, bird watching and sightseeing excursions, or through less explicit activities, such as the Tuesday morning networking meetings or monthly potluck dinners, the residential tourist community fails to transcend its alienated experience of Boquete if it does not meaningfully and actively engage the world around it. Isolated from exposure to alternative experiences of and meanings for Boquete, residential tourists' alienated understanding of Boquete as an aesthetic and commodified landscape only becomes reinforced through homogeneous, intra-community social interaction.

Residential tourist growth and development only compounds this social and experiential divide. As the residential tourist community continues to grow larger, the burden to learn the other group's language begins to shift from the residential tourist community to the native Boqueteño community. Given residential tourists' socioeconomic status as the new class of super-rich in Boquete, businesses and workers alike are racing to accommodate the residential tourist community's every need, preference and desire; this, of course, necessitates that service workers in Boquete learn English. On a broader level, the implication of residential tourists' elite socioeconomic status means that they are generally exempt from traditional obligations for outsiders, which generally dictate that they assimilate with the local community's cultural traditions, behavioral norms and social conventions.

The overall implication of residential tourists' social isolation and high socioeconomic status holds that there is little, if any, imperative to motivate this emerging and isolated community to strive towards bridging the social experientially divide; to endeavor to understand the native community's experiences of and meanings for Boquete as a multidimensional place and dynamic community. While the social segregation existing between the native and foreign residential communities is a reality that neither group entirely creates or chooses, it nonetheless is the prevailing social system which effectively prohibits the frequency and intensity of meaningful interaction necessary for residential tourists to transcend their alienated experience of Boquete as landscape.

Conclusion

Based on their motivations, intentions, identities and social interactions, residential tourists have both personally and socially constructed a way of seeing Boquete as landscape. This dominant experience of Boquete as landscape is 'molded and mirrored', to use McHugh's (2000) vocabulary, by the attitudes and values of the promotional grand image of Boquete. Of particular significance are the tropes of the natural ideal and the authentic village, both of which resound strongly in individual residential tourists' own articulations of their experiences of Boquete as a glorified natural and social landscape.

Fundamental to the landscape experience of Boquete by residential tourists are three ingredients: the primacy of aesthetic tastes as a basis for creating meaning, which is overwhelmingly personal and selectively created; the primary of visual perception as a basis for passively and remotely engaging the surrounding world; and the primacy of landscape as an expendable and degradable commodity, which tenuously and unstably binds them to this place. Residential tourists demonstrate a strong tendency to remotely imbue the natural and human landscapes with personal meaning from a distance. As such, in order to authenticate their desired meanings for these natural and human surroundings, residential tourists selectively imagine meaning out of simple gestures, trivial observations and other small kernels of empirical knowledge. This fundamental experience of Boquete as landscape helps create – and is reinforced by – residential tourists' homogeneous patterns of intra-community socialization and, by extension, their social isolation from the native community at large. Simply stated, their collective process of worldmaking in Boquete has created a world apart, alienated from the local contexts of meaning.

Nonetheless, concomitant with the residential tourist experience of Boquete as landscape is a collective respect for the native community and a desire, on some level for acceptance and belonging. However cursory these feelings may be, they create promising opportunities and hopeful possibilities for residential tourists to explore and strive to understand Boquete beyond the curtain of landscape.

Yet as promising as these desires may be to acculturate with the greater Boqueteño community and establish roots in this place, growth and development also expose residential tourists' precarious and somewhat shallow relationship with Boquete. As the carefully crafted image of Boquete as a landscape of paradise begins to reveal itself as precariously unsustainable, many residential tourists, after just a few short years of living in the district, have begun to consider pulling up stakes in Boquete in order to reclaim their ideal landscape of residential tourism elsewhere. The ease with which many of these foreign residents are willing to abandon their professed 'place of home' in Boquete ultimately betrays rather superficial motivations for making a 'home' in Boquete in the first place, and reveals extremely fragile ties binding residential tourists to this place.

What is certain is that residential tourists are experientially and socially alienated from many of the subtle senses of and meanings for Boquete as a living place. With time, it is quite possible that residential tourists may penetrate the landscape curtain, begin to acquire a meaningful understanding of Boquete and become invested caretakers of this field of care. However, it is just as easy to imagine that, as growth and development continue to crush the image of Boquete as a landscape of natural paradise and social utopia, many of these foreign residents will leave to chase after this elusive landscape elsewhere, abandoning Boquete to an uncertain future. We shall explore some considerations regarding the uncertain futures of residential tourism and Boquete in the concluding chapter.

Note
1. In accordance with informant participation agreements, all informants' names have been changed to protect confidentiality.

Chapter 5

The Estranging Place: Assessing Native Residents' Experiences of Boquete

Introduction

Behind the facade of landscape there exists a distinct identity for Boquete and a wholly different reality for life in this place. For the native Boqueteño community, Boquete was not 'discovered' as a residential tourist destination in the late 1990s; rather, it has been an established place of home, work and community for generations, as detailed in Chapter 3. While the aesthetic qualities of the surrounding landscape certainly do not go unrecognized by Boqueteños, these aesthetic elements are neither the reason they live in this place nor in the forefront of their minds on a daily basis.

This chapter serves to complement the previous chapter by establishing how native residents fundamentally experience Boquete, and by exploring how the development of residential tourism is affecting these experiences. Significantly, native Boqueteños express experiences of Boquete that stand in marked contrast to those expressed by residential tourists. Unlike residential tourists, who principally experience Boquete as a consumable landscape of residential tourist paradise, native inhabitants fundamentally relate to Boquete on a deeply meaningful level in which people and place are profoundly fused together into a unified identity. Native Boqueteños articulate experiences of Boquete as an irreplaceable center of their individual and social identities, a foundation for their daily existence, and an inimitable place of work, family, community and home.

However, as the institution of residential tourism increasingly permeates the fabric of the Boqueteño community and imposes changes to and upon the land, the historically strong bonds between community and place are dissolving for native inhabitants. Owing to efforts to remake Boquete into an international destination for residential tourism, three distinct processes of estrangement acutely affecting the native community have begun to emerge, gradually yet perceptibly. These estranging processes are: the experiential alienation of individual inhabitants from their ties to community and place; the commodification of familial land into marketable real estate property; and, in the most extreme, permanent residential displacement from the district. These dislocating processes are shaking the foundations of established identities, homes, livelihoods and senses of place and community among Boqueteños. Together these processes threaten to disunite native inhabitants from place and, ultimately, to transform their experiences of Boquete into that of a placeless, unknowable landscape.

Boqueteños and Place

For the overwhelming majority of its native-born inhabitants, Boquete exists as an existential field of care. This, as Relph (1976) contends, is the 'central reference point of human existence;' the place in which residents' lives and identities are fundamentally invested. When compared to residential tourists' social networks, which are diffusely scattered across space in postmodern fashion, Boqueteños' social networks are relatively insular and dense; only infrequently do they extend beyond the limits of the immediate region. In contrast to the former group of residents, for which Boquete is a destination, this place for its native inhabitants is a deeply meaningful home. Unlike the transplantable value of home evinced by many residential tourist informants, for Boqueteños home is intimately associated with this particular place. Their identities are inextricably bound to Boquete to a degree that, without the intense vinculum to this place, little remains of native residents' identities.

Thus, the known universes, or social realities, experienced by residential tourists and native Boqueteños are dramatically distinct. While well-traveled and highly mobile residential tourists characteristically possess 'thin' knowledge about a variety of places, the relatively immobile Boqueteños' knowledge of the world is spatially limited but experientially profound. Boqueteños' 'thick' knowledge about their place of home, or field of care, is due to the fact that most of these native residents are third-, fourth- and fifth-generation residents, many of whom have never traveled beyond the province, and only an elite few who have ventured outside the borders of Panamá. What Boqueteños lack in spatial knowledge of a larger world is compensated by concentrated, existential knowledge about Boquete as a 'small world' (Tuan, 1996). With deep roots in a particular place, as Relph notes, one has a 'secure point from which to look out on the world, a firm grasp of one's own position in the order of things, and a significant spiritual and psychological attachment to somewhere in particular' (1976: 38).

In contrast to the 'high imageability' (Tuan, 1996) of the promotional grand image of Boquete, native residents' sense of place is not conspicuously displayed but rather quietly articulated through quotidian acts of community. The essence of Boquete as an existential place subtly resides in unceremonious daily routines; behind closed doors and along narrow dirt roads removed from the paved main streets of downtown; and as a largely unwritten record of family and community histories which are archived in the collective consciousness of the community.

The insiders' experience of Boquete fits comfortably with Relph's notion of existential insideness, as discussed in Chapter 2. This is because, despite changes over the years to the socioeconomic composition of Boquete, the local community has been successful in preserving the vitality and values of its customs, traditions and collective identity. Certainly the ascendancy of Boquete into the national and international economies, and the introduction of Ngobe Bugle labor forces are notable examples of modernizing and transformative changes which have recently occurred in Boquete. However, despite these and other changes, Boquete has been highly successful in retaining its provincial, agricultural and community-oriented identity.

Boquete is an irreplaceable home*place* for its native residents in that it is, as Relph writes, the 'foundation of [their] identity as individuals and as members of a community' (1976: 39). Boqueteños' known world is relatively limited, with the existential epicenter located in the district, fading in intensity with increasing radial distance outwards. This means that for Boqueteños their identities as social beings are fundamentally place dependent: transplanted or displaced outside the immediate region, the average Boqueteño becomes wholly uprooted from his identity, his social networks and his place in the world.

As roughly half of economically active individuals in the district are supported by the primary industry of agriculture, Boqueteños' engagement with the land far exceeds that of workers in more advanced societies, such as those from which residential tourists originate. As such, among the Boqueteño community, land is certainly regarded as a commodity, but its value is objectively and concretely tied to its productive – not aesthetic – value. However, among the Boqueteño community, agriculture possesses more than simply an economic value. It further holds symbolic value as the glue binding individuals to place and community; the common denominator around which community forms (Figure 5.1). The land and the products created on and derived from the land are sources of great pride for the Boqueteño community. The community takes very seriously its collective roles as stewards of the land and producers of the high quality coffee, fruits, vegetables and flowers grown here.

In describing Boquete from the insider's perspective, native residents speak of an organic fusion between people and place, community and land. Their characterizations of Boquete evince a perspectival depth that greatly surpasses landscape appraisal. For example, Rufino,[1] the youngest

Figure 5.1   Sign promoting Boquete as 'land of excellent quality produce' (photo by author, 2005)

generation in one of the district's most prominent coffee families, spoke to me in depth about Boquete's strong roots as an agricultural community. Elaborating on this topic, he told me:

> Being an agricultural community means that people have an associa-
> tion to the land, a *strong* association to the land. The way I see it, the
> association to the land had to be economical [and] it had to be sustain-
> able. So that's how we come in with this coffee concept. From my
> perspective, being from a fourth generation coffee family, the only
> place that can sustain some identity of [Boquete] … would be to farm
> a crop because we are farmers. (emphasis in original)

Similarly, commenting on the strong bond between Boqueteños and the land, Lucia, a third-generation matriarch of a family-owned coffee processing enterprise, spoke of a balanced symbiosis between people and place which has developed over time. Reaching back to the community's rustic origins, she reasoned that:

Since this town was created [in] a small valley, it has a lot of sense ... of survival. So you live out of whatever it is around you ... and you will be provided [for] by taking care of those surroundings. Because the Boqueteños understand that you live [off] of nature, you must respect [that] nature too.

Similar to residential tourists, Lucia also evokes the presence of 'nature' in describing Boqueteños' collective experience of their place of residence. However, whereas residential tourists speak of this 'nature' as something apart – some fantastic and discrete entity to be encountered, Lucia speaks of it as something with which Boqueteños actively engage and utilize as a resource to survive. 'Nature' is seen as a part of them, and they a part of it. While native residents obviously regard their natural surroundings with much respect, a pragmatic understanding of it – based on their working relationship and connectedness with these natural surroundings – prevents them from glorifying the natural environment to ethereal heights as many residential tourists are inclined to do.

Both of the above statements regarding the general character of Boquete typify the collective sentiments of most Boqueteño informants with whom I spoke. The collective self-reflection of Boqueteños evokes the community's deep-rooted history in order to imbue modern-day Boquete with meaning and identity. In statements about their community, Boqueteños emphasize, in one way or another, the importance of agriculture and a strong land-community bond as essential ingredients of the Boqueteño identity. In this way, a fourth-generation, elderly Boqueteña named Almira told me that, 'for us, we were taught [by our parents] give special care to the land, to love the place in which you live'.[2]

Boqueteños are certainly not oblivious to the natural beauty of their surroundings; in fact, they are often downright proud of the district's uncommonly breathtaking scenery and frequently boast of the community's environmental stewardship and care for the land. Expressing a moment of frustration over outsiders' inability to recognize the Boqueteño community's role as careful stewards of the land, Lucia explained:

It used to be that people would come and then just see how green [Boquete] was. But then I was feeling that they were not appreciating that [Boquete] is green because *somebody has kept it green*. ... And for me it was, wait a minute, why do you think we have what we have? [Boquete] is green because somebody has been taking care of it. ... [My] first reaction was, why not appreciate and say, wow, you have really done a good job here in keeping what [you] have found here? (emphasis in original)

Indeed, native insiders are well aware of Boquete's breathtaking natural landscape and should be credited for several generations' conscious and coordinated efforts to preserve the district's natural environment. However, unlike outsiders who place a premium on landscape aesthetics as a desired product, for the native insiders of Boquete landscape aesthetics are but a by-product of a much more important end: that of maintaining the environmental conditions which have long allowed them to make a sustainable home in the highland valley.

This affirms the idea that for insiders, landscape aesthetics is an acknowledged, yet relatively inconsequential, aspect of their home*place*. Lending weight to this idea, Carmen, a second-generation Boqueteña and matriarch of a large, family-owned orange grove, related to me an eloquent story about the preservation of a forested mountainside above her family's property. Learning about the functional importance of this preserved forested land when she was a young child, Carmen recalled:

> Our father asked us never to touch [the forested mountain]. I was very little when he told me, and he said you should never touch that mountain. I said why? He said because there are many little arroyos … [or] springs, that come down from there.

The necessity of water to irrigate the family's orange grove motivated Carmen's family to preserve the verdant mountainside, a scene which I admittedly found myself admiring from her patio during our interview. However, while I was only able personally to value the mountain for its aesthetic beauty, for Carmen this beautiful landscape was but a window into a deeper meaning for the land. For Carmen this mountain not only provided physical subsistence, in the form of natural springs, from which her family irrigates their orange grove; on a deeper level, this mountain recalled past memories and experiences, effectively symbolizing part of her family's living history in this place. As an outsider, here for me was a glimpse into the insider's world of Boquete; a world which I could only vicariously comprehend through native residents' articulated experiences.

Native residents' way of life in Boquete is the practical result of generations of local knowledge about the land and its natural surroundings. Their way of life evokes an intimate understanding between people and place that greatly surpasses superficial concerns for landscape aesthetics. As such, Lucia explained:

> you see most of the [residential tourist] construction taking place in places where they will have a nice view, which is higher up. Most of the [Boqueteños] here in town [do] not have that kind of culture. We

choose a place because of its functionality. So for instance, I [have] been taught by my family [that] you don't build beside the river. It's very nice but here in Boquete you don't build there [because] you will get flooded out and lose everything.

Another informant, in fact, related to me the story of a residential tourist who – against the well-intentioned advice of several of her Boqueteño neighbors – purchased a particular piece of property along the cedar-lined banks of the Rio Caldera; a river widely known among the local community to flood during exceptional periods of heavy rainfall. (Supposedly, the real estate agent, either out of sheer ignorance or greed, assured the buyer that the property was not at risk of flooding.) Before construction on the residential tourist's house was completed, several days of heavy rainfall initiated a series of events that ultimately destroyed the house's foundation, not to mention the buyer's dreams of living along the banks of the river.

In contrast to residential tourists' superficial knowledge of the local environs, which rarely penetrates the facade of visual appearance, native Boqueteños' knowledge of the area is profoundly broad and penetrating; a level of knowledge that may only be gained through generations of family and community rooted in place over time. In a place where the present generation often cultivates the same land on which their great-grandparents farmed, the consciousness of the Boqueteño community extends well beyond its lifetime, back to the origins of Boquete's settlement. Their collective identity evinces a place molded by a history of 'a humble and simple people, a people who had only their hands and their strength with which to create an *hogar*[3] in the middle of the virgin mountain',[4] as Sánchez Pinzón states in her account of Boquete's living history (2001: Introducción).

However, with the recent development of residential tourism and related efforts to remake the physical spaces of Boquete into an idyllic residential tourist destination, a new, other-directed identity for Boquete is quickly gaining momentum. In a very real, perceptible sense, as Boquete is increasingly being remade, the Boqueteño community's intimate relationship with this place is deteriorating into an estranged experience of Boquete as an unknowable landscape.

Place into Landscape

As Boquete continues to develop into a residential tourist destination, three distinct processes are occurring that threaten to alter the native community's experience of Boquete from that of knowable place into alien landscape. While most Boqueteños have remained rooted in place throughout this turbulent period of physical and social transformation, the physical spaces and identity of Boquete nonetheless are changing around them. These changes, which might otherwise be thought of as being part of a process of 'development', are for much of the Boqueteño community an uncontrollable process of alienation that is gradually dislocating deep-rooted ties between people and place. This first estranging process of alienation concerns residents' experiential, emotional and social ties to familiar people and places within their community. A second process estranging insiders from place in Boquete is land commodification. With impressive increases in real estate demand and land prices throughout the district, a new way of seeing and evaluating the land has begun to compete with the community's long-held, collective values for land as the productive and sustaining foundation of life in Boquete. With this process Boqueteños become obliged to see the land as a saleable good with a quantifiable market value, rather than an inalienable place imbued with an indeterminable amount of personal, familial and productive values. This process of commodification often leads to the third and final process of estrangement: that of permanent residential displacement. Certainly the most drastic of the three processes, displacement involves the complete physical uprooting of inhabitant from homeplace, causing emotional and social ties to be irrevocably severed.

Amidst the perceptible changes – the sea of real estate signs, the clamor of new construction, the growing presence of English-speaking residential tourists roaming the streets of Bajo Boquete – there remains a bewildering public silence regarding the issue of residential tourism growth and development among the native community. In private, native informants tell me that the public silence is the product of the community's collective uncertainty and ambivalence in the face of the myriad of bewildering and disorienting transformations occurring in Boquete. While in the public realm Boqueteños may be reticent to openly express a definitive opinion for or against residential tourism and its far-reaching effects, in the private realm behind closed doors there is ample talk – and strong feelings – about the changes affecting their community. As such, the majority of Boqueteños' expressions about their experiences of place and community at this critical juncture in Boquete's history are private and deeply personal articulations.

If one word could adequately describe native residents' reaction to residential tourism, it would be ambivalence. On the one hand, residential tourism development is seen by the native community as providing an immediate and visible economic boost to the district. In a community that recorded almost 15% unemployment during the year 2000, Boqueteño informants report that, at present, there is virtually zero unemployment in Boquete; in fact, several informants have reported labor shortages in the local service and construction sectors (DEC, 2003). However, on the other hand, Boqueteños – always gracious and accommodating hosts, as their cultural norms dictate – hold tightly guarded concerns regarding the changes that residential tourism development has created and will continue to create for their community. In this way, residential tourism presents something of a conflict of interest for Boqueteños, generating feelings of uneasy ambivalence within the native community. Collectively, Boqueteños cannot seem to decide whether residential tourism settlement and development ultimately will have a net positive or negative effect on their lives.

While residential tourism now bolsters Boquete's economic livelihood, this same force threatens to destroy its community and rooted identity. The oppositional duality of residential tourism's effect on the equilibriums of community and place presents a very apparent dilemma for Boqueteños, and exposes subtle cracks of intra-community conflict, as well as a tangled web of complex power relations within this community. For instance, only after I went to great lengths to ensure her anonymity did Graciela, a Boqueteña mother and cashier at an American-owned coffee shop, agree to speak to me about her impressions of residential tourism. Rightly so, she was extremely hesitant to openly express her thoughts about residential tourism settlement and development for fear that she might lose her job at the coffee shop, whose customers are overwhelmingly residential tourists. Once in private, however, she freely expressed great concern for her son's future in Boquete and told me of her fear that Boqueteños were quickly becoming second-class citizens in their own community. 'I suppose that in five years Boquete will no longer be Boquete. Boquete will be an American colony,' Graciela flatly told me in private. 'Perhaps there is an economic benefit [from residential tourism], but at the same time it is hurting the district'.[5]

Similarly, it is most often only in private conversations that Boqueteños remove the cordial facade to reveal the wounds of estrangement that are occurring in conjunction with residential tourism development. Another common, yet quietly expressed sentiment among native residents is the idea that two separate communities of residents have developed in Boquete. Like many native informants, Almira, a third generation Boqueteña, explicitly drew a sharp distinction between the present wave of residential tourists and the founding wave of foreign pioneers over a century ago:

It is very different what is taking place today. The people who come today already have a family; they are retired and so forth, and they live in a world apart from the Boqueteños. Those who came here to establish Boquete married Boqueteñas or, if they brought their wives, they lived together with the native community. Today there is a separation. ... Those who have come here recently, they want to live...far away from us, and this is *very* bad in a town as small as Boquete. (emphasis in original)[6]

The distinct social divide that native residents perceive to exist between themselves and their contemporary foreign counterparts is important because it establishes the preconditions for native informants' feelings of growing estrangement from Boquete. Rather than viewing residential tourism development as a beneficial and progressive advancement, native informants generally express in private the sentiment that, in the long run, it will manifest itself as a destructive force destined to rob them of their place-based identities and remake Boquete into something decidedly *not theirs*. Remarkably, the themes of alienation, commodification and displacement surface again and again in the expressions of Boqueteño informants' appraisal of how residential tourism is affecting their experiences of place and community.

Alienation

The first thematic process of estrangement that native Boqueteños articulate to be occurring in conjunction with residential tourist development is a growing sense of alienation: experiential alienation from the land and social alienation from one another within the community. This alienation is expressed as an emotional and psychical, rather than physical, dissociation. The perceptions of alienation create a general fear that Boquete altogether is becoming an unknowable landscape of other-directed spaces. As is a common human reaction to external threat, this perceived alienation from place and community has functioned to strengthen and intensify many Boqueteños' sense of place. An 'acute' sense of place, Tuan contends, often occurs in conjunction with loss of place, however:

the loss of place need not be literal. The threat of loss is sufficient. Residents not only sense but know that their world has an identity and a boundary when they feel threatened, as when people of another race wants to move in, or when the area is the target of highway construction or urban renewal. Identity is defined in competition and in conflict with others: this seems true of both individuals and communities. We owe our sense of being not only to supportive forces but also to those that pose a threat. (1996: 453–55)

The native residents' awareness of Boquete's unique and rooted identity has sharply intensified as they increasingly sense that residential tourism development threatens to irrevocably alter this place. More and more they fear that the identity of their community is dying as a new, other-directed Boquete is born out of the destruction of their field of care.

This collective sentiment is perhaps best demonstrated by a rare public display of local animosity towards residential tourist development which appeared in Boquete in 2005. On a solemn and unadorned eight by ten foot sign anonymously erected along the main highway leading into Boquete, a message mournfully warned approaching vehicles: 'He who wishes to know Boquete come now, already it is coming to an end' (Figure 5.2).[7] That no individual or group, presumably within the native community, claimed ownership for this most public form of protest against residential tourism only emphasizes the sensitive, cautious and ambivalent

Figure 5.2   Anonymously placed sign located along the main highway connecting Boquete to the provincial capital of Davíd. The sign reads: 'He who wishes to know Boquete come now, already it is coming to an end'. (photo by author, 2005)

public face of the Boqueteño community's reaction to residential tourism and its effects.

While this sign was the subject of much conversation among native informants during my visit, it ostensibly went unnoticed by residential tourist informants, none of whom made any mention of it to me during our interviews. That residential tourists were oblivious to this stark symbol of animosity – by which many of these foreign residents likely passed in their automobiles on a daily basis – not only confirms their lack of linguistic competency to read and understand Spanish; on a more profound level this lack of awareness demonstrates the great degree to which residential tourists are socially and experientially isolated from the native community.

Interestingly enough, as the foreboding sign implies, native residents often convey a growing sense of alienation by describing Boquete as a dying organism. This expression of Boquete as an organic life form is further exemplified in an unpublished short story written by Ulices Urriola, a native of Boquete (see Appendix 1). Titled, 'Boquete: A Pueblo That is Living the Last Days of Its History', the story provides a valuable window into the guarded, innermost fears of Boqueteños regarding the process of alienation. With a bold and raw style the author begins by writing:

> The above title could be considered a little exaggerated and outside the reality of many persons who do not have knowledge of this sad situation that we as Boqueteños are suffering, as day by day we watch our pueblo die. Superficially one observes an economic boom; diverse activities, such as construction and commerce, have flourished that in the end give the false image of economic prosperity. But in reality this revival is nothing more than the dark veil that hides our approaching and inevitable destruction.[8]

The figurative language of Boquete as a dying pueblo lends credence to Relph's (1976) contention that, 'place is essentially its people'; for what truly is expiring here are the intangible qualities of place, which reside in the collective reservoir of consciousness in its native residents, yet carry such weight and volume as to give life to the notions of place and community.

This notion that the insider's place is rapidly being dispropriated and remade into something wholly unknowable by outside forces is shared by many Boqueteño informants (Figure 5.3). For example, during my interview with Carmen, the orange grove owner, she told me that much discussion among locals centered on guarded but growing fears of losing Boquete. Speaking about the conversations concerning residential tourism

Figure 5.3   The physical remaking of downtown Bajo Boquete (photo by author, 2005)

and its effects that Boqueteños are having behind closed doors, Carmen told of the native community's collective anxiety, remarking that a common sentiment among Boqueteños is: 'Oh, my goodness, Boquete will never be Boquete again. We are losing Boquete; Boquete is gone.'

In distinguishing between place and placelessness, intimate attachment and alienation, Boqueteños categorically returned to the symbolic importance of the land to their individual and social identities. For instance, when I asked Lucia, the coffee processing matriarch, if the first wave of residential tourism was a blessing to Boqueteño farmers, who at the time were sinking into economic ruin during an international coffee crisis, she responded by saying:

> [It was] a sad blessing. … [Land] in Boquete has been passing on, generation after generation, and the last thing you want to do is not to leave anything for your generation. Now you lose everything [if you sell your land]. I mean the money is money, and it will end at some

time. But here in Boquete you could see coffee farms that have raised one generation, have raised another generation, have raised another generation, and could raise as many generations as you could like to, as long as you take care of the farm.

Echoing these sentiments, Urriola states in his short story: 'Our one and irreplaceable resource is the land, or, said another way, "Boquete without its fields for cultivation will die"'.⁹ This further reiterates not only the vital importance of the land to the economic survival of the native community, more profoundly it tells of how critical the land is symbolically to the stability of the Boqueteño identity. The land mediates and bridges relationships within the community and provides a spatial context for place and community to thrive. Boqueteños fear that without the land they are sure to lose their collective and individual identities, turning them into alienated strangers in a place which is becoming less and less knowable as residential tourist growth and development continue.

The value of the land for its productive and symbolic values is similarly articulated by J.B. Jackson (1997) in his essay from 1952 entitled, 'The Almost Perfect Town'. In this poignant essay, the Chamber of Commerce of a fictional, rural American town named Optimo convenes to discuss the future of its town, which, like Boquete, has reached a crossroads between an agricultural past and a possible, other-directed future oriented around heavy industry and tourism. Jackson tells us that the collective sentiment of the committee in Optimo is: 'If we want to get ahead, the best thing to do is break with our past, become as independent as possible of our *immediate* environment, and at the same time become almost completely dependent for our well-being on some remote outside resource' (39–40, emphasis in original). Considering Optimo's momentous crossroads – which, incidentally, bears striking similarities to Boquete's own reality – Jackson writes:

For almost a hundred years – a long time in this part of the world – [Optimo] has been identified with the surrounding landscape and been an essential part of it. Whatever wealth it possesses has come from the farms and ranches, not from the overalls factory or from tourists.

Now, if Optimo suddenly became a year-round tourist resort, or the Overalls Capital of the Southwest, what would happen to that relationship, do you suppose? It would vanish. The farmers and ranchers would soon find themselves crowded out and would go elsewhere for those services and benefits which they now enjoy in Optimo. And as for Optimo itself, it would soon achieve the flow of traffic, the new store fronts, the housing developments, the payrolls, and bank accounts it cannot help dreaming about; and in the same process it would achieve a total social and physical dislocation, and a loss of its own identity. (40–41)

Like the changes that Jackson imagines for his fictionalized community, in Boquete the process of reorienting the town's physical spaces as well as its identity around residential tourism causes insiders to suffer the painful experience of watching their field of care and their knowable community disappear before their eyes. This insider-to-outsider reorientation is what Relph (1976) calls the 'other-directedness in places', and it is the first criterion he lists for the manifestation of placelessness, which was discussed in Chapter 2. In the case of Boquete, other-directedness is eliminating the identity of place from the physical spaces of Boquete so that this space may become, as Relph sets forth, a 'landscape made for tourists' (p. 118). As the organic bonds between a place and its invested caretakers are severed, the meaningful link of identity between a people and a place also disappears. As the spirit of place gives way to vacated space, a contrived, other-directed image of landscape comes to occupy this space where a living place used to be. The more unknowable and other-directed Boquete becomes, the more acute the feeling of alienation will be for Boqueteños. This process of alienation is akin to crossing the threshold from existential insider to existential outsider; from a knowable experience of place into an estranged experience of landscape.

Stopping by a hardware store in Bajo Boquete for an informal chat with the staff, a middle-aged Boqueteña woman working at the counter told me that she foresees Boquete becoming a 'tumba' – signifying both a tomb and a clearing of felled trees – with 'a golf course here, a mansion there, and a restaurant over there',[10] as she pointed her finger along the horizon of verdant mountain slopes appearing in the distance through the storefront window. This vision of Boquete as an alienated landscape of other-directedness captures the fear of many Boqueteños: that they are quickly losing touch with their field of care, becoming alienated from the spatial foundation on which their collective identity is built. Already Boqueteños collectively express an existential feeling of estrangement and an ominous threat of place destruction as they articulate a feeling that the intangible essence, the lifeblood of Boquete is suffering a slow death. It is as if each parcel of land contains a small fragment of the identity and essence of this place. With every transfer of land from the local to the foreign domain of ownership, a small part of Boquete dies in the eyes of the local community.

Commodification

Despite all of the changes imposed upon Boquete from outside, the processes estranging native residents from place and community also are somewhat fueled by the individual choices made by Boqueteños. In both the creation and destruction of place, space is absolutely essential in order for the physical manifestations of change and transformation to occur. In the context of Boquete, residential tourist growth and development exists fundamentally because there is a replenishing pool of native landowners who are willing to sell their land to the foreign interests of residential tourism. In light of this consideration, a clear-cut narrative of innocent native residents who unwillingly fall victim to place destruction by outside forces becomes direly problematic, exceedingly hollow and fallaciously naive. To be sure, many native Boqueteños are willing and active participants in the development of residential tourism and, by relation, agents of their own collective estrangement from place and community. Indeed, the extreme yet not entirely unreasonable argument could be made that Boqueteños facilitate or even contribute to the remaking of Boquete into an alienated landscape of residential tourism and, by extension, the demise of their field of care. In support of this argument, one could point not only to Boqueteños who sell their land to foreign interests, but also to Boqueteños who cooperate, even in the smallest capacities, to remake Boquete and to promote the image of a residential tourist paradise.

Amidst this large, complex web of destruction and construction in Boquete, however, a fundamental and important shift in natives' attitudes towards the land has taken place; a shift that greatly alters their relationship with the land and their experience of Boquete as a field of care. This is the process of land commodification and it serves as a bridge linking experiential estrangement (alienation) with physical estrangement (displacement).

As outside interests have increasingly demanded *space* onto which the grand image of residential tourism may be projected (and offered up unimaginable sums of money for the rights to own and remake these spaces), many landowning Boqueteños have obliged them by selling fragments of Boquete – their homes, their familial lands, their places of social gathering – for princely sums of money. In the process, real estate value and the aesthetic value upon which the former value is based, has begun to crowd out the personal, social and (re)productive values that formerly gave meaning to the land among the Boqueteño community. Quite simply, land commodification functions to further disassociate insider from place, transforming land into landscape.

Landowning Boqueteños have acquired an alienable relationship with the land as they have come to *see* it from the outsider's perspective as a transferable commodity with great commercial value. While there are many popular tales circulating through the Boqueteño community of landowners striking it rich by selling their coffee fincas to foreign real estate developer-brokers, informants told me that many landowners categorically refuse to sell their land. (In fact, for several informants their refusal to 'sell out to the gringo' was a source of immense pride and satisfaction.) Regardless, though, it is doubtful that there exists even one landowner in the district who does not know what his land is worth in the residential tourist real estate market.

Rufino, the fourth-generation coffee farmer in his early thirties, is one of the landowners who staunchly refuses to sell his land. Addressing the pressures and dilemmas that land commodification has placed on local landowners, he reasoned that Boqueteño families are better off in the long run not selling their land to foreigners:

> This is your piece of land. It's not a hundred thousand dollars like [the real estate broker says] that it [is] worth. But you [plant] ten thousand [coffee] trees and you will have one hundred thousand dollars in ten years for your kids.

However, Rufino's farsighted, patient approach to the red-hot land speculation bonanza seems to be the exception rather than the rule among Boqueteño landowners. I also spoke with one of the district's half-dozen taxi drivers, a third-generation Boqueteño in his thirties, who told me that he did not own any land in Boquete, but if he did, he would surely sell it. 'If I had a big chunk of property and somebody was to give me a million bucks, and I know it's worth it, I'll sell it', he told me with an imaginative smile. 'You only going to live once.'

However, given the economic disparities between the local economy and the foreign economies out of which residential tourists essentially operate, a foreigner's offer of US$100,000 or US$200,000 for a landholder's modest, six-hectare coffee finca is, quite literally, equivalent to winning the lottery in Panamá. Simply stated, foreigners' real estate offers are too good to refuse for many Boqueteño landowners. In a related discussion, one of Boquete's more affluent native residents related to me the following anecdote:

> [There are many] poor people [in Boquete] that have a very humble house, but they own it. They own the land, they own that whole house … and they only work as farm workers, and you come to them and you say, I'll buy your land for $50,000. They have never seen that amount of money and they say, 'oh yes, yes, I'll sell it [to] you.' … With that money they can no longer [afford to] buy another piece of land or

build another house … But it's tempting … the money you offer them, and that's why they sell their properties [without] considering that it's going to be very hard to get another piece of land or to build a house with that money. Because you know the money goes quick.

Considering the jackpot-like stakes, it is understandable to see how the decision to sell one's land is often made.

However most older Boqueteño informants with whom I spoke adamantly denounced the trend of selling out. Their reasoning behind this stance was partially based on economic principles, but primarily based on moral appeals to preserve the cultural traditions of Boquete. Many in this older generation of native residents perceive land commodification and the nouveau riche Boqueteños who sell out as direct affronts to the traditional Boqueteño identity and way of life. Septuagenarian Almira, for example, told me:

My father would always tell me, 'one must work every day.' My father, [the land] he owned, it was worked. But today, the youth [of Boquete] do not see the life we [elders] live. We study, we work, and then we keep working. The youth are preoccupied with having a nice house, a nice car, although they cannot [attain them]. … So, if foreigners come and buy [your land] for $100,000, the family is happy, right? [The parents] buy a car for each of their children; [as a result] they are without land, but they are now also without money. And now where are [they] going to go?[11]

While multiple outside forces – stretching beyond the scope of residential tourism – are certainly intervening to estrange the younger generations in Boquete from the traditions of an agriculturally oriented way of life, residential tourism is undoubtedly the most immediate and impactful force shaping younger generations' attitudes about their desired identity and way of life in adulthood.

In Boquete there appears to be a process of negotiation taking place between a large and relatively vocal faction of (mostly older) Boqueteños who seek to preserve and continue a modest, agriculturally centered way of life in Boquete, and a smaller, relatively inarticulate faction of (mostly younger) Boqueteños who are willing to sell some or all of their land in order to move beyond a direct dependency upon the land for their financial livelihoods. For the former 'preservationist faction', the land has assumed a previously unimagined level of symbolic value in the face of threats to Boquete as a field of care and to its traditional way of life. Specifically, native ownership of the land and resistance to the temptations to sell one's land to foreigners are the preservationist faction's battle cry for saving their community and field of care from irrevocable destruction.

In a second short story that the decidedly preservationist proponent Ulices Urriola penned in 2004, he tells the anecdote of a 'laborious and honest' but 'naive' Boqueteño farmer named Antonio, who is approached by two foreign visitors who offer him $200,000 for his family's finca (see Appendix 2). For Antonio, 'this was the deal of a lifetime',[12] the author writes. Antonio immediately agrees to sell his land to the foreigners. However, Urriola tells us:

> After a few days he began to dispel the dream of the big deal. This occurred because in the rush to vacate his land, he forgot about several family keepsakes such as the portrait of his ancestors and other objects [of personal value]. Consequently he did not think twice about returning to his land in order to recover his forgotten items, but to his surprise, upon arriving he encountered an electric fence and a sign in another language that seemed to say 'Do Not Enter'; but more eloquent was the painted skull on the sign. [It was then that Antonio] noticed a great bonfire which was slowly consuming the remains of what once was his house and the memories of his deceased loved ones.[13]

Beneath the theatrical facade of this anecdote, there lies a deep conviction held by the preservationist faction: that without the land, there is no *place* for Boquete, as a community of inhabitants and reservoir of shared traditions and histories. Without control of the land, Boquete becomes but a voided space to be razed and remade into something entirely new and unknowable.

This is the exact sentiment that the anonymous erectors of another sign – on display during summer 2005 on a grassy slope at a major intersection in Bajo Boquete – intended to convey. In the heart of Bajo Boquete, the black and white sign squared off like a soldier preparing for impending battle opposite an oversized, English language real estate sign located across the street (Figure 5.4). The former sign direly pleaded:

> Boqueteño, in your hands is the life of your community. If you sell your land, it will die. If you do not, it will live. Think of this for yourself and for your country.[14]

Displacement

Urriola's second short story continues to tell of a series of misfortunes that afflicts the protagonist, Antonio, following his regrettable decision to sell his finca to foreigners. Shortly thereafter his wife and children

Figure 5.4 Anonymously placed sign erected near the main square in downtown Bajo Boquete, in 2005. The sign reads: 'Boqueteño, in your hands is the life of your community. If you sell your land, it will die. If you do not, it will live. Think of this for yourself and for your country' (photo by author, 2005)

abandon him and he loses most of his capital gains through a series of unsound business investments. Striving to impress a stark moral warning upon Boqueteño landowners who consider selling their lands, the author concludes his story thus:

> [O]ur respected farmer [has] lost all of his money and today, without family [or] friends, he lives in the capital city of the Province, doing errands and asking for small loans from acquaintances, all of whom know he will never repay them. The saddest part of this story is that it occurred to someone just like you and I, kind reader. In all sincerity, we ask you that if you know the identity of the person who has lived this story, never reveal his name for the sake of solidarity. Take into serious account that which happens to those who sell their land, so that you do not become the protagonist of the next tragic story.[15]

The implication of selling one's land, according to this anecdote, ultimately culminates in complete territorial displacement from home. Once removed from the physical context of Boquete, the protagonist is stripped of his personal, familial and social identities, his dignity, his independence and his livelihood. Through the act of displacement he becomes a stranger to his former place of home and community, estranged from the social and emotional bonds that once made him part of a larger familial and community fabric. He is left to wander an existential twilight zone of misfortune and suffering in a strange land.

Despite the exceedingly dramatic nature of this anecdote, it nonetheless provides a suitable context for exploring displacement, the third and final process of estrangement that native residents articulate. Residential displacement is a consistently documented outcome in case studies that involve cohorts of socioeconomic actors similar to those in Boquete, and in case studies which focus on vacation and residential tourist-related growth in 'high-amenity' areas (e.g. Forsythe, 1980; Gober *et al.*, 1993; Martín, 2004; Nelson, 1997; Smutny, 2002; Torres & Momsen, 2005). Broadly speaking, the establishment of residential tourism in Boquete has initiated a number of – primarily economic – consequences that have induced the permanent displacement of local residents from Boquete.

However, residential displacement in Boquete is neither fully forced nor chosen. Its causes are a nebulous chemistry of voluntary and involuntary actions, systemic and endemic factors. As Boquete is quite literally remade into a residential tourist destination, many Boqueteño landholders may 'choose' to sell their land to foreigners. However, taking into consideration both the patriarchal hierarchy and the legacy of land inheritance in the Boqueteño family structure, women, children and future generations have little to no say in these decisions. In addition, to examine displacement solely at the individual and family levels neglects to take into consideration larger, intervening socioeconomic factors at work. These factors include: local economic restructuring (from an agriculture-based to a service-based economy); inflating costs of goods and services, such as groceries, entertainment and construction materials; shrinking rental property availability and increasing rental property costs; and, especially, the astounding increase in district-wide land prices, which effectively prohibits residents operating within the local economy from purchasing land in the district ever again.

While the actual number of Boqueteños displaced from Boquete thus far remains small relative to the district's total population, the imminent threat of significant displacement in the near future is a very distinct and powerful force shaping native residents' present attitudes. A common attitude regarding the very real threat of displacement is reflected in Urriola's first short story regarding the apocalyptical 'last days' of Boquete. In this story the Boqueteño writer warns:

> In a span of two years [foreigners] have succeeded in buying a third of the total land area in the district, which signifies for the nation that this land already is dead or [at least] completely sterile since it will produce not one coffee bean, nor even one vegetable, nor will it serve as a settlement for a Boqueteño family. This we affirm given that the land is bought in order to build residences for retirees from the most developed countries;[16]

Regardless of whether this semi-fictional outlook is ultimately deemed hyper-exaggerated or farsightedly accurate, most Boqueteños share the essence of this belief: that land appropriated by the foreign domain is land that, evermore, will be lost to the local community. Boqueteño informants anticipate that, with time, foreigners will take possession of the majority of the district's land, parcel by parcel, until native residents are forced either to leave the district or submit to becoming 'the gardeners and housekeepers' of residential tourists, as one native informant expressed to me. Considering all of the foreign wealth being invested in the development of first-rate, luxury homes and residential communities in Boquete, it is not difficult to understand how Boqueteños have come to view the land being sold to foreign ownership as 'dead land' from which they will be forever estranged.

Foreseeing that residential tourism will occupy center stage in Boquete's future, many native residents envision that the district is well on its way to becoming a colony of foreigners. In this widely shared vision of the future, native inhabitants have been displaced from their homes in Boquete and the former identity of Boquete has been scoured from the land, leaving behind a sanitized void of space over which the grand image of residential tourism has been projected. This bleak vision is shared by Graciela, the Boqueteña coffee shop employee, who told me:

> I suppose that in five years Boquete will no longer be Boquete. Boquete will be an American colony. It will no longer be the district of Boquete and one will no longer see Panamanians [here]. One will see more Americans than Panamanians, and [Boquete] will never be the same again. In fact, Boquete already is not the same [place] that it was ten years ago.[17]

Without land, this 40-year-old informant and mother of a teenage son worried that her son faced an uncertain future, in which having a home in Boquete and a secure place in the community became less likely with each passing day. However, at the time of our interview, her son was currently studying English at a vocational school in Davíd, and expressed dreams of opening a business to offer translation and interpretation services to the growing population of residential tourists in Boquete. In contrast to his mother's generation, he elicited optimism for a lucrative future in Boquete and conveyed the vision of hopeful opportunity that his adolescent generation perceived residential tourism to offer the community.

Graciela, meanwhile, was convinced that her son's generation did not fully understand the irreversible and estranging implications that she perceived residential tourism to present. In a culture that prizes land ownership as the benchmark of family, independence, and socioeconomic prosperity, the mother expressed near certainty that her son and most of his peers would never have the privilege of owning land in the district. Highlighting an inter-generational difference in perspective, Graciela was convinced that her son's generation would carelessly sell off the remainder of Boquete's land to foreigners before realizing the error of their ways. She expressed conviction that the lure of a large payout offered for these properties was, in her words, a 'trap disguised by opportunity' that would be all too alluring for her son's generation to resist.

During my interview with Rufino, the fourth-generation coffee farmer, his adult sister and her teenage daughter agreed to come over to his house to participate in the discussion. At one particularly emotional point during the interview, when our conversation approached the inevitable topic of Boquete's future, Rufino stood up from his chair and pointed to his niece, who was sitting on a nearby couch. Speaking of the girl's future in Boquete, Rufino said:

[T]en years, twenty years ago – she could have [had] a hectare of land for a thousand dollars. [If] she had saved a thousand dollars, she could [have] bought land in [the neighborhood of] Palmira, here in Boquete. You think she can buy a hectare of land in Boquete today? Never.

Given these present circumstances, it is entirely possible to understand why many Boqueteños interpret the present rumblings of transformation as the ominous beginning of a large-scale process of displacement, which threatens to physically sever native residents' ties with their field of care, as well as their bonds with community.

As evidence of this nascent process of displacement, many informants pointed to the growing number of other-directed restaurants, grocery stores and gated residential communities which are effectively dispropriating both space and fragments of place from the native community. The most prominently cited example of these other-directed spaces, from which virtually the entire native community has been displaced, is Valle Escondido, the first gated community established in Boquete.

Situated in a narrow pass, which leads into an extensive, canyon-walled inner valley, the construction of Valle Escondido several years ago effectively blocked Boqueteños' route of access to the inner valley beyond the gated development's property. Following the completion of Valle Escondido, its non-residents were initially outrightly denied right-of-way access through the gated community to reach the inner valley. Only after a lawsuit compelled the American owner to change this policy, did Valle Escondido agree to open up access to this pre-existing thoroughfare to non-residents. However, this consolation literally came at a price, as non-residents now are required to pay US$1 entry fee to pass through the development's main gate (Figure 5.5). As Graciela conveys below, Boqueteños flatly resent that they are losing access to certain spaces which formerly held significance for them as a meaningful part of their field of care:

In Valle Escondido right now it is practically an American colony. Everyone who lives there is an American. This, in a place where there has always been Boqueteños working [and] living, okay? Now, it is an American colony. The Boqueteño now has to *pay* to enter and I don't think that is just. ... The Boqueteño has lived here all his life. Why should a foreigner come here and impose a fee upon him for that which he has lived with his whole life?[8] (emphasis in original)[1]

Although Boqueteños technically are not prohibited from passing through the gated community, the strictures of having access only during visiting hours, and having to submit to inspection at the guard house and pay the

Figure 5.5   Gated entrance to Valle Escondido, Boquete's first master-planned community completed in 2001 (photo by author, 2005)

prohibitively expensive entrance fee, impose de facto and symbolic restrictions upon the native community's access to a piece of Boquete which is a meaningful part of their collective home and history. In essence, as the native community is displaced from this land, it becomes but an estranged landscape to them: an inaccessible and voided space emptied of the personal and social meaning it once held for them and replaced with the unknowable, alien image of residential tourism. While these acts of physical dispropriation certainly do not, nor cannot, take away Boqueteños' memories and emotional ties to the land, they nonetheless serve to sever real, meaningful connections between a people and place as a field of care, causing the significance of the latter to begin to weaken and erode.

Conclusion

Native residents certainly see the beauty of Boquete's landscape; they see this beauty but they see beyond this aesthetic facade as well. For the native community, the visible, surrounding environment ultimately serves as a window into deeper collective and symbolic meanings for Boquete as a unique, living place. Their value for the land and surroundings is fundamentally interwoven into a larger fabric of deeply personal meaning, which is suffused with the distinct character of shared traditions, histories, collective memories, social ties and the community's unified dependence on the land for sustenance.

The history and identity of this place are both literally and symbolically built upon the land. Literally this relationship is exemplified by the practice of agriculture, which represents one of the most fundamental and self-evident ties between a people and their environment. Symbolically, land is the common denominator around which the social organization of community and its collective identity are formed and maintained in Boquete.

However, native informants articulate perceptible changes that are beginning to alter the deep-rooted relationship between inhabitants and place. As the transformative processes of residential tourist growth and development continue to remake Boquete, the native Boqueteño community has begun to express three distinct processes of estrangement that threaten to reorient inhabitants' experiential, emotional and, perhaps, even their physical ties to Boquete as both a place and a community. An abstract manifestation of this estrangement is occurring through the process of alienation. This process implies the increasing loss of Boquete's traditional identity to forces of other-directedness, which are serving to create feelings of experiential and emotional dissociation between inhabitants and place. Boqueteño informants express this alienation as a sense of being closed off from place as a meaningful extension of their being, and as a sense of isolation from their known worlds, the social and spatial contexts of their existence.

Furthermore, the unbridled land speculation taking place in Boquete has initiated a process of land commodification within the native community. This is manifest as the literal disunion of subject from object, as landholders step outside their traditional relationships with the land in order to reconceptualize it in commodifiable and aesthetic terms as alienable real estate property. This process of commodification appears to have created an intra-community debate between those wishing to sell their lands to foreign interests and to oblige the development of residential tourist amenities and services, and those seeking to preserve the traditional identity and way of life in Boquete by retaining domain over their lands and, in the process, preserving the cultural traditions of Boquete. Fundamentally this social debate centers around two different perspectives concerning which values best constitute a desirable quality of life. For the primarily older faction of preservationists, quality of life means preserving Boquete's cultural integrity and traditions of familial land ownership, agriculture and the tight-knit social bonds of a knowable community. To preserve these socio-cultural values of Boquete, the preservationist faction has sought to frame the issue of land ownership in impassioned moral terms, campaigning for Boqueteño landowners to resist 'selling out' to foreign interests and, by extension, to the demise of their valued way of life. For a smaller, primarily younger faction of Boqueteños, who generally are more hopeful and optimistic about the changes residential tourism is creating, quality of life means improving the Boqueteño community's overall standard of living by striving for greater opportunities for socio- economic and geographical mobility, and by providing Boqueteños with the chance to pursue livelihoods beyond agriculture. In essence, the existence of this subtle intra-community tug of war between moral-cultural values and socioeconomic values only underscores how the highly pervasive issue of land commoditization has fundamentally come to play such a critical role in the larger process of estrangement, which rings loudly and clearly from the collective voice of the Boqueteño community.

This process of commodification serves as a critical link between experiential estrangement, characterized by the former process of alienation, and physical estrangement, characterized by the third estranging process of residential displacement. While relatively few Boqueteños have yet to be physically displaced from their homes in the district, the overwhelming majority of Boqueteño informants express palpable anxiety concerning the threat of displacement, as well as an acute perception that Boquete is slowly dying with the continued losses of both the symbolic identity and the spatial context of this place.

Ultimately, as place is fundamentally a social creation, the true yardstick for measuring changes to a place lies not in its visible and material transformations; rather, it rests in residents' experiential sense of place. In Boquete, the loss of place that Boqueteños express is enough to make this loss real to them and real for the entity of place itself. Amidst the clamoring of destruction and construction in the physical contexts of Boquete, the quiet and elusive spirit of Boquete, as a unique place of existential insideness, struggles to survive for those who know no home other than here, for those who know no community other than this.

Notes

1. In accordance with informant participation agreements, all informants' names have been changed to protect confidentiality.
2. 'Para nosotros, nos enseñaron a querer la tierra principalmente, a querer el lugar donde vives.'

3. A Spanish word without a directly corresponding English counterpart. The word translates as 'hearth, fireplace, or home'; it connotes a meaning of home which greatly surpasses the word 'casa'.

4. '...gente humilde y sencilla, gente que sólo tenía sus manos y su fuerza para levantar un hogar en medio de la montaña virgen.'

5. 'Supongo que en unos cinco años Boquete no va a ser Boquete. Boquete va a ser colonia americana. ... Tal vez haya una recurso económico que ayuda, pero a la vez está dañando al distrito.'

6. 'Es muy diferente lo que está pasando ahora. Ahora viene la gente ya con su familia, jubilados y eso, y viven en un mundo aparte de los Boqueteños. Los que vinieron aquí a poblar Boquete se casaron con Boqueteñas o, si traía[n] su[s] esposa[s], vivían junto [con la comunidad nativa]. Ahora hay como una separación. ... Los que han venido aquí, quieren vivir ... lejos de nosotros, y eso es *muy* mal en un pueblo tan pequeño.'

7. 'El que quiera conocer a Boquete venga, ya se acaba.'

8. 'El título anterior podría ser considerado un poco exagerado y fuera de la realidad a muchas personas que no tienen conocimiento do esta triste situación por la que estamos pasando los boqueteños, que día a día vemos morir nuestro pueblo. Superficialmente se observa un auge económico; han florecido diversas actividades como la construcción, comercio, etc. que a la postre dan la falsa imagen de una bonanza económica pero en realidad este resurgir no es mas que el oscuro velo que oculta nuestra próxima e inevitable destrucción.'

9. '...se desprende que nuestro único e insustituible recurso es la tierra o, dicho de otra forma, "Boquete sin sus campos de cultivo, morirá".'

10. '...con un campo de golf aquí, un mansión allí, y un restaurante allá.'

11. 'Mi papá me decía, "hay que trabajar todos los días". Mi papá, él lo que tuvo, fue trabajado. Pero hoy día muchos jóvenes no ven la vida que nosotros llevamos. Estudiamos, trabajamos, y seguimos trabajando. Y la gente [joven] se ilusiona mucho con tener una bonita casa, un carro muy bonito, aunque no pueda. ... Entonces si [los extranjeros] vienen y te compran en cien mil dólares, la familia es feliz, "no? Le compran un carro a cada hijo; se quedan sin tierra, pero se quedan sin plata también. "Y para adónde nos vamos a ir?'

12. '...ese era el negocio de su vida.'

13. 'A los pocos días se empezó a desvanecer el sueño del gran negocio y este ocurrió porque en la prisa por abandonar su tierra se olvidó de algunos recuerdos familiares como el retrato de los antepasados y alguno que otro objeto de uso personal. Como es normal, no dud[ó] el regresar a su tierra para recuperar lo olvidado, pero cual sería la sorpresa, que al llegar encontr[ó] una cerca de alambre ... y un letrero en otro idioma que parecía decir 'prohibido el paso'; pero más elocuente era la calavera pintada en el mismo y por último observ[ó] una gran fogata donde se consumían lentamente lo que una vez fue su casa y los recuerdos de su seres queridos ya fallecidos.'

14. 'Boqueteño, en tus manos esta la vida de tu pueblo. Si vendes tu tierra, morirá. Si no lo haces, vivirá. Piénsalo por ti y tu país.'

15. '...nuestro apreciado agricultor perdió todo su dinero y hoy en día, sin familia, ni amigos vive en la ciudad Cabecera de la Provincia, haciendo mandados para vivir y pidiendo pequeños préstamos a conocidos, que todos saben que nunca pagará. Lo triste de esta historia es que ocurrió a una persona como usted y yo, amable lector. De todo corazón, le pedimos que de poder identificar la persona

que ha vivido esta historia, nunca revele su nombre por solidaridad humana y tomen muy en cuenta lo sucedido a quienes venden su tierra, para que no sea usted actor de la próxima historia trágica.'

16. 'En un lapso de dos años han logrando [sic] comprar un tercio de la superficie total del distrito lo que significa que para la nación este terreno ya esta muerto o sea que es completamente estéril, ya que no dará un solo grano de café, una sola legumbre, ni servirá de asiento para ninguna familia boqueteña. Afirmamos esto ya que la tierra se compra para construir residencias para jubilados de los países mas desarrollados;...'

17 'Supong[o] que en unos cinco años Boquete no va a ser Boquete. Boquete va a ser colonia americana. No va a ser distrito de Boquete y no va a ver panameños. Va a ver más americanos que panameños, y ya no va a ser lo mismo. Es que ahorita mismo Boquete no es lo mismo que era diez años atrás.'

18. 'En Valle Escondido ahorita mismo [es] prácticamente colonia americana. Todos los que viven [allí] son americanos. Eso en lugar en donde todo el tiempo estuvo las personas de Boquete trabajando, viviendo, ¨verdad? Ahora ... es colonia americana. El boqueteño tiene que *pagar* para entrar y creo que no es justo. ... El boqueteño radicó todos sus años aquí. ¿Por qué un extranjero va a venir a imponerle pagar por lo que toda su vida vivió?'

Chapter 6
Conclusion

Introduction

In this concluding chapter, I begin by refuting the problematic image of residential tourism as a place-wrecking force by discussing some of the positive changes and progressive developments that it has spawned in the case of Boquete. I also begin a segmented discussion regarding the ultimate socio-spatial impacts that residential tourism is creating for Boquete, a discussion which I resume at the conclusion of this chapter. Next, taking into consideration all of the findings regarding residents' experiences of Boquete, their patterns of social interaction and the overarching socio-spatial implications of residential tourism growth and development, I briefly explore three theoretical scenarios for the future relationship between Boquete and residential tourism. This section then flows into a theoretical exploration of a particular subtype of the residential tourist identity, who demonstrates highly mobile, footloose behavior in his nomadic quest for distinctly 'authentic' landscapes of residential tourist paradise as they sporadically emerge and deteriorate around the globe. Towards the conclusion of this chapter, I offer some broad guidelines for future research into this line of inquiry before closing with some final thoughts on the main ideas presented in this work.

Rethinking Residential Tourism

Reflecting on the notion of nostalgia Raymond Williams rhetorically ponders: 'Is it anything more than a well-known habit of using the past, the "good old days", as a stick to beat the present' (1973: 12)? When change occurs, the instinctual human response is to seek out what is being lost, what will be missed. Change generates uncertainty, and uncertainty generates fear. The overwhelming response to residential tourism by native Boqueteño informants in the previous chapter is no exception. This is partially justifiable, as residential tourism irrefutably has created a number of significant negative consequences for the Boqueteño community; consequences which are likely to be compounded as residential tourism growth and development pursue a path of progression towards saturation. These negative consequences can be generalized as the estranging processes of alienation, commodification and displacement; processes which are unraveling place's meaningful union of land, individuals and community.

143

In Boquete, there is demonstrable evidence of physical destruction, such as the disappearance of the family-owned, agricultural fincas, which are giving way to unknowable, gated communities, as well as the remaking of places of home and community into contrived, other-directed landscapes. Then there is the unseen symbolic destruction of place: perceived threats to the established Boqueteño identity; the scouring of tradition and socio-cultural meaning from the spaces of Boquete, effectively whitewashing over the essence of place as a field of care; and native residents' sense of loss as they articulate the demise of a living entity which is Boquete. Ultimately, while the destruction of place is evident in changes to the vessels and vestiges of place in a physical context, its true impact is measured in changes to the meaning existing beneath these symbolic shells and structures.

Nevertheless, Williams' philosophical inquiry raises some important questions regarding nostalgia and, by extension, change. Can change – as measured by the perceived difference between the past and present, and by the anticipated difference between the present and future – be morally objectified as good or bad? What about agents of change, such as residential tourism? Plainly speaking, the issue of residential tourism, in the context of Boquete, is such a dynamic, unprecedented and unconsummated phenomenon as to evade a simple, straightforward moral judgment. Furthermore, there is a dilemma of representation, if one were to attempt to morally brand residential tourism. From whose perspective would this judgment be made?

On a theoretical level, to perceive the realities of Boquete prior to residential tourism as morally superior to the present realities of Boquete as an international destination for residential tourism would be to fall prey to a distorted and romanticized image of the past, which, incidentally, is not much different from the ideology of landscape as a way of seeing. This type of idealization is what Williams describes as the 'myth of the happier past.' In several important regards, residential tourism should not be wholly shunned as 'bad', just as pre-residential tourist Boquete should not be wholly glorified as 'good' and worthy of complete preservation.

Indeed, a thorough examination of pre-residential tourist Boquete draws to the surface a host of characteristics which easily refute the myth of the happier past in Boquete: high rates of unemployment; marginal educational and healthcare systems; pronounced periods of political instability and regional neglect; systematic exploitation of and racial discrimination towards the indigenous underclass; and unforgiving waves of economic instability, marked by pronounced periods of crisis. While residential tourism is far from being the cure-all for Boquete's traditional woes, as an agent of globalization and modernization, residential tourism is in many ways a beacon of economic and political stability, of social progress and of an overall improvement in the standard of living for residents of the district. Since the arrival of residential tourism, the unemployment rate in the district has dwindled virtually to zero, modern healthcare facilities and services in the district are being aggressively developed and, abstractly, residential tourists represent new agents of international diplomacy and accountability for an adolescent democracy in Panamá. Furthermore, from a provincial and regional standpoint, the increasing presence of residential tourism should prompt the central government to engage more aggressively in pursuing regional development initiatives beyond the scope of the urbanized canal corridor.

Most significantly, residential tourists inject hundreds of thousands of dollars into the local economy each month. The positive economic impact of their direct and indirect investments into this local economy cannot be understated. These economic contributions have helped to fuel robust economic growth in Boquete. Furthermore, they have ushered in greater overall economic stability for the district as a whole, as the sources of revenue within the local economy have been diversified into a greater number of industries, which extend well beyond the traditional base of agriculture. Indeed, without the direct and indirect economic contributions of residential tourism, Boquete would probably be left to struggle for its financial survival through agricultural trade in increasingly erratic and competitive international markets. Underscoring the economic volatility that Boquete likely would have faced in this hypothetical, alternative reality had residential tourism not become intertwined with the destiny of Boquete, Gayla Smutny finds that: 'Global economic restructuring has meant that a relative degree of economic stability is difficult to achieve in communities tied to a single economic base (e.g. mining, farming or lumber harvesting) because these places are vulnerable to changes in international commodity prices and demands' (2002: 440). Undoubtedly, residential tourism has helped the local economy rebound from the most recent economic crisis triggered by global restructuring in the international coffee economy during the last decade. Since that time, residential tourism has effectively widened and stabilized Boquete's economic base so that the community is no longer mercilessly vulnerable to fluctuations in international markets.

Furthermore, as we continue rethinking residential tourism's overall impact on Boquete, I find it necessary to dispute the metaphor that residential tourism is a species of parasite destroying its host. For residential tourism to grow and develop in Boquete, it continually requires new space into which it may be annexed. To an extent, the native community chooses to allow residential tourism to take root and prosper in the district. In an abstract sense, the issue of whether or not to allow residential tourism to develop in Boquete is a public referendum in which individual landholders vote with their land titles. By this logic, the resulting implications of residential tourism are, to an extent, the consequences of individual choice that landholding powers in Boquete freely make. Given that the majority of Boqueteño families own the land on which they live, this 'vote' for the continual growth and annexation of residential tourism is a somewhat democratic process within the native community. As evidence of the democratic nature of this process, take, for instance, the 'political campaigning' against selling one's land that the preservationist faction has launched through public campaign messages posted throughout the district, as well as through morally appealing literature, both of which were discussed in the previous chapter.

Thus, in addition to the quantifiable business and employment opportunities that residential tourism has created, it also has afforded a growing number of Boqueteños new opportunities for their lives; a luxury of choices which otherwise would not have been available. Relph writes that for insiders of a place, 'there is not merely a fusion between person and place, but also a tension between them.' Insiders' experience of place 'is a dialectical one – balancing the need to stay with the desire to escape' (1976: 42). In this light, what may be negatively interpreted by some native Boqueteños as 'residential displacement' may be positively interpreted by others as a liberating and empowering opportunity for mobility; the chance to escape the drudgery of place. The greater opportunities for geographical and socioeconomic mobility that residential tourism directly and indirectly makes accessible to the native community may ultimately provide Boqueteños with the chance to pursue greater educational and professional opportunities beyond the spatial confines of Boquete. In line with these opportunities, Bjørn Kaltenborn and Daniel Williams argue that residential displacement during this era of globalization need not automatically be judged as a negative consequence:

> [W]hile strong place bonds are seen as having a positive effect on psychological wellbeing, from the humanistic perspective such bonds may also be maladaptive as low mobility is strongly associated with low economic and social well-being. The humanistic tradition has also been criticised for its overly romantic if not anti-modern and exclusionary view of place as constituted by authentic social relations. Rather than protecting authentic places from the eroding forces of commodification and globalization, the desire to maintain an authentic, insider's relationship to a place may perpetuate social inequalities. (2002: 190–1)

Informants' accounts of the estranging processes alienating them from community and place beg us to blame residential tourism for these ostensibly 'negative' consequences. Yet even Tuan, an emotive patriarch of humanist geography, finds displacement to be surmountable:

> Should destruction occur we may reasonably conclude that the people would be thoroughly demoralized, since the ruin of their settlement implies the ruin of their cosmos. Yet this does not necessarily happen. Human beings have strong recuperative powers. Cosmic views can be adjusted to suit new circumstances. With the destruction of one 'center of the world,' another can be built next to it, or in another location altogether, and it in turn becomes the 'center of the world'. (1977: 150)

Furthermore, on a different note, it is impossible to say what Boquete would be like today had residential tourism never developed here. Having pre-established links to the global currents of international trade through coffee, one might argue that the forces of globalization, commodification and modernization were already being sown in Boquete prior to the arrival of residential tourism.

However, while the above considerations may allow us to reconsider the *significance* of residential tourism and its effects on the development/ destruction of Boquete, these considerations do little to directly confront and address the context-specific realities that residential tourism poses for the future of Boquete.

Future Scenarios

Below I explore three possible scenarios for Boquete's future as a residential tourist destination. The first presents the promise of what a cosmopolitan version of residential tourism might hold for Boquete. In this hopeful scenario, residential tourists slowly develop meaningful roots in Boquete as the aesthetic veil of landscape is pulled back to reveal Boquete as a field of care for which these foreign residents become invested caretakers. Alternatively, the second scenario explores latent sources of potential conflict, which could arise between the native and residential tourist communities as growth and development creates new demands, pressures and threats to the status quo in Boquete. In this scenario, increasing intercommunity tension and animosity rise to the surface as continued growth and development function to consolidate social isolation, effectively accelerating the other-directedness of Boquete and inhibiting residential tourists from acquiring a meaningful understanding of place. In the final scenario, I apply Butler's (1980) and Cohen's (1972) resort and tourist evolution models to the case study of Boquete in order to understand what these theoretical models might forecast for the future of Boquete.

The transcendental promise: Cosmopolitan residential tourism

In a sense, despite their many differences, established residential tourists and native Boqueteños share a mutual desire to preserve many of the traditional and natural qualities of Boquete. While the former group's intentions for maintaining the status quo are founded upon a desire to preserve its status of exclusive distinction and its perceived landscape of natural paradise and social utopia, the latter group's intentions are to preserve their way of life, their strong attachment to place and their bondedness as a community. Oddly enough, despite having different sets of motivations, both groups share similar conservative values: an appreciation of the rural, agricultural identity of Boquete; a desire to preserve and care for its natural environment; and a general opposition to unrestrained growth and development. Indeed, Kaltenborn and Williams suggest that: 'With much of the literature and thinking organised around the insider-outsider distinction … it becomes easy to assume that insiders and outsiders have different types of values and that they will take different stands on policy issues and attitudes towards management priorities' (2002: 196). However, to an extent, this is not the case. Because of these groups' shared, conservative values, there exists meaningful common ground yet to be realized by these socially isolated groups. There exists the possibility that, as growth and development increasingly threaten the status quo, residential tourists – particularly, those of the first and second waves – and native Boqueteños will find themselves rallying for the same preservationist/anti-growth causes.

These shared values could potentially serve as a social link to bridge the great experiential divide between the residential tourist and native Boqueteño communities; and, thus, open the door for the now-alienated and distanced residential tourist community to discover Boquete as a meaningful field of care. This is particularly promising given that there are already some indications on both sides of the social divide that these diverse residential groups seek meaningful interaction. For example, there are residential tourists, such as Susan, the Valle Escondido resident, who have acquired over time a desire to experience other aspects of Boquete beyond the walls of their residential enclaves, and outside the comfort of their socio-spatial bubbles of high-amenitied isolation. There also is hope to be found in indications that the younger generations of Boqueteños regard residential tourism more as a promising opportunity for upward mobility than as a threat to a cherished way of life. This sentiment is exemplified by Graciela's teenage son who, in contrast to his mother's demonstrable anxiety and concern towards residential tourist growth and development, viewed these very same processes as propitious and welcome mechanisms of progress. Both of these developments are promising indications that these disparate groups may bridge the social and experiential divide over time to evolve towards a shared understanding of place and community, towards shared values and towards a shared vision for the future of Boquete.

Through bridging this divide, there exists the opportunity for residential tourists to transcend their outsider experience of Boquete as a landscape of paradise in order to acquire an empathetic insideness of Boquete as a meaningful place. Concerning this particular type of cultivated, self-conscious sense of place, Relph writes:

> Empathetic insideness demands a willingness to be open to significances of place, to feel it, to know and respect its symbols – much as a person might experience a holy place as sacred without necessarily believing in that particular religion. This involves not merely looking at place, but *seeing* into and appreciating the essential elements of its identity. … Such identity of place does not present itself automatically, but must be sought by training ourselves to see and understand places in themselves. (1976: 54–5)

A particularly relevant parallel to this meaningful and open attitude towards place can be found in Hannerz's (1990) discussion of cultural cosmopolitanism. Although these two scholars are fundamentally concerned with different theoretical foci – Relph writes of place, Hannerz, of culture – both essentially share a concern for exploring the transcendental path from alienated outsideness to empathetic insideness. Like the empathetic insider, Hannerz writes of cosmopolitans who, 'tend to want to immerse themselves in other cultures, or in any case to be free to do so … They want to be able to sneak backstage rather than being confined to the front stage areas' (pp. 241–2). Just as Relph allows for his outsider personality the opportunity to deliberately cultivate a meaningful sense of place, Hannerz also allows for his stranger personality to 'build up competence' (p. 242) over time to achieve a cosmopolitan attitude towards alien experience and meaning. What is particularly interesting about Hannerz's theory of cosmopolitanism is that out of all the stranger personality's modern-day forms of identity (e.g. the tourist, the exile, the labor migrant, the business traveler and so forth) he explicitly singles out the expatriate as the identity 'most readily associa[ble] with cosmopolitanism' (p. 243). This is because, Hannerz hypothesizes, the expatriate voluntarily chooses to live abroad and, thus, 'can afford to experiment' with new lifestyles, cultural practices and identities; yet all the while he retains possession of the means of mobility: the luxury to return home or, as the

Boquete case study has demonstrated, relocate to a different destination, whenever he chooses. Because of this, Hannerz contends, the expatriate approaches alien cultures with the most openness and willingness to engage the Other.

This theoretical proposal concerning the expatriate's fitness to assume a cosmopolitan identity provides hope that, with time, residential tourists will acquire a cosmopolitan attitude towards Boquete and its native community. Discovering, interacting and caring are forms of investment, which bond individuals to a deeper relationship with community and place. By investing in place as cosmopolitan residential tourists, these foreign residents could continue to appreciate the landscape and enjoy the pleasures of leisure and consumption in balanced moderation; however, these experiences would be tempered, and greatly enriched, by a deeper awareness for the shared, negotiated values and meanings for this place as a field of care.

Problem of inter-community conflict

Despite the appealing possibility for a cosmopolitan style of residential tourism, which would strengthen Boquete's base of invested caretakers, this hopeful scenario neglects to consider how the dynamic processes of growth and development are intervening at present to remake Boquete and, in the process, drive out many residents, both native *and* foreign. For the former group, growth and development are initiating the processes of alienation, commodification and displacement, creating the estranging effects discussed in the previous chapter. For the latter group, growth and development are shattering their carefully constructed image of Boquete as a residential tourist paradise, and destroying their imagined, exclusive status as novelty personalities in a Juan Valdez romance set among an Edenic landscape. Significantly, as discussed in Chapter 4, many residential tourists of the first and second waves have already begun to consider pulling up stakes in Boquete after just a few short years of residence in order to reclaim their ideal landscape of residential tourist paradise in more pristine and less developed areas of Latin America.

The undeniable reality is that, ongoing residential tourist growth and development very likely will serve to place added pressure upon already limited resources in Boquete. This, in turn, may very likely serve to exacerbate both intra- and intercommunity tensions, conflicts, and animosities, which presently simmer just below the cordial facade of social civility in Boquete. Among residential tourists, the established residents of the first and second waves already demonstrate unabashed resentment towards their newly arriving peers of the third wave; while among native residents, the preservationist faction resents that many landowners are selling out to foreign interests. Meanwhile, native Boqueteños are beginning to blame residential tourists for fuelling the processes that are estranging them from place and community. Cast in this light, the possibilities of cosmopolitan residential tourism, empathetic insideness and a common, middle ground of shared values all begin to appear as naively romantic aspirations.

In their case study of British expatriates' residential experiences in rural France, Buller and Hoggart rightfully anticipate that, regarding intercommunity tension and animosity, 'the question of scale is important, for it is possible that an enhanced British presence will bring any "isolationist" behaviour into sharper focus (especially if increased British numbers raise competition over housing and other local resources)' (1994: 112). In Boquete, issues of scale, as well as issues concerning the carrying capacities of basic public utilities, services and infrastructures are extremely relevant concerns. Potable water infrastructures, telecommunication networks, electrical power grids and sewage treatment systems in the district are already overwhelmed and utterly insufficient to accommodate the new demands that added residential tourist growth and development promise to engender in the not too distant future. In fact, already residents report of frequent water shortages in the district, as well as a waiting list for landline telephone service, given that this network presently operates at maximum capacity. On top of these problems, the basic layout of Bajo Boquete, the commercial center of the district, is ill-equipped to handle the growing number of vehicles, literally increasing by the day, which have begun to jam the narrow streets and overwhelm the preposterously limited number of parking spaces available in the commercial center (Figure 6.1). In a district without even one traffic signal, traffic congestion is becoming a frustratingly common phenomenon. Alone, these resource and infrastructure crises, whether impending or already a reality, represent a basis for intergroup tension; however, considering that residential tourists do not provide direct financial contributions to the provision of these resources and infrastructures – as they do not pay property or income taxes – animosity towards residential tourists is especially likely to increase among the native community. The socioeconomic status of residential tourists as Boquete's super-rich certainly will do nothing to assuage Boqueteños' resentment of these foreigners' special status as non-tax paying residents, regardless of their indirect economic contributions to the district's public coffers. Quite possibly, this point of tension will only be confounded if the dominant settlement pattern of residential tourism

Figure 6.1   Traffic congestion on the main street of downtown Bajo
Boquete on a Saturday night (photo by author, 2005)

continues moving in the direction of isolated residential enclavism. Much of the marketing appeal of these residential tourist-directed gated developments accentuates the privatized 'first-world' or 'American-standard' amenities, resources and infrastructures that they provide for their affluent residents' exclusive use. While this privatization of services and utilities may alleviate some of the public resource and infrastructure demands, the negative social consequences of progressive isolationism by the residential tourist community ultimately would greatly outweigh any practical benefits.

The incapacity of public services and infrastructures to meet current and future growth is only part of a larger deficiency of governmental planning and oversight, both locally and regionally; this despite the issuance of over 2000 residential building permits in circulation and the development of no less than eight large-scale gated residential communities within the district, as of 2005. The implication of these developments is that profit-driven real estate developers and brokers and the unfettered style of global free market capitalism they represent may ultimately destroy any semblance of traditional Boquete as a field of care before residential tourists have adequate time to cultivate a sense of insideness. While there are many hands stirring the pot of residential tourist growth and development in Boquete, there simply exists no unified development plan, nor any significant governmental oversight or controlling organization to ensure that Boquete's growth and development are socially responsible and environmentally sustainable.

What is direly needed is a local task force – comprised of invested local residents and stakeholders who represent the many different constituencies and interests in Boquete – which would work with municipal and regional governmental agencies to create and enforce a strategic plan for sensible growth and development in the district. However, before this can happen, the Panamanian government must do more to educate the public and equip them with the adequate resources so that they may understand and confront the wide-ranging implications of the government's neoliberal strategy to attract foreign residents as a means for increasing foreign investment and development in the republic. Indeed, it is quite apparent that much of the Boqueteño community's ambivalence towards residential tourism derives from the simple fact that, as a collective body, the community is profoundly under-prepared, under-informed, and under-resourced to fully grasp and respond to this powerful and complex phenomenon.

Additional to these material concerns, disparities in lifestyle, class and core values existing between the native and residential tourist communities also contain the seeds for intercommunity animosity, particularly as growth and development create additional pressures and threats to the established identity of Boquete. Despite these groups' common, conservative values regarding preservation of the natural and traditional qualities of Boquete, continued growth and development threaten to expose and exacerbate fundamental differences that exist beneath the thin surface of these rather superficially shared values. Ultimately, conflicts may arise as residential tourists seek to preserve the aesthetic facade of traditional Boquete, while native Boqueteños seek to preserve the symbolic meaning of place, regardless of its appearance.

From this perspective, it appears that the pace and scale of continued residential tourism growth and development will likely be the decisive factor in determining not only the nature of relations between the two communities of Boquete in future years, but also the ability of established residents to preserve traditional Boquete, both in appearance, as a landscape, and in meaning, as a place.

The future identity of residential tourism

In the final of three scenarios exploring the future relationship between residential tourism and Boquete, I turn to Butler's (1980) and Cohen's (1972) theoretical models regarding, respectively, the evolutionary developments of tourist destinations and a typology of international tourist identities, in order to explore what applicable insights these theories might hold for the future development of residential tourism in Boquete. In Chapter 2, I identified the progression of residential tourism in Boquete to be at the stage of 'development' in Butler's theoretical model. Residential tourism in Boquete clearly has matured beyond the 'involvement stage', the period preceding full-scale development during which time the marketing of (residential) tourism and (residential) tourist services begins to acquire basic definition; however, undoubtedly, it has yet to mature into the following stage of consolidation, the period following aggressive development during which time the pace of new growth slows appreciably. What is most significant about Butler's model, as applied to the context of this case study, is that it affirms an important finding occurring in Boquete: that a significant proportion of first and second wave residential tourists have begun to consider relocating away from Boquete as continued foreign growth and development function to destroy the very image of paradise that originally attracted them to Boquete. As the development stage evolves, Butler theorizes that: 'The type of tourist will [change], as a wider market is drawn upon, representing... Cohen's institutionalized tourist' (1980: 8).

Cohen's theoretical analysis of the phenomenon of international tourism is particularly complementary to Butler's model because it provides a linear model for the social evolution of the tourist identity in the spatial context of a particular host destination, as that destination mutates over time. Cohen proposes a typology of four tourist roles, whose identities range from 'non-institutionalized' to 'institutionalized' depending upon each role's level of preference for experiences of novelty and familiarity. Chronologically, the first type of tourist-oriented contact with a particular destination is made by non-institutionalized 'explorers' and 'drifters'. However, as the host destination grows and develops as a market for tourism due to the 'spearheading' efforts of the explorers and drifters, the non-institutionalized tourist identity gradually gives way to an institutionalized identity of less adventurous, mass tourists.

Applied to the context of residential tourism in Boquete, the resulting implication is that the established first and second waves of residential tourists – those expressing an urge to relocate as the landscape deteriorates – likely embody the role and preferences of Cohen's non-institutionalized tourist identity. *If* Cohen's and Buter's models are applicable to these contexts, what presently is occurring in Boquete is a tidal shift in the identity of the residential tourist population from non-institutionalized to institutionalized, as the spearheading explorers and drifters give way to an infantry of mass residential tourists. Regarding the practices and development of mass tourism, Cohen theorizes that:

> The main purpose of mass tourism is the visiting of attractions, whether genuine or contrived. However, even if they are genuine, the tendency is to transform them or manipulate them, to make them 'suitable' for mass tourist consumption. They are supplied with facilities, reconstructed, landscaped, cleansed of unsuitable elements, staged, managed, and otherwise organized. As a result, they largely lose their original flavor and appearance and become isolated from the ordinary flow of life and natural texture of the host society. (1972: 170)

Applying Cohen's theory to the context of residential tourism in Boquete, the implication is that, as mass residential tourism materializes, the value of Boquete's main attraction – its promoted and glorified landscape – will only become more essential to maintaining its appeal as a world-class destination for residential tourism. According to Cohen, the character of this main attraction will become increasingly artificial, contrived, staged and sanitized; or, to use Relph's (1976) vocabulary, it will grow into an 'inauthentic landscape'.

Similarly, applying Butler's (1980) model to his case study of the North American expatriate community in Lake Chapala, Mexico, Truly (2002) discovers that as the area's foreign growth and development continues, its foreign residents perceive a distinctive decrease in native-foreign residential interaction. In fact, his research findings indicate that the newer arriving expatriates are negatively perceived by the established expatriate community as 'importing a lifestyle' from North America.

Perhaps most troubling for Boquete's future, as inferred from these theoretical models, are Cohen's final thoughts concerning the impacts of mass tourism:

> As tourism is eagerly sought for by the developing nations as an important source of revenue, it may provoke serious disruptions and cause ultimate long-range damage in these societies. The consequences cannot yet fully be foreseen, but from what we already know about the impact of mass tourism it can safely be predicted that mass tourism in developing countries, if not controlled and regulated, might help to destroy whatever there is still left of unspoiled nature and traditional ways of life. In this respect, the easy-going tourist of our era might well complete the work of his predecessors, also travelers from the West – the conqueror and colonialist. (1972: 182)

Although an era of mass residential tourism has yet to fully materialize in Boquete, many of Cohen's dire warnings resonate in the estranging effects of alienation, commodification and displacement that native residents already vocalize.

What is particularly interesting about the ongoing social experiment of residential tourism, and what distinguishes it from all other varieties of tourism, are the idealistic and grandiose stated intentions of its practitioners: to make a lasting home in the same type of environments and destinations that other types of tourists wish to visit only temporarily or seasonally. However, considering the theoretical models for, as well as the practical nature of international tourism – with its steady march towards mass commodification, development and inauthenticity – might it be that the stated intentions of residential tourists tend to be unrealistic? Is the notion that residential tourists may be able to make a meaningful and sustainable home abroad really realistic? Perhaps it is still too early in this grand social experiment to tell.

Landscape Nomadism

What are we to make of the residential tourists who, after just a few short years of residence in Boquete, have become disenchanted with the illusions of paradise perceived in its landscape; and who express a nomadic desire to pack up their belongings and venture forth on a quixotic quest to recapture their desired, utopian landscape elsewhere? Among the findings to come out of this research there is a strong indication that the great majority of established residential tourists are fervently opposed to additional growth and development precisely because these processes directly threaten to destroy – or rather expose the illusion of – the natural and social landscape of residential tourist paradise in Boquete. The primacy of this valued aesthetic landscape is so integral to the residential tourist experience, overshadowing emotional ties to place and social bonds with community, that without it a significant number of established residential tourists express little motivation to continue living here. Indeed, as the dynamics of mass residential tourist growth and development intervene to fell the image of Boquete as a landscape of natural paradise and social utopia, a significant number of residential tourist informants desire to rid themselves of this place in order to regain this preferred residential landscape elsewhere.

These residential tourist 'landscape nomads' appear to be enamored with a particular, romanticized image of landscape – as conveyed through the tropes of the natural ideal and the authentic village – as well as with the concomitant social status of exclusivity and elitism that this particular residential tourist fantasy affords them. Fundamentally, for these landscape nomads, 'home' is not spatially confined to a particular place but rather ideologically oriented around a particular, desired landscape; an idealized residential setting, which is independent of the spatial constraints of place, and which is recreatable in any number of spatial contexts, provided that they are favorable settings for this imagined residential tourist landscape.

Not unlike history's long record of nomadic peoples, who throughout time immemorial have imbued their collective quests for life-sustaining resources and the experience of the journeys themselves with the meaning of 'home', these landscape nomads may be an emergent form of aesthetic- and consumption-oriented peripatetics, arising out of the particular globalizing, socioeconomic and demographic contexts of the 21st century. Although these landscape nomads may present themselves more in the image of 'landscape refugees' – ostensibly forced by the 'destructive' pressures of growth and development to uproot themselves and migrate from place to place in search of some 'peace and quiet' – their nomadic lifestyles are, undeniably, quite voluntary.

If indeed there is such a thing as landscape nomadism emerging out of the escalating practices of residential tourism and, more generally, consumption-oriented migration, then on an international scale these landscape nomads are destined to play an extremely significant role as reconnaissance scouts spearheading the frontier of consumption-oriented settlement and development further into new regions and localities.

Suggestions for Further Research

Concerning future research into the issues explored in this book, first and foremost, it is imperative that residential tourism and related forms of consumption-oriented migration, such as IRM, be explored from the greatly underrepresented perspective of the host communities whom these phenomena directly and indirectly affect. Implicitly related to this suggestion, there also exists a great need to qualitatively understand these issues from the perspectives and based on the experiences of the participants whose lives are affected by these phenomena, whether voluntarily or involuntarily. Residential tourism manifests itself to be an awesome, transformative force capable of creating both constructive and destructive impacts on a local level; however, we must be wary not to assume that we may easily observe or infer the nature of these impacts, as they are liable to be highly subjective and not overtly manifest. Indeed, the physical, economic, social or cultural changes one individual or community may regard as progressive development another may perceive as calamitous destruction. Certainly, this difference of subjective perception and qualitative experience may be evident not only between diverse groups, such as foreign and native inhabitants sharing a common place of residence, but even within relatively homogeneous groups who, for instance, may be split along generational or socioeconomic lines. Now that we have begun to gain a quantitative and demographical foothold towards a greater understanding of these phenomena, it becomes necessary to expand the scope and sharpen the definition of our qualitative inquiries into residential tourism and related forms of consumption-oriented migration.

As residential tourism begins to mature in the destinations in which it is now developing, there are a host of longitudinal questions that deserve to be explored. These include investigating how the socio-cultural identities of these destinations and their residential communities, as well as how the nature of social interaction between diverse residential groups in these places, evolve over time. In addition, we must continue to explore both the practical and theoretical links between short-term vacation tourism and long-term residential tourism. In particular, it remains to be fully seen how well Cohen's and Butler's theoretical models relate to the practical development and maturation of the destinations and practitioners of residential tourism over time, on the ground. Furthermore, the practical and highly dynamic nature of residential tourism, which in the case study of Boquete draws human migration into the district as well as threatens to initiate significant residential relocation and displacement in the near future, begs us to explore the larger temporal and spatial patterns of migration associated with this phenomenon.

Perhaps one of the most intriguing questions yet to be fully explored concerns the notions of landscape nomadism and of an evolving, global frontier of residential tourist settlement and development. Of particular interest here are the long-term patterns of mobility and the social behaviours of non-institutionalized, residential tourist landscape nomads, who, at least in theory, effectively function to spearhead the advance of consumption-orientated settlement and development into new territories. If or when these landscape nomads abandon their primary destinations of residential tourism, to where do they relocate and how do their patterns of migration affect larger processes of settlement and development?

Among the wide range of issues that remain to be explored, I would greatly urge researchers always to approach residential tourism as a phenomenon fundamentally involving and affecting three co-related entities: voluntary and involuntary participants, interacting in a meaningful physical context. Indeed, to neglect to explore this phenomenon without taking all three entities into equal consideration would be to create an egregiously incomplete snapshot of its effects. Finally, with regard to our conceptual understandings of residential tourism and related forms of consumption-oriented migration, especially IRM, we must endeavor towards constructing more complex and nuanced frameworks for exploring these practical phenomena. In practice, these phenomena are not merely rational, anesthetic pursuits in search of relative affluence, a warmer climate, sun and sand. Indeed, we must take into account that these phenomena also represent modern-day, socio-spatial manifestations of our persistent and quixotic human desires for escapism, nostalgia, fantasy, aesthetic harmony, experiences of exotica and landscapes of natural paradise and social utopia.

Conclusion

The temptation here is to reach a final moral judgment on residential tourism and either glorify it as progressive development or condemn it as wrongful destruction. However, there simply is no way to reduce such a complex phenomenon down to a straightforward moral conclusion, nor is there any one actor or group of actors who we could even credit or blame for the wide-ranging effects of this phenomenon. In line with what Don Mitchell (1996) conveys in the conclusion of his study of landscape, to look back upon the body of this qualitative work and the varied collection of human expressions which underwrite it and attempt to reach a unified, overarching conclusion would be to level the dimensionality of this complex phenomenon and to selectively promote some observations and expressions over others. By now, this temptation to look back and *see* residential tourism in simplified, manifestly coherent terms should sound familiar to the illusions of landscape, as a way of seeing.

Indeed, residential tourism is what it is: but one of the many faces of the ubiquitous and nebulous globalizing processes acting on a variety of levels to create new forms of social, cultural and economic interaction, greater interconnectedness and significant transformations to our many notions of place and community. Even in the localized context of Boquete, the scope of the actors involved in actively shaping and sustaining residential tourism is incredible. To name just a few of these parties consider: the Panamanian politicians and economists who create the neoliberal economic policies that attract residential tourism; the residential tourists who migrate to Boquete; the Boqueteños who oblige the annexation of residential tourism into new spaces and who provide desired residential tourist accommodations, services and amenities; the marketers and advertisers who package and promote Boquete in the image of a world-class destination for residential tourism; and the real estate developers and brokers who oblige this image through the physical remaking of Boquete.

Rather than wrestle with the morality of residential tourism, what we can do as invested and considerate students, scholars, observers and participants is to understand the practical effects of residential tourism as best we can, by listening to those parties whose everyday lives are directly affected by this phenomenon. Then, armed with this practical information, we can affect positive change by promoting the progressive outcomes of residential tourism, while simultaneously highlighting and acting to minimize its undesirable outcomes.

As detailed earlier in this chapter, there is cause for celebrating the many progressive developments that residential tourism engenders. These positive outcomes may be generalized as effectuating a higher standard of living in Boquete: better healthcare services and facilities, economic diversification, new opportunities for socioeconomic and geographical mobility, increased economic stability and political accountability and so forth. Furthermore, residential tourism provides the possibility for new forms of meaningful and enduring intercultural exchanges to occur. Finally, we must not overlook or discount the expressed pleasure and meaning that these new residential experiences have brought to the residential tourists themselves. By aspiring for beauty, comfort and belongingness in their lives, they are simply seeking to fulfill a basic human desire that has moved mankind since time immemorial. However, with regard to the destructive outcomes of residential tourism, what immediately comes to mind are the processes of estrangement that are working to disjoin the meaningful union of caretakers from their field of care and from a knowable community. While many in the Boqueteño community express optimism and gratitude for the new socio-economic opportunities and higher standards of living that residential tourism has effectuated, the lasting impression of their collective expression during this transformative era of residential tourist growth and development resonates not as celebration but as mourning and loss. Like Ulices Urriola's anecdote of the Boqueteño farmer who traded his land for material wealth, the unseen personal value he forfeited in the process was utterly devastating to his identity, his quality of life, his independence and his dignity. Ultimately, this perceived estrangement from the meaningful entities of place and community and the related expressions of loss that reverberate from the collective voice of the Boqueteño community during this process of 'development' are troubling indeed.

Just as there is no one identifiable cause to blame for initiating the events contributing to this profound and collective cry of estrangement, there are no simple remedies to correct it. However, there do exist two real opportunities to make residential tourist development and practices more sustainable in the immediate future. The first opportunity relates to governmental policy. It is incumbent upon the central government to counterbalance its neoliberal economic policies, which result in highly localized pockets of residential tourist development in western Panamá, with proportionally equal investments in public infrastructures, community planning initiatives, and land use oversight in these areas so as to ensure that this new form of development is sustainable. In other words, the Panamanian government must accept a greater responsibility to regulate real estate development and to ensure that the provinces and districts bearing the unequal burdens of its national economic development initiatives are fairly compensated with commensurate levels of funding and resources.

The second opportunity, which relates back to the main thesis of this book, concerns residential perception. Fundamentally, if residential tourism is to be sustainable as an individual lifestyle and as a social practice, it will require that residential tourists penetrate the alluring facade of landscape as an illusion of natural paradise and social utopia. Simply put, this collectively conditioned experience is a self-indulgent way of seeing that allows its participants to shirk their responsibilities to their human and natural surroundings by seeing themselves as disconnected, uninvolved and unaffecting entities.

While the image of landscape is *real* and meaningful for its makers, it is also a highly unstable and individualistic construction of reality that is quite often grossly out of touch with deep-rooted and negotiated constructions of reality held by those immersed in the intimate, everyday experiences of that environment. Landscape, as a way of seeing, creates an *un*real context of consumption in which the meaningful contexts of its production are mystified. And in a greater sense landscape is a consumption- and aesthetic-oriented way of seeing which seeks to escape the bonds of humanity; bonds which obligate us to be considerate and willful participants in the world around us. Landscape as a way of seeing ultimately excuses its participants from their implicit responsibilities to this immediate world by obscuring their inescapable interconnectedness *with* this world. Seeing one's surrounding world as a landscape of leisure and consumption inevitably creates not only a misunderstanding about this world, but also a misunderstanding about one's role in this world and the consequences of one's presence and actions in this environment.

Residential tourists flock to Boquete, prompted by provocative heralds who proclaim that here a worldly, residential paradise may be found. Here, buying into the grand image of Boquete as a utopian landscape of leisure and consumption is facilitated by the burgeoning industry and growing community of residential tourism, both of which function to define and propagate this illusory representation of place. This fantastic image of Boquete is sustained in the minds of residential tourists, at least initially, as they do not yet know enough about the everyday realities of Boquete as a living place to bring these ethereal fantasies down to earth; to expose the myth of exclusive distinction as a seductive image that is truly unsustainable under the pace of residential tourism growth and development occurring in Boquete.

Ultimately, residential tourists must be willing to acquire some degree of disillusionment from the way of seeing their place of residence as a landscape of natural paradise and social utopia if they are to have any real chance to create a meaningful and enduring home here. Residential tourists have the choice either to embrace the experiential process towards discovering their immediate surroundings as a flawed but real living place, or to flee from this inevitable truth which awaits them behind the veil of landscape. As outsiders who voluntarily introduce themselves into an established *place* and a vibrant *community*, residential tourists have an implicit humanitarian responsibility to strive to understand the histories and experiences of the native community and to respect and preserve the values and way of life that they so cherish.

Appendix 1

Boquete: A pueblo that is living the last days of its history[1,2]

ULICES URRIOLA

The above title could be considered a little exaggerated and outside the reality of many persons who do not have knowledge of this sad situation that we as Boqueteños are suffering, as day by day we watch our pueblo die. Superficially one observes an economic boom; diverse activities, such as construction and commerce, have flourished that in the end give the false image of economic prosperity. But in reality this revival is nothing more than the dark veil that hides our approaching and inevitable destruction.

Boquete is a pueblo that has survived for close to one hundred years on its base in agriculture which is Boquete's principal resource and is predominated by the coffee sector. [This industry] generates dozens of thousands of jobs directly and indirectly and is one of the few sources of foreign currency for the nation by means of the exportation of the coffee which has an excellent quality which is renowned on an international level. Continuing in the same direction, we can mention other products like flowers, vegetables, and others of great success. From this one infers that our one and irreplaceable resource is the land or, said another way, 'Boquete without its fields for cultivation will die'. It is on this point where the problem resides. A few years ago a group of foreign investors redis- covered us not for the good but rather for the contrary: as an object of busi- ness. They found a district that was completely urbanized at the cost of the sacrifice of all Panamanians because with our taxes the national govern- ment constructed highways, aqueducts and electrical installations, with the hope of modernizing agriculture, for the development of the country. As well as fertile, urbanized lands, the modern discoverers encountered land owners overwhelmed by debt and frustrated by the antinational politics characteristic of most governmental regimes. The land owners had minimal knowledge of the real value of their lands and even less knowledge of the full benefits that could be derived from these lands. [It is in] these circumstances that the modern freebooters have taken maximum advantage, having come forth on the global scene, on the ardor of global- ization, and the actual neoliberal theories. The success obtained by these businessmen is appalling. In a span of two years they have succeeded in buying a third of the total land area in the district, which signifies for the nation that this land already is dead or [at least] completely sterile since it will produce not one coffee bean, nor even one vegetable, nor will it serve as a settlement for a Boqueteño family. This we affirm given that the land is bought in order to build residences for retirees from the most developed countries. Although their retirement pensions are of little worth in their places of origin, with those same finances here in Panamá they can lead a pleasant life at the cost of our extinction. These retirees are among millions; enough to occupy all the nation's lands, displacing the Panamanians and depriving them of their greatest resource, which is the land given that we are not an industrialized country and we have hardly begun to exploit other resources.

Despite the little time that has passed, the experience in Boquete with the new colonists is terrible. They try to suffice as much as possible [shopping] in retail stores outside of the region, preferably in foreign-owned franchises, and only in exceptional occasions when they do utilize local services, they haggle over prices and wages. They keep themselves separate from the activities of the [Boqueteño] population, towards whom they express an obvious contempt, perhaps [because] they consider us inferior. Well, on this point perhaps they are right because by selling them paradise for a few dollars we should not expect even the most minimal consideration from them or from anyone. We hope that that these small considerations serve to move something in the conscience of Boqueteños so that they don't sell their lands. We make a call to the appropriate authorities who are called-upon to safeguard the integrity of the nation. It will not be that we intend to do something when, all the same, we find ourselves on the path towards a common grave, which is the ultimate fate for all who forget the sacred duty to fight every day [given] by God for one's life and one's liberty.

Notes

1. Boquete, un pueblo que esta viviendo los últimos días de su historia por Ulices Urriola: El título anterior podría ser considerado un poco exagerado y fuera de la realidad a muchas personas que no tienen conocimiento de esta triste situación por la que estamos pasando los boqueteños, que día a día vemos morir nuestro pueblo. Superficialmente se observa un auge económico; han florecido diversas actividades como la construcción, comercio, etc. que a la postre dan la falsa imagen de una bonanza económica pero en realidad este resurgir no es más que el oscuro velo que oculta nuestra próxima e inevitable destrucción.

Boquete es un pueblo que ha sobrevivido por cerca de cien años a base de la agricultura que es su principal recurso, predominando el sector cafetalero que genera docenas de miles de empleos directos e indirectos y que es una de las pocas fuentes de divisas para la noción por medio de la exportación del café, que tiene una excelente calidad la cual es reconocida a nivel mundial. Siguiendo en la misma dirección podemos mencionar otros productos como las flores, legumbres y otros de gran aceptación. De esto se desprende que nuestro único e insustituible recurso es la tierra o, dicho de otra forma, 'Boquete sin sus campos de cultivo, morirá.' Es en este punto donde radica el problema. Hace unos pocos años un grupo de inversionistas extranjeros nos redescubrieron no para bien sino por el contrario, como objeto de negocio. Encontraron un distrito completamente urbanizado a costa del sacrificio de todos los panameños porque con nuestros impuestos el gobierno nacional construyó carreteras, acueductos, tendidos eléctricos, con la esperanza de modernizar la agricultura, para el desarrollo del país. Además de tierras fértiles urbanizadas los modernos descubridores encontraron unos propietarios agobiados por las deudas y frustrados por las políticas antinacionales de casi todos los gobiernos de turno y como si fuera poco los dueños de las tierras contaban con un mínimo conocimiento del valor real de las mismas y menos del provecho que le pudieran sacar. Circunstancias estas que han aprovechado al máximo los modernos filibusteros contemporáneos surgidos a la escena mundial al color de la globalización y las actuales teorías neoliberales. El éxito obtenido por estos comerciantes es aterrador. En un lapso de dos años han logrado comprar un tercio de la superficie total del distrito lo que significa que para la nación este terreno ya esta muerto o sea que es completamente estéril, ya que no dará un solo grano de café, una sola legumbre, ni servirá de asiento para ninguna familia boqueteña. Afirmamos esto ya que la tierra se compra para construir residencias para jubilados de los países mas desarrollados; que aunque sus jubilaciones sean pequeñas en su lugar de origen, aquí en Panamá, con estos recursos pueden llevar una vida placentera a costa de nuestra extinción. De estas personas se cuentan por millones, como para llenar todas las tierras nacionales, desplazando por supuesto a los panameños y privándolos de su mayor recurso que es la tierra, ya que no somos un país industrializado y apenas empezamos a explotar otros recursos.

A pesar del poco tiempo transcurrido la experiencia en Boquete con los nuevos colonos es terrible, tratan de autoabastecerse hasta donde sea posible en almacenes fuera de la región preferiblemente en franquicias extranjeras y solo en ocasiones excepcionales utilizan los servicios locales, regatean precios y salarios, se mantienen ajenos a las actividades de la población por la cual expresan un menosprecio notorio o sea que nos consideran inferiores.

Bueno en esto quizás tengan razón ya que al venderles el paraíso por unos dólares más no podemos esperar ni la más mínima consideración de ellos ni de nadie. Esperamos que estas pequeñas consideraciones muevan en algo la conciencia de los boqueteños en primera instancia para que no vendan sus terrenos. Hacemos un llamado a las autoridades correspondientes que son las mas llamadas a salvaguardar la integridad de la nación, y no sea que intentemos hacer algo cuando todos por igual nos encontremos en el camino de una fosa común que es el destino final de todo pueblo que olvida el sagrado deber de luchar todos los días de Dios por su vida y su libertad.

2. English translation provided courtesy of the author.

This is the story of a farmer who sold his land to a foreigner for a great amount of money[1,2]

ULICES URRIOLA

In the fertile and marvelous highlands of Chiriqui lived Antonio, a laborious and honest farmer [who] was very well-known and well-respected in his pueblo. He supported his family by means of coffee and vegetable cultivation on a six hectare plot of land which he had inherited from his father who was also a farmer. Antonio was not a rich man, but he and his family survived despite the great problems presently confronting the agricultural industry. In certain occasions Antonio complained about his bad situation but even so he considered himself fortunate, since the immense majority of Panamanians lived in an acute state of poverty. Like this, Antonio's life passed day by day without great troubles until one awful day in his destiny there appeared a familiar local accompanied by a foreigner who offers Antonio a great amount of money for his land. It was not very difficult for the visitors to convince the naive farmer of the benefits of selling his land for a great sum of money, to be more precise, two hundred thousand dollars, an unimaginable sum of money to Antonio for a piece of land that, according to him, had only provided for a life of [financial] constraints. As such, this was the deal of a lifetime. The deal went through and Antonio had to abandon his land and rent a house in the pueblo for him and his family to inhabit. After a few days he began to dispel the dream of the big deal. This occurred because in the rush to abandon his land, he forgot about several family keepsakes such as the portrait of his ancestors and other objects [of personal value]. Consequently he did not think twice about returning to his land in order to recover his forgotten items, but to his surprise, upon arriving he encountered an electric fence and a sign in another language that seemed to say 'do not enter'; but more eloquent was the painted skull on the sign. [It was then that Antonio] noticed a great bonfire which was slowly consuming the remains of what once was his house and the memories of his deceased loved ones. Faced with this very eloquent reality, Antonio decided to take drastic measures and put his money earned [from the land sale] to good use so that he could provide for himself and his family. With this end in mind he did the following:

(1) He ignored the wishes of his children: to buy a car, to attend university, to acquire a new house, etc. This was an appropriate measure for his reality as a farmer without land, which should have been to conserve his money at all costs. This measure put him at odds with his family, who could not understand why, having so much money, their father would not give them these small luxuries. For this they opted to abandon him and leave him alone with his money.

(2) Alone and without family, Antonio thought clearly. He decided to invest the money in various business ventures to generate an income, since the money itself did not produce earnings. This action, theoretically of good logic, brought on catastrophic consequences. He lost more than half of his investment because in the real world to invest in any kind of business venture is very risky and made so even more when one does not possess the necessary experience; remember that Antonio had always been a farmer.

(3) But as our farmer still had some money left, he did not think twice in heading in the direction of the bank. He had heard that many people live off the money they kept in accounts with fixed terms, so he decided to do the same. Like this he visited the branches of various banks looking for a reasonable interest rate, which he could not find since all the banks offered meager interest rates that would not support him. As with all experiences, there was a lesson learned. Antonio learned, although a little too late, a sad lesson, which is that the banks make all the earnings and the client takes all the losses and that we should keep as far away as possible from such dangerous institutions.

(4) Finally, the inevitable occurred. Antonio had spent all of his money, which really did not take much time given the high cost of living and the lack of income that helped him in achieving this end.

To get to the point with this story, we will tell you that our respected farmer lost all of this money and today, without family, nor friends, he lives in the city of Cabecera in the province, doing errands and asking for small loans from acquaintances, all of whom know he will never repay them. The saddest part of this story is that it occurred to someone just like you and I, kind reader. In all sincerity, we ask that if you know the identity of the person who has lived this story, never reveal his name for the sake of human solidarity. Take into serious account that which happens to those who sell their land, so that you do not become the protagonist of the next tragic story.

Notes

1. Esta es la historia de un agricultor que vendió su tierra a un extranjero por
    mucho pero mucho dinero por Ulices Urriola: En las fértiles y maravillosas
    tierras altas chiricanas vivía Antonio un laborioso y honrado agricultor era
    muy conocido y respetado en su pueblo, sostenía su familia mediante el
    cultivo de café y hortalizas en una superficie de terreno de seis hectáreas que
    había heredado de su padre que al igual que él fue un agricultor. Antonio no
    era un hombre rico, pero sobrevivía con su familia a pesar de los grandes prob-
    lemas que enfrenta el agro hoy en día. En ciertas ocasiones Antonio se quejaba
    de su mala situación pero aún así contaba con más, que una inmensa mayoría
    de panameños que viven en una pobreza muy acentuada. Así transcurría día
    tras día la vida de Antonio sin mayores trastornos hasta que un día fatal en su
    destino apareció un conocido lugareño acompañado de un extranjero que
    andaba ofreciendo grandes cantidades de dinero por los terrenos de esas áreas.
    No les fue muy difícil a los recién llegados convencer al ingenuo agricultor de
    la conveniencia de vender sus tierras por una gran suma de dinero, para ser
    más preciso, doscientos mil dólares, una suma jamás imaginada por Antonio,
    por un terreno que según él, solo le había servido para vivir con muchas
    limitaciones. Por lo tanto ese era el negocio de su vida. La venta se realizó y
    Antonio tuvo que salir de su tierra y alquilar una casa en el pueblo para vivir él
    y su familia. A los pocos días se empezó a desvanecer el sueño del gran
    negocio y este ocurrió porque en la prisa por abandonar su tierra se olvidó de
    algunos recuerdos familiares como el retrato de los antepasados y alguno que
    otro objeto de uso personal. Como es normal, no dudaron el regresar a su tierra
    para recuperar lo olvidado, pero cual sería la sorpresa, que al llegar encon-
    traron una cerca de alambre electrificada y un letrero en otro idioma que
    parecía decir 'prohibido el paso', pero más elocuente era la calavera pintada en
    el mismo y por último observaron una gran fogata donde se consumían lenta-
    mente lo que una vez fue su casa y los recuerdos de su seres queridos ya falle-
    cidos. Ante esta realidad tan elocuente Antonio decidió tomar medidas
    drásticas para dar el mejor uso al dinero recibido de manera que le pudiera
    garantizar la existencia propia y familiar y para tal fin hizo lo siguiente:

    (1) Desolló las pretensiones de sus hijos, para comprar carro, ir a la univer-
         sidad, adquirir una casa nueva, etc. Esta fue una medida muy apropiada
         para su realidad de agricultor sin tierra, el cual debía conservar su dinero
         a toda costa. Esta medida le trajo grandes diferencias con sus familiares,
         que no podían entender, que, teniendo tanto dinero, so padre no pudiera
         darle esos pequeños lujos, por lo cual optaron por abandonarlo y dejarlo
         solo con su dinero.
    (2) Solo y sin familia Antonio pensó correctamente: decidió invertir dinero en
         varios negocios para tener una entrada, ya que el dinero estático no
         produce ganancias. Esta medida, si bien lógica, le trajo consecuencias
         catastróficas, perdió más de la mitad del dinero, porque en las condiciones
         actuales hacer inversiones en cualquier empresa es muy arriesgado y más
         a£n cuando no se tiene la experiencia necesaria, recuerden que Antonio
         había sido un agricultor.
    (3) Como aún le quedaba algún dinero a nuestro agricultor no dudó en dirigir
         sus pasos en dirección a los bancos. Él había escuchado que muchas

personas vivían del dinero que tenían en cuentas a plazo fijo y él no sería la excepción de no poder hacerlo y así de esta forma recorrió todas las sucursales bancarias buscando el interés más razonable y conveniente, cosa que no logró, ya que en todas partes le ofrecían un interés como para morir de hambre. Como en toda experiencia, hay un aprendizaje. Antonio aprendió aunque un poco tarde una triste lección y es que los bancos llevan todas las ganas de ganar y el cliente las de perder de lo que se desprender que debemos mantenernos en lo posible alejados de tan peligrosas instituciones.

(4) Al final ocurrió lo inevitable. Antonio tuvo que gastar todo su dinero, que por cierto no le tomo mucho tiempo, ya que el alto costo de la vida, y la falta de entradas le ayudaron mucho a tal propósito.

Para no cansarlos con esta historia les diremos que nuestro apreciado agricultor perdió todo su dinero y hoy en día, sin familia, ni amigos vive en la ciudad Cabecera de la Provincia, haciendo mandados para vivir y pidiendo pequeños préstamos a conocidos, que todos saben que nunca pagará. Lo triste de esta historia es que ocurrió a una persona como usted y yo, amable lector. De todo corazón, le pedimos que de poder identificar la persona que ha vivido esta historia, nunca revele su nombre por solidaridad humana y tomen muy en cuenta lo sucedido a quienes venden su tierra, para que no sea usted actor de la próxima historia trágica.

2. English translation provided courtesy of the author.

Appendix 3

Methodological Notes

Theoretical Framework

Gareth Morgan and Linda Smircich make a solid case urging qualitative researchers to 'approach discussions of methodology in a way that highlights the vital link between theory and method – between the world view to which the researcher subscribes, the type of research question posed, and the technique that is to be adopted as a basis for research' (1980: 499). As such, I find it necessary to elucidate a few thoughts regarding my epistemological approach to this research endeavor. Going into this project, I hypothesized that, given the great social, cultural and economic differences existing between native and foreign residents, their experiences of and meanings for this place would greatly differ. However, how they would differ, or even *if* they would differ, remained uncertain.

My epistemological approach to this research is based upon a constructivist world view which conceives that social groups actively create a *perception* of reality; a reality that is both 'pluralistic and plastic,' as Thomas Schwandt alleges. Constructivism places an 'emphasis on the world of experience as it is lived, felt, [and] undergone by social actors.' As such, constructivists are 'deeply committed to the … view that what we take to be objective knowledge and truth is the result of perspective. Knowledge and truth are *created*, not discovered by the mind' (Schwandt, 1994: 125, emphasis added). Applied to human geography, this implies that while the physical and environmental characteristics of the external world certainly influence our human experience of this world and what it means to us (as place, landscape, etc.), ultimately the meaning and experiences are human creations that reside with us rather than 'out there'. In other words, the objective qualities of the external world contribute to a variety of subjective realities or experiences that human groups actively create, negotiate and share.

The constructivist believes that, '[t]hrough our nonverbal and verbal symbol systems we create many versions of the world in the sciences, the arts, and the humanities' (Schwandt, 1994: 126); this is what Nelson Goodman (1978) has termed the process of 'worldmaking'. Regarding this construction of experience, Schwandt writes that the 'frames of interpretation (versions) belong both to what is interpreted (world/reality) and to a system of interpretation (beliefs/views)' (1994: 126; parenthetical notations added). According to this epistemological perspective, social groups who participate in the creation of a shared world or reality share a common ground (perspective) and a common ideological position in the world (identity). As such, constructivism allows not only for multiple *interpretations* of a particular place, but also for a particular place to have multiple *lived-in realities*. Communication is essential to 'worldmaking', as it is the social process through which perspectives and interpretations are shared, negotiated and normalized among social groups. Ultimately, the chief concern for constructivists is to evaluate how different social groups undergo the process of 'making and judging world versions,' as Schwandt writes, and to understand the implications of these world versions or perspectives.

Case Study Selection

From approximately half a dozen prospective field research sites in Mexico and Central America that were considered, in early 2005 I selected Boquete as my case study. My decision to select Boquete was theoretically influenced by R.W. Butler's (1980) groundbreaking model for resort cycle development and, importantly, by subsequent applications of this resort development model to retirement destinations (Foster & Murphy, 1991; Hovinen, 1982; Truly, 2002).

While there certainly are valuable insights to be gleaned from a qualitative analysis of residential tourist destinations at all stages of Butler's development model, I elected to focus on a residential tourist destination currently undergoing the development stage of Butler's model, which is discussed in greater detail in Chapter 3. Much of my decision to select a destination in the development stage arose purely based on logistical considerations. While choosing a less developed residential tourist destination might very well mean a dearth of research subjects or an unnucleated, diffuse settlement pattern of informants, selecting a more developed residential tourist destination might create too large a research pool to be adequately sampled by an independent researcher.

In addition to the typological value of Butler's resort development model to my case study selection process, Butler's model also rightly situates the analysis of my case study as but a temporal and partial snapshot of a living, mutable place. This idea supports Jennifer Hyndman's belief that, while qualitative fieldwork may be able to capture a 'thick' experiential description, it nonetheless is but a partial slice of a larger experience or reality. '[O]ne's findings in the field never capture the whole picture. In fact, no whole picture exists' (2001: 267), she contends. As such, I fully expect that residents' experiences of and meanings for Boquete will evolve with time to change the identity of this place from what it is today. In addition, as I further address below, I cannot claim to have represented the experiences of all residents in Boquete. In this way, I hope that the case study findings presented in this work will be received as a thick, but necessarily partial slice of residential experiences of Boquete during this era of residential tourist development.

Methods

As Norman Denzin and Yvonna Lincoln (1994) prescribe in their *Handbook of Qualitative Research*, my research methods resulted from a 'bricolage' of various qualitative techniques: participant observation, semi-structured individual and group interviews and textual analysis. My research in Boquete began 'from a distance' in the early spring of 2005, when I began remotely gathering contextual information about both the district's history and the evolution of residential tourist growth and development. By the beginning of that summer, I was utilizing online discussion forums to establish contacts with residents – albeit primarily foreign residential tourists – and soliciting informants to participate in interviews during my upcoming field visit to Boquete.

Surprisingly, learning about and connecting with Boquete's residential tourists proved to be a relatively simple task. As most residential tourists maintain a transnational identity, they rely heavily on Internet communications in order to keep in touch with friends and family in their countries of origin, network with other expatriates around the world, and publish personal accounts of their experiences in blogs and in other types of online journals. In general, residential tourists in Boquete were eager to participate as informants; as such, before I ever stepped foot in the district, I had already secured contacts with over a dozen residential tourists whom I was scheduled to interview. In addition, a short public announcement, which I delivered on the morning of my arrival in Boquete at an informal weekly residential tourist gathering (known as the Tuesday Morning Networking (TMN) meeting), ultimately generated more interest from residential tourists than I had time to fully pursue.

Of course, in order to work towards understanding as many residents' place experiences as possible, I was also committed to devoting equal time to exploring native residents' place experiences. Even though I had cleared the first communication hurdle, being a fluent Spanish speaker, I experienced significant early difficulties establishing contacts within the native community prior to my visit. Mainly, this was because most native Boqueteños spend little, if any, time communicating via the Internet.

However, upon arrival in Boquete, I quickly gained entrée into a number of diverse native social networks within the native community. This was accomplished with relative ease, first by knocking on doors, so to speak, and then later branching out into the native community through my core informants' network of friends, family and work associates.

Interviews

During the course of my fieldwork in Boquete during the summer of 2005, I conducted 24 formal interviews with a total of 40 informants. Of this total number of informants, 25 were foreign-born residential tourists, comprising 14 formal interviews. As most residential tourists in Boquete are married, empty-nester couples who migrate together from their country of origin, roughly two-thirds of these interviews were conducted with married couples. As such, the male-to-female ratio of residential tourist informants was nearly even (13: 12).

The remaining 15 informants, comprising 10 formal interviews, were conducted with native-born residents of Boquete. Unlike the residential tourist interviews, which were most frequently conducted in pairs, interviews with native residents typically were conducted individually; however, two of these interviews were conducted with families consisting of two or more related informants. One obvious limitation of the data gleaned from interviews with native informants, which I will further address below, results from a significant gender imbalance. Unlike the relatively even male-to-female ratio in the foreign-born sample, the ratio in the native-born sample (4: 11) underrepresents males and overrepresents females. However, while this limitation certainly deserves to be noted, I am confident that the bricolage of various qualitative techniques adequately compensates to correct the gender imbalance of the native-born informant sample.

These formal interviews usually took place at residents' homes, with only a handful of interviews taking place at non-residential locations, such as a workplace, a coffee shop or, on one occasion, a small meeting room at my boarding house. In addition, due to time constraints and my personal desire to survey the largest possible sample, most informants participated in only one interview. However, these interviews typically were rather lengthy, lasting anywhere from one to two hours. Furthermore, the interviews were often either preceded or followed by several additional hours of informal socialization with informants and their friends and families over meals, tours of their residences and properties, and the like.

All formal interviews were tape recorded and semi-structured around one of two 'scripts' of predetermined questions, that varied depending on whether the informant or informants were native or foreign born residents. Despite my labeling of these interviews as 'formal' (in order to differentiate from a relatively more informal set of 'street' interviews described below), I not only permitted informants to liberally interpret and respond to my questions in open-ended fashion, I also allowed informants the opportunity to ultimately guide the direction of the interview. By allowing the informants to shape the course of the interview, albeit within predetermined boundaries that I dutifully enforced, I discovered that this flexible, open approach, as John Eyles attests, 'allow[s] people to describe and talk about their own lives in their own words' (1988: 8). My interviewing philosophy and experiences greatly mirrored those described by Hyndman: 'Listening and probing proved more insightful than any of the interview schedules I had circulated to the research ethics committee prior to my departure. By engaging people in their terms, doors were opened and invitations extended' (2001: 268).

In addition to these formal interviews, I also conducted several informal 'street' interviews exclusively with native-born inhabitants in an attempt to widen my native-born interview sample, albeit with less depth than those acquired through the more formal interviewing techniques. Unlike formal interviews, these informal sessions were neither pre-arranged, nor tape recorded, nor did they follow a predetermined script of questions. In total, I conducted six informal interviews with a total of eight native-born informants, six of whom were male. While these informal interviews are not regarded as carrying the same weight as formal interviews, nonetheless I succeeded in enriching my understanding of the native-born male perspective.

Participant observation

During my fieldwork in Boquete, my role as both participant in and observer of daily interactions took place during all waking hours. As such, virtually all of my experiences and activities during my temporary residence in the district became subject to critical, introspective analysis and reflection. My more explicit and resolute attempts to assume the role of the participant–observer included: sitting in on TMN meetings; frequenting both 'local-oriented' and 'foreign-oriented' restaurants, coffee shops and bars; spending time in Boquete's main square; and choosing to walk as my preferred method of transportation. In addition, I gained valuable insights from complementary observations, which, according to

Robin Kearns, constitute the gathering of 'additional descriptive information before, during or after other more structured forms of data collection' (2000: 105). Mostly these valuable complementary observations were circumstantially related to formal interviews, which, as mentioned above, often gave me the opportunity to visit residents' homes and participate in other, less structured forms of social interaction with informants.

Textual collection

In addition to interview transcripts, field notes and a field journal that I kept, I accumulated a rather large collection of various 'texts' during the research process. Notable among these 'texts' are several short stories written by a native-born resident and given to me by an informant; Sánchez Pinzón's (2001) historical monograph about Boquete; various e-mails, online discussion forum threads, blogs, and the like written by residential tourists; Internet web page text and images concerning real estate and master-planned residential communities in Boquete; and a collection of personal photographs capturing a variety of visual narratives, images and symbols, some of which are presented in this work.

Analysis

In casting a wide net of qualitative techniques, all of which I conducted with an ever-constant and -conscious loyalty to my primary research questions, I succeeded in harvesting a large data set, including, but by no means limited to, over 40 hours of interview audio tape. I adopted the process of analytic induction to slowly sift through this mound of qualitative data in order to identify the common threads and prevailing themes. Eyles describes this process as one in which 'the "results" at the outset of data analysis are no more than hunches to be revised and refined by repeated checking and combing through the data' (1988: 4). For this process I conceived of three duties for my role as the researcher. In chronological order, they are: (1) to identify common place experiences, meanings and identities; (2) to understand how and along what lines these experiences, meanings and identities are created; and (3) to explore the implications of these socially shared and created experiences, meanings and identities. Fulfilling these duties required me to cycle through the data repeatedly, each time employing a different lens to scrutinize the information according to a specific idea or hypothesis. This process is what Eyles describes as the 'progressive categorization and refinement' of the data. In the end I am confident that my findings and observations rightfully reflect common place experiences and meanings shared among groups of residents in present-day Boquete.

Critical Issues of Reflexivity

A growing number of scholars urge qualitative researchers to situate their knowledge by implicating themselves in the research process as active and influential participants (e.g. Berg & Mansvelt, 2000; Crang, 2003; Evans, 1988; Hammersley, 1998), or at least attempt to do this (see Rose, 1997). As such, I feel it necessary to briefly and introspectively explore my own issues of positionality in the research process and my (re)presentation of the research findings. This is an especially important component of this research enterprise given that the constructivist worldview implicates me, the researcher, as a social actor helping to shape the realities or worldviews in which the research is conducted, interpreted, analyzed and presented (Denzin & Lincoln, 1994). My identity as a white, American male not only affects my initial position from which I perceive, interpret and participate; it also undoubtedly affects how informants relate to me and respond to my inquiries. While I agree with Gillian Rose (1997) regarding the impossibility of the researcher to achieve a full and transparent position of self-reflexivity, it nevertheless is important for me to explore several implications of my own position within the research endeavor.

I am certain that both my personal identity (as an American and English-speaking male) and my professional identity (as a graduate student from a respected university) helped me to quickly and easily network and connect with my foreign-born, residential tourist informants. Armed with little knowledge about me beyond superficial information about my identity, residential tourists overwhelmingly accepted me as a stranger into their homes. I suspect that most participated because they felt they could trust a person in my position, and because they had a genuine desire to participate in a research endeavor concerning their lives and experiences. For better or worse, many residential tourist informants, often unconsciously, treated me as one of their own; often saying things like, 'as you know, back in the United States *we* do x, but here in Panamá *they* do y.'

In contrast, I am certain that my identity equally made me an outsider in the eyes of the native-born Boqueteño population. From their perspective I surely was seen as an American *gringo*, an outsider, who – if not for my age, my Spanish-language abilities and my unusual predilection to walk everywhere, with notebook in hand – otherwise would have been mistaken for a residential tourist. This position presented me with a number of challenges, some of which proved to be surmountable, others of which proved to be unconquerable. First, as mentioned previously, I initially encountered challenges tapping into social networks among the native community. However, I fortuitously overcame much of this social barrier by quickly establishing relationships of trust and respect with several well-respected pillars of the native community, who opened many doors for me. In the end, though, just like residential tourist informants, native Boqueteño informants were extremely outgoing, gracious, and accommodating hosts.

A second challenge that I encountered regarding my position vis-à-vis the native-born population ultimately culminated in my inability to elicit an ideal level of formal participation from the native-born male population. Given that I had significantly less difficulties communicating with native-born females, I attribute this participation impediment to the restrictive social norms regarding the male identity and male-to-male interaction in Latin American cultures. Under the legacy of machismo, which Octavio Paz describes as an 'ideal of manliness ... never to "crack"' or open up (1985: 30), Latin American males, Panameños included, are disinclined to speak introspectively about their personal feelings and experiences, least of all in public, to a stranger who is also male. While I was successful in gaining detailed insight into the experiences of several native-born men, perhaps the inability to gain more was the greatest limitation of this research endeavor.

A third and final challenge concerns qualitative and emotional access to native-born residents' inner thoughts, feelings and place experiences. In addition to fully anticipating being perceived as an outsider by the native community, prior to my field visit I also wondered whether I would be able to adequately grasp, interpret and represent the 'insider's experience'. Would these 'insiders' privilege me with a glimpse into their world? And, assuming that I was privileged with this insider knowledge, would I be able to empathize with their place experiences and meanings? Despite these initial mental challenges and internal preoccupations, I encountered in Boquete a diverse group of native-born informants who were eager to make their feelings, perspectives and experiences known and, importantly, informants who were also aware of my limited knowledge as an outsider. In fact, native informants were thrilled to have someone from outside their community show an interest in their lives and experiences. By showing interest in their lives, and having the ability to communicate with them in their own language, the native-born residents with whom I interacted were eager to make their perspectives and experiences known to the outside world via my research.

This final point relates to the ambiguities of 'insiders' and 'outsiders' and the problems and the promises of representation across this dichotomy. In the case of native-born Boqueteños (the 'insiders'), my identity as an 'outsider', I am convinced, actually benefited my research, as this group saw me as an agent capable of representing their experiences to a larger audience beyond their community.

References

Andrews, M. (1999) *Landscape and Western Art*. New York: Oxford University Press.
Berg, L. and Mansvelt, J. (2000) Writing in, speaking out: Communicating research findings. In I. Hay (ed.) *Qualitative Research Methods in Human Geography* (pp. 161–82). South Melbourne, Victoria: Oxford University Press.
Berger, J. (1977) *Ways of Seeing*. New York: Penguin Books.
Beyers, W.B. and Nelson, P.B. (2000) Contemporary development forces in the non-metropolitan west: New insights from rapidly growing communities. *Journal of Rural Studies* 16, 459–74.
Buller, H. and Hoggart, K. (1994) *International Counterurbanization: British Migrants in Rural France*. Aldershot: Avebury.
Burgess, J.A. (1982) Filming the fens: A visual interpretation of regional character. In J.R. Gold and J.A. Burgess (eds) *Valued Environments* (pp. 35–54). London: George Allen and Unwin.
Burnett, A.D. (1975) *Areas for Statutory Neighborhood and Community Councils in Cities*, 6–7. Department of Geography, Portsmouth Polytechnic.
Butler, R.W. (1980) The concept of a tourist area cycle of evolution: Implications for management of resources. *Canadian Geographer* 24 (1), 5–12.
Casado-Diaz, M.A. (1999) Socio-demographic impacts of residential tourism: A case study of Torrevieja, Spain. *International Journal of Tourism Research* 1, 223–37.
CIA World Factbook (2005) *The World Factbook* Database. On www at https://www.cia.gov/library/publications/the-world-factbook/geos/pm.html. Accessed 16 March 2006.
Clavé, S.A. (1998) Residential tourism development. From the conquest of travel to the restructuring of tourist cities. *Documents d'Analisi Geografica* 32, 17–43.
Cohen, E. (1972) Toward a sociology of international tourism. *Social Research* 39 (1), 164–82.
Compite Panamá (2005) Cluster de Turismo Residencial: Boquete. Powerpoint presentation. Boquete, Panamá, 12 July.
Cosgrove, D. (1984) *Social Formation and Symbolic Landscape*. Madison, WI: University of Wisconsin Press.
Cosgrove, D. (1985) Prospective, perspective and the evolution of the landscape idea. *Transactions of the Institute of British Geographers*, 10 (1), 45–62.
Cox, G. (1988) 'Reading' nature: Reflections on ideological persistence and the politics of the countryside. *Landscape Research* 13 (3), 24–34.
Crang, M. (2003) Qualitative methods: Touchy, feely, look-see? *Progress in Human Geography* 27 (4), 494–504.
Cronon, W. (1995) Introduction: In search of nature. In W. Cronon (ed.) *Uncommon Ground: Toward Reinventing Nature* (pp. 23–67). New York: W.W. Norton and Co.
Daniels, S. and Cosgrove, D. (1988) Introduction: Iconography and landscape. In D. Cosgrove and S. Daniels (eds) *The Iconography of Landscape* (pp. 1–10). Cambridge: Cambridge University Press.
Davies, C. (2005) 2005 travel and adventure report: A snapshot of boomers' travel and adventure experiences. Washington: AARP, Knowledge Management.

Denzin, N.K. and Lincoln, Y.S. (1994) Introduction: Entering the field of qualitative research. In N.K. Denzin and Y.S. Lincoln (eds) *Handbook of Qualitative Research* (pp. 1–17). Thousand Oaks, CA: Sage Publications.

Duncan, J.S. and Duncan, N.G. (2004) *Landscapes of Privilege: The Politics of the Aesthetic in an American Suburb*. New York: Routledge.

Elliott, R.C. (1970) *The Shape of Utopia: Studies in a Literary Genre*. Chicago, IL: University of Chicago Press.

Evans, M. (1988) Participant observation: The researcher as a research tool. In J. Eyles and D.M. Smith (eds) *Qualitative Methods in Human Geography* (pp. 118–35). Cambridge: Polity Press.

Eyles, J. (1988) Interpreting the geographical world: Qualitative approaches in geographical research. In J. Eyles and D.M. Smith (eds) *Qualitative Methods in Human Geography* (pp. 1–16). Cambridge: Polity Press.

Forsythe, D.E. (1980) Urban incomers and rural change: The impact of migrants from the city on life in an Orkney community. *Sociologia Ruralis* 20, 287–305.

Foster, D.M. and Murphy, P. (1991) Resort cycle revisited: The retirement connection. *Annals of Tourism Research* 18, 553–67.

Gober, P., McHugh, K. and Leclerc, D. (1993) Job-rich but housing-poor: The dilemma of a western amenity town. *The Professional Geographer* 45 (1), 12–20.

Goodman, N. (1978) *Ways of Worldmaking*. Indianapolis, IN: Hackett.

Gordon, B.L. (1957) *Notes on the Chiriquí Lagoon District and Adjacent Regions of Panama*. Berkeley, CA: Department of Geography, University of California, Berkeley.

Hammersley, M. (1998) *Reading Ethnographic Research: A Critical Guide*. (2nd edn) London: Longman.

Hannerz, U. (1990) Cosmopolitans and locals in world culture. In M. Featherstone (ed.) *Global Culture* (pp. 237–52). London: Sage Publications.

Hansen, A. (2002) Discourses of nature in advertising. *Communications* 27, 499–511.

Hay, R. (1998) Sense of place in developmental context. *Journal of Environmental Psychology* 18, 5–29.

Henríquez, J.A. (1909) *Chiriquí: lo que hoy es esa provincia de la República de Panamá, y el porvenir que le espera*. Panama: Diario de Panamá.

Hovinen, G.R. (1982) Visitor cycles – outlook for tourism in Lancaster County. *Annals of Tourism Research* 9 (4), 565–83.

Hyndman, J. (2001) The field as here and now, not there and then. *The Geographical Review* 91 (1–2), 262–72.

Jackson, J.B. (1997) *Landscape in Sight: Looking at America*. H.L. Horowitz (ed.). New Haven, CT: Yale University Press.

Kaltenborn, B.P. and Williams, D.R. (2002) The meaning of place: Attachments to Femundsmarka National Park, Norway, among tourists and locals. *Norwegian Journal of Geography* 56, 189–98.

Kavanagh, K.H. (2005) 'The whole land is sacred' – story and the Navajo sense of place. In G. Backhaus and J. Murungi (eds) *Lived Topographies and their Mediational Forces* (pp. 31–47). Lanham, MD: Lexington Books.

Kearns, R. (2000) Being there: Research through observing and participating. In I. Hay (ed.) *Qualitative Research Methods in Human Geography* (pp. 103–21). South Melbourne, Victoria: Oxford University Press.

King, R., Warnes, A.M. and Williams, A.M. (1998) International retirement migration in Europe. *International Journal of Population Geography* 4 (2), 91–111.

Kratz, E.F. (2005) Paradise found: Where to retire abroad. *Fortune*, 11 July.

Lefebvre, H. (1991) *The Production of Space*. (D. Nicholson-Smith, trans.). Oxford: Basil Blackwell.

Leiss, W., Kline, S. and Jhally, S. (1986) *Social Communication in Advertising: Persons, Products and Images of Wellbeing*. Toronto: Methuen.

Lowenthal, D. (1962–3) Not every prospect pleases. *Landscape* 12 (2), 19–23.

Lowenthal, D. (1982) Revisiting valued landscapes. In J.R. Gold and J.A. Burgess (eds) *Valued Environments* (pp. 74–99). London: George Allen and Unwin.

MacCannell, D. (1976) *The Tourist: A New Theory of the Leisure Class*. New York: Schocken Books.

Martín, L.M. (2004) Tourist expansion and development of rural communities: The case of Monteverde, Costa Rica. *Mountain Research and Development* 24 (3), 202–5.

McCullough, D.G. (1977) *The Path Between the Seas*. New York: Simon and Schuster.

McHugh, K.E. (2000) The 'ageless self'? Emplacement of identities in Sun Belt retirement communities. *Journal of Ageing Studies* 14 (1), 103–15.

McHugh, K.E. (2003) Three faces of ageism: Society, image and place. *Ageing and Society* 23, 165–85.

Meagher, T.F. (1861) The new route through Chiriquí. In M. LaRosa and G.R. Mejía (eds) (2004) *The United States Discovers Panama: The Writings of Soldiers, Scholars Scientists and Scoundrels, 1850–1905* (pp. 103–24). New York: Rowman and Littlefield.

Meinig, D.W. (1979) The beholding eye: Ten versions of the same scene. In D.W. Meinig (ed.) *The Interpretation of Ordinary Landscapes* (pp. 33–48). New York: Oxford University Press.

Melvin, J. (ed.) (2004) Meaning, mapping and making of landscape (A forum with M. Andrews, A. Linklater, S. Callery, H. Fulton, P. Keiller and F. Moussavi). *Architectural Review* 215 (1283), 81–8.

MetLife Mature Market Institute (2005) Demographic profile: American baby boomers. Online document: http: //www.metlife.com/WPSAssets/ 19506845461045242298V1F-Boomer%2Profile%202003.pdf>.

Mitchell, D. (1996) *The Lie of the Land*. Minneapolis, MN: University of Minnesota Press.

Morgan, G. and Smircich, L. (1980) The case for qualitative research. *The Academy of Management Review* 5 (4), 491–500.

Nelson, P.B. (1997) Migration, sources of income, and community change in the non-metropolitan Northwest. *The Professional Geographer* 49 (4), 418–30.

Nelson, V. (2005) Representation and images of people, place and nature in Grenada's tourism. *Geografiska Annaler* 87B (2), 131–43.

O'Reilly, K. (1995) A new trend in European migration: Contemporary British migration to Fuengirola, Costa del Sol. *Geographical Viewpoint* 23, 25–36.

Osorio, A.O. (1988) *Chiriquí en su historia, 1502–1903, tomo II*. Panamá: ENAN.

Panamá. Contraloria General de la Republica (1945) *Censo de población, 1940*. Panamá: Imprenta Nacional.

Panamá. Dirección de Estadística y Censo (DEC) (2003) *Chiriquí y sus estadísticas, años 1996–2000*. Panamá: Imprenta Nacional.

Panamá. Ministerio de Agricultura, Comercio e Industrias (MACI) (1947) *Censo agropecuario de la Provincia de Chiriquí*. Panamá: Imprenta Nacional.

Paz, O. (1985) *The Labyrinth of Solitude*. New York: Grove Press.

Perkins, H.C. (1989) The country in the town: The role of real estate developers in the construction of the meaning of place. *Journal of Rural Studies* 5 (1), 61–74.

Porteous, J.D. (1996) *Environmental Aesthetics*. London: Routledge.

Punter, J.V. (1982) Landscape aesthetics: A synthesis and critique. In J.R. Gold and J.A. Burgess (eds) *Valued Environments* (pp. 100–23). London: George Allen and Unwin.

Raya, P. (1994) El turismo residencial en Andalucía. *Boletín Económico de Andalucía* 17, 21–31.

Relph, E.C. (1976) *Place and Placelessness*. London: Pion.

Riger, S. and Lavrakas, P.J. (1981) Community ties: Patterns of attachment and social interaction in urban neighborhoods. *American Journal of Community Psychology* 9 (1), 55–66.

Robinson, T. (1907) *Panama: A Personal Record of Forty-Six Years, 1861–1907*. New York: Panama, Star and Herald Co.

Rodriguez, V. (2001) Tourism as a recruiting post for retirement migration. *Tourism Geographies* 3 (1), 52–63.

Rose, G. (1997) Situating knowledges: Positionality, reflexivities and other tactics. *Progress in Human Geography* 21 (3), 305–20.

Sack, R.D. (1992) *Place, Modernity, and the Consumer's World*. Baltimore, MD: Johns Hopkins University Press.

Sánchez, R.A. (2004) *Boquete: rutas de aventura*. Map. Panamá: Arte Digital.

Sánchez Pinzón, M.O. (2001) *Boquete: rasgos de su historia*. Panamá: Culturama Inter-nacional.

Sauer, C.O. (1967) *Land and Life*. J. Leighly (ed.). Berkeley, CA: University of California Press.

Schwandt, T.A. (1994) Constructivist, interpretivist approaches to human inquiry. In N.K. Denzin and Y.S. Lincoln (eds) *Handbook of Qualitative Research* (pp. 118–37). Thousand Oaks, CA: Sage Publications.

Smith, N. (1990) *Uneven Development: Nature, Capital, and the Production of Space*. Oxford: Basil Blackwell.

Smutny, G. (2002) Patterns of growth and change: Depicting the impacts of restructuring in Idaho. *The Professional Geographer* 54 (3), 438–53.

Solc, V. (1970) *Chiriquí Culture*. Prague: Nàprstek Museum.

Thrift, N. (1987) Manufacturing rural geography? *Journal of Rural Studies* 3 (1), 77–81.

Torres, R.M. and Momsen, J.D. (2005) Gringolandia: The construction of a new tourist space in Mexico. *Annals of the Association of American Geographers* 95 (2), 314–35.

Truly, D. (2002) International retirement migration and tourism along the Lake Chapala Riviera: Developing a matrix of retirement migration behavior. *Tourism Geographies* 4 (3), 261–81.

Tuan, Y.F. (1977) *Space and Place: The Perspective of Experience*. Minneapolis, MN: University of Minnesota.

Tuan, Y.F. (1996) Space and place: Humanistic perspective. In J. Agnew, D.N. Livingstone and A. Rogers (eds) *Human Geography: An Essential Anthology* (pp. 444–57). Oxford: Blackwell.

Tuan, Y.F. (1998) *Escapism*. Baltimore: Johns Hopkins University.

Urry, J. (1990) *The Tourist Gaze*. London: Sage.

Urry, J. (1995) *Consuming Places*. London: Routledge.

Vakis, R. and Lindert, K. (2000) Poverty in indigenous populations in Panama: A study using LSMS data. *World Bank LCSHD Paper Series*. Washington, DC: World Bank.

Vera, F. (ed.) (1997) *Análisis Territorial del Turismo*. Barcelona: Ariel.

Varela, R.L., Bernat, M.V. and López, V.R. (2005) *Economía de Panamá para Todos*. Panamá: Intracorp.

Warnes, A.M. (1992) Migration and the life course. In T. Champion and T. Fielding (eds) *Migration Processes and Patterns Volume I* (pp. 176–87). London: Belhaven Press.

Warnes, A.M. (1994) Permanent and seasonal international retirement migration: The prospects for Europe. *Netherlands Geographical Studies* 173, 69–81.

Williams, A.M., King, R. and Warnes, A.M. (1997) A place in the sun: International retirement migration from northern to southern Europe. *European Urban and Regional Studies* 4(2), 115–34.

Williams, A.M. and Hall, C.M. (2000) Tourism and migration: New relationships between production and consumption. *Tourism Geographies* 2 (1), 5–27.

Williams, A.M., King, R., Warnes, A.M. and Patterson, G. (2000) Tourism and international retirement migration: New forms of an old relationship in southern Europe. *Tourism Geographies* 2 (1), 28–49.

Williams, A.M. and Patterson, G. (1998) 'An empire lost but a province gained': A cohort analysis of British international retirement in the Algarve. *International Journal of Population Geography* 4, 135–55.

Williams, R. (1973) *The Country and the City*. New York: Oxford University Press.

Index